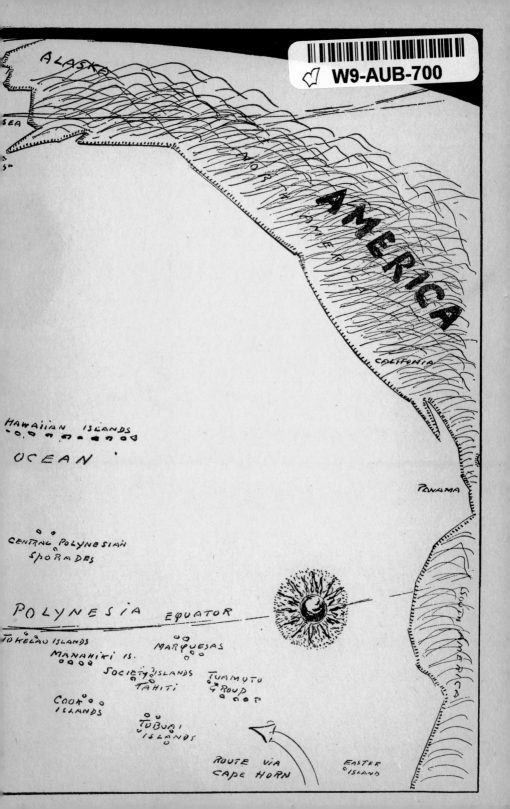

EX LIBRIS

Norman G. Rhode

# THE STORY OF THE PACIFIC

THE GREAT DISCOVERERS OF THE PACIFIC

HENDRIK WILLEM VAN LOON

# THE STORY OF
# THE PACIFIC

HARCOURT, BRACE AND COMPANY, NEW YORK

*Typography by Robert Josephy*

PRINTED IN THE UNITED STATES OF AMERICA
BY QUINN & BODEN COMPANY, INC., RAHWAY, N. J.

# TO HELEN

# CONTENTS

# THE STORY OF THE PACIFIC

# 1. THE PANAMA CANAL

WHY IS it that the truly great experiences of one's life are apt to be so exceedingly simple?

As a child I had heard all about the Panama Canal. Early in the fifties a brother of my grandmother had moved to Brazil. He had survived yellow fever and revolutions and had amassed a considerable fortune. When I was six or seven years old he had come back to Holland, bringing his family—his wondrous family of dark-eyed, dark-haired daughters. They had made such a stir in our little Dutch town that soon they had felt obliged to escape to the delights of Paris and the Riviera, which were much more to their rather exuberant Latin tastes than the simple pleasures of an evening at home with some unknown cousin, who in his Spartan simplicity had felt rather awkward before this over-generous display of feminine beauty and charm.

I am afraid that these French peregrinations were not an unlimited success. For one day they had suffered a humiliation from which they never fully recovered. They were mighty proud of their jet-black hair and wore it in long braids that almost reached to their feet. Well, one fine morning they had climbed to the top of a bus to proceed to Fontainebleau. The bus was crowded and they had been pushed hither and yon, and when they reached their destination—oh, ghastly discovery!—their hair was gone!

It was of course quite a common occurrence during the late eighties of the previous century to have one's hair stolen. It was needed for the manufacture of those chignons which were then highly popular and were contraptions of human hair meant to be worn underneath those crazy little hats which now, after an absence of almost fifty years, have once more made their appearance. The supply of false hair being necessarily limited (for no living Chinaman would then have dreamed of divesting himself of his queue), a class of professional hair-stealers was then successfully operating not only in Paris but in every large city of the continent. The poor Brazilians had been easy victims and the labor of twenty painful years of brushing and combing had been rapidly undone by the quick clip of a sharp pair of scissors.

Somehow or other, that event made a very deep impression upon my youthful mind and it made me conscious of the existence of a people called the French. The Eiffel Tower, coming to me at about the same time (it was the year of the great Paris exhibition) in the form of an inkstand, a watch charm and a paperweight, also helped the good work along, and finally the Indian suits which generous uncles and aunts brought back to me from Buffalo Bill's contribution to the *Grande Exposition* turned me into an ardent Francophile.

THE DISCOVERY OF THE PACIFIC

Alas, the only way in which I could give evidence of my feelings at that time (I was all of seven years old) was by a close application to my studies of the noble French tongue. I bravely struggled with *j'ai, tu as, j'eusse, je fusse* and all the other perplexing problems of a language so infinitely more complicated than my native Dutch, in which, as all of us knew, the good Lord had originally written the Major Catechism of our Reformed Church, and soon I had acquired a sufficient facility in this queer idiom to fish the Paris *Illustration* out of that cardboard "portfolio" which the bookstore used to send us once a week and to be able to translate the simpler captions of its fascinating and intriguing pictures. And in that way I learned a good deal about a gentleman by the name of Ferdinand de Lesseps, who having dug the Suez Canal had now set bravely out to repeat his success on the Isthmus of Panama but who, in some mysterious way, had got no further than the door of a French jail.

The details of the "Panama scandal" did not become clear to me until many years later but at least I learned a lot about the geographical aspects of that narrow strip of land which separates the Atlantic from the Pacific and which appeared to be a region of inaccessible mountains and deep ravines, all of them inhabited by wild natives and wilder crocodiles.

You know how it goes with such childish recollections. They are as persistent as the weeds in the grass of your garden. You can plow them up, poison them, burn them down, and a few days later, behold! there they are again as if nothing had happened. As a result, for almost half a century, the Isthmus of Panama remained to me just that—a region of high mountain peaks, dense forests, wild natives and even wilder crocodiles.

Therefore, when at an ungodly hour, the steward knocked on the door and said, "In a few moments we will be in Cristobal, Sir," I quickly slipped into a dressing-gown, put on a pair of sandals and hastened to the deck, to hear me say to myself, "Lord help us all! the Captain took the wrong course! We are going into the Hook of Holland!" For the distant landscape was about as exciting as the coast of my native land and what I supposed to be the entrance to the canal looked as impressive as the mouth of the river Maas or the Scheldt.

Of course, when we came a little closer, I noticed certain differences. Everything was not entirely flat. There were a few low hills, but for the rest, I would not have been in the least surprised if the vessel had landed me in Rotterdam instead of the city which the ever-courteous and obliging American Government so generously called after the great Italian discoverer when it erected its own harbor at the northern entrance of the proposed canal to avoid any direct contact with the plague-hole which since the middle of the last century had been known as Colon.

Of that old Colon very little seems to remain. William Aspinwall had founded it as a terminal for his railroad across the Isthmus and during the hopeful days of that enterprise (A.D. 1850) it had been known as Aspinwall. This name being a little too complicated for the contemporary Panamanians (then in full possession of this tract of land), it had shortly afterwards been changed into the much simpler and easier Spanish name of Colon (Columbus to us). It had also been most magnificently neglected. Soon its streets had become marshes, ideally suited for the purpose of breeding yellow fever mosquitoes, and when in the year 1903 our government, after a most efficiently stage-managed one-night revolution, had acquired the right to a narrow strip of land leading from the Pacific to the Atlantic, one of the stipulations of the famous treaty of peace had granted the United States full sanitary control over the big cities of the newly established Republic of Panama.

The rest of the story can best be summed up in one single word—Gorgas. For without the thoroughgoing ministrations of this modern miracle-man, there never would have been any canal. There would have been (as there had been in the days of poor de Lesseps) a vast variety of cemeteries, hiding the pathetic remains of those faithful Spaniards and Frenchmen and Cubans who had so valiantly struggled to dig this little trench in this Godforsaken land of malaria and yellow fever while it was still under control of the French Canal Company.

Whereas today, the canal region is a health resort, where a mosquito has no more chance to survive than the proverbial snowball in Hades. In less than two years, this quiet-spoken Southern gentleman had performed his herculean task and could thereupon leave it to another officer of the United States Army to do the actual digging and to give us that short cut from the Atlantic to the Pacific which had been one of man's most cherished dreams ever since that evening of the twenty-fifth of September of the year 1513, when Vasco Nuñez de Balboa, from his silent "peak in Darien" had solved the problem of the Great South Sea, of which shortly afterwards he was to become the "Grand Admiral and Commander-in-Chief."

Alas for poor Balboa! poor, serious, hard-working and incompetent Balboa! Restlessly he had crossed and re-crossed his isthmus, founding cities, erecting forts, sending glowing descriptions of his conquest to His Most Catholic Majesty in far-off Spain. Others, less delicate in their methods (to indulge in a slight understatement), had wanted his job. And one of them had got it. He had got it by the simple expedient of having Balboa arrested on trumped-up charges. A packed tribunal had thereupon done the rest and less than four years after he had first climbed his famous peak and had shouted his triumphant "There it is!" the discoverer of the Pacific Ocean had been decapitated as a traitor and an enemy to the crown.

One often hears it said that republics are ungrateful. Within the domain of the Canal (as I shall hereafter call it), this statement is not borne out by the facts. Both Goethals, who did the digging, and Gorgas, who made the digging possible, were duly honored by the governments they served so faithfully and so efficiently and at an annual salary which must have horrified all believers in "private enterprise." For these sound businessmen regarded the income of a major of the Medical Corps, U.S.A., and of a colonel of the Engineering Corps, U.S.A., as mere cigarette money and made no bones about saying as much. I am not enough of an economist to know whether they were right or wrong, but I would like to stop here for a moment and say something that has been on my mind for a considerable number of years.

I have, during a fairly long life as a newspaperman, come in contact with a great many officers of both our army and our navy. I am, of course, familiar with the objection of so many of our modern and enlightened minds whose personal dislike for physical exertion (or lack of courage or anything you like to call it) is rather apt to make them scoff at the products of both Annapolis and West Point. They talk about the uselessness of so much meaningless drilling. They complain of the rigidity of the curriculum and denounce the mental restrictions imposed upon those who live by the rule of thumb of the War Department. I have come to a quite different conclusion. Except perhaps for the fact that as a rule these graduates of our two military institutions have much better manners than their academic colleagues, I have invariably found them to be much like the professors in our better-class universities, simple and direct, gentlemen who uncomplainingly accept whatever task is wished upon them and ask for no mercy.

Today they may be called upon to administer a couple of islands in the Pacific. Tomorrow they may be told to dig a trench through twenty miles of mountains or to fish an aviator out of the sea or to prevent Japanese poachers from putting a complete end to the race of the nimble seal without at the same time provoking the wrath of the very sensitive gentlemen who are now in control in Tokyo. The applause they receive in case they are successful is usually a little less than nothing at all. On the other hand, the blame they get in case they fail is almost always much more than they deserve. Yet there never seems to be any lack of candidates for this sort of a career. Those who do not like the "military idea," explain this by pointing to the ease and the regularity of the officer's existence. It is true, the profession gets scandalously underpaid, but it promises a regular income to all those who care to observe a few very elementary rules connected with the idea of "being a gentleman." And—come good times, come bad times—the check is there on the dot and unless Uncle Sam himself should go bankrupt, there is no danger that any of our gold-striped officials will ever be told that the firm cannot meet its obligations.

Furthermore, promotion, although slow, is completely automatic and the most ambitious of young men will not proceed much more rapidly than some mediocre pen-pusher in an obscure office somewhere on the top floor of the Navy Department, whose only claim to fame rests in his proud boast that he has never made a mistake.

That is what we are apt to hear when we listen to our pacifists and many of our intellectuals. But my own recollections of the sort of men who wear the United States uniform (a recollection now covering a period of some thirty

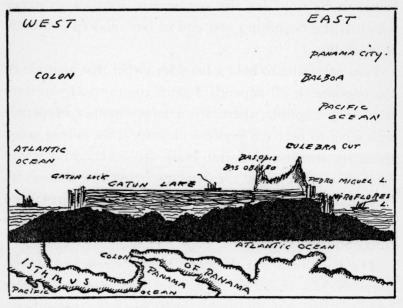

CROSS-SECTION OF THE PANAMA CANAL

years) do not quite bear this out. On the contrary, I found most of these men quite eager to do whatever they had been told to do, with that extra touch of devotion and loyalty which constitutes the difference between just another job and a piece of craftsmanship.

I have often wondered why it should be that way and why so many exceedingly bright and capable young men should be perfectly willing to forego the possible rewards

inherent in business and in the professions when they must
have known that, financially speaking, they could never
get anywhere at all. I think that I have found the answer.
They preferred that sort of career because they felt themselves to be unfit for the competitive form of existence
which is the beginning and end of our modern economic
form of life.

I am not going to hold a brief for either that attitude or
the opposite. It all depends, I think, on the way you were
born. For example, there are a large number of people
who seem to derive a positive pleasure from selling something to someone else. But there are others who would
rather starve to death than try to persuade a stranger to
buy something he neither wants nor needs. And these poor
fellows are at their very worst whenever they are obliged
to try and sell themselves.

The army man and the naval officer belong to the cate-
gory which is under no obligation to do this in order to
go about their allotted tasks. Their work is forever being
observed and scrutinized by invisible eyes. Their character
is well known to all their superiors, who for years have lived
with them in close harmony in some army post or on board
a battleship. Their habits and customs and manners are
known to all their colleagues. There may of course be a
certain amount of favoritism in the services, for personal
likes and dislikes are unavoidable as long as we are men and
not angels. But that evil, too, seems to have been reduced
to a minimum by an elaborate set of checks and counter-

checks. In short, once a military man has made up his mind
to eschew the fleshpots of our present competitive system
and has ordered his tailor to provide him with a uniform
and brass buttons displaying an eagle or an anchor, he
knows that his future will depend almost entirely upon his
own efforts and that he will not be forced to enter into
that rather disheartening (not to say disgusting) pushing
and crowding and kicking-the-other-fellow-in-the-pants
which is an inevitable part of life in the market place.

A few timeservers and a few lazy and careless brethren
may occasionally slip by and enjoy a few years of comparative leisure at the expense of the taxpayers, but their number is very small. The others are honorable and decent
fellows, often of outstanding ability, who happen to prefer
a non-competitive existence to one that would undoubtedly
offer much greater financial rewards but at the risk of their
being obliged to sacrifice part of their personal integrity.

So much for the men who built the Canal, and now let
me give you a few facts for the benefit of those who like a
few statistics with their geography.

Most people of course are vaguely familiar with the fact
that the Panama Canal is not really a canal in the accepted
sense of the word, as a *canna* or reed or tube through which
water can freely pass, as it does through the pipes in the
bathroom. It has not even been dug into the soil, as most
ordinary canals have been. On the contrary, it has been
made to run through the attic, for with the exception of
short stretches near the Atlantic and the Pacific, the Panama

Canal runs well above sea level and in the region of the Gatun Lake it reaches the respectable height of eighty-five feet.

The famous Culebra Cut (now called the Gaillard Cut in honor of the man responsible for this difficult engineering feat) is forty-five feet deep but its bottom is situated forty feet above sea level. Incidentally, the width of the Canal itself now makes it possible for every ship, with the exception of the *Queen Elizabeth, Queen Mary* and the *Normandie,* to sail through this narrow gap. As some 29,-000,000 tons are moved through the Canal every year (which is only 7,000,000 less than pass through the Suez Canal) we need not for the moment worry about these three aquatic monsters, who may well have been the last of their kind, for unless all present indications are entirely misleading, the days of the super-super-luxury greyhounds are numbered. They will disappear together with the civilization which mistook quantity for quality and considered the dinosaur as the proudest product of all creation.

The Canal runs through a strip of United States territory which is five miles wide on both sides of the centre of the waterway itself, but which fails to include the cities of Panama and Colon, which have remained in the possession of the sovereign republic of Panama ever since Theodore Roosevelt established that puppet state. None of this land can belong to private owners. It is government domain and a silent but highly eloquent argument in favor of govern-

ment ownership. For nothing strikes the visitor to this part
of the world quite as much as the excellent way in which

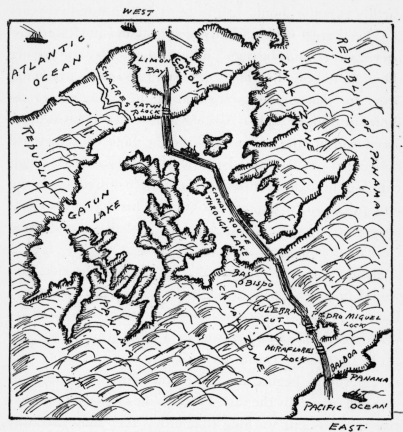

THE PANAMA CANAL

the whole of this region is administered by government
officials rather than by private enterprise.

The very air seems filled with a quiet efficiency which
extends from the little electric cars, which pull your ship
into the locks with a minimum of fuss and a minimum loss

of time, to the sanitary measures which make you feel as if every one of the forty thousand people who inhabit this earthly paradise should live to be at least a hundred years old. Yet a great deal of highly technical and intricate engineering work must be done both during the day and during the night to keep the Canal in constant and perfect running order for that endless procession of ships which use this short cut from Europe to Asia and whose owners insist upon speed and accuracy in return for the high tolls they are obliged to pay. For this is no Suez Canal—a wide trough running through a flat desert where eternal dredging is the only price you have to pay for safety. This third-story canal offers entirely different problems, as I shall try and make clear by drawing you a picture.

Should you enter the Canal from the Atlantic side, you would first of all pass through the Limon Bay, on which the city of Colon is situated. Soon the shores begin to approach each other and you enter a canal which leads you up to the famous Gatun locks. There the interesting part of the voyage begins, for there your ship starts upon its skyward career. By the way, I would like to give all prospective travelers fair warning that unless they most carefully watch every moment of the hoisting operation, they will miss the whole thing, for all the operations necessary to drag your vessel into the locks and to lift it some forty feet up in the air are performed with such skill and ease that you will find yourself peacefully sailing across Gatun Lake while you are still waiting for the show to begin.

Take first of all this matter of going up in your watery elevator. Little electric cars, running on rails parallel with the Canal itself, have quietly pulled the ship into the first lock. At once invisible hands have closed the gates behind you and your vessel begins its upward course. This experience is repeated twice more and before you realize how the thing is done, you are on the top floor, eighty-five feet above sea level.

On the day I passed through the Canal, we were very fortunate in having a perfect day. I can, however, imagine what it must look like when it rains. Soon afterwards I was to learn all about tropical showers, rains, deluges and cloudbursts, but on that particular morning, the sun was shining brightly and I was grateful, for once you have arrived in the actual lake, the scene becomes very depressing. Indeed, you will then begin to understand how Noah must have felt when on the thirty-ninth day of his voyage the earth had practically disappeared from view. On all sides you have evidence of steaming merrily across an inundated wilderness. Here and there the top of a tree, deader than any tree one has ever seen before, sticks out from the surface of the waters, looking like something one remembers from Doré's illustrations of the Deluge. Once upon a time, and not so very long ago either, those trees were enjoying life, liberty and an arboreal pursuit of happiness, fighting no doubt a million plagues and perils but nevertheless deriving considerable contentment from the fact that they existed. And around their bases there clustered the huts of happy little natives, dancing the rumba and the tarantella and the fandango to the merry strumming of their guitars, living on luscious tropical fruit and dying like flies—they, their loving wives and their loving children—dying like flies from every form and variety of preventable disease, from leprosy to psoriasis and from typhoid to phthisis. Nevertheless, like the trees which they were too lazy to cut down, they too were exercising their constitutional rights of life, liberty and the pursuit of happiness. I add this for the benefit of those sentimental citizens who are always able to weep bitter tears upon the fate of their poor little brown brethren who lived lives of unsoiled innocence until the wicked White Man broke rudely into their beautiful paradise and forced them to wear pants and made them brush their teeth and send their children to the Red Cross to be inoculated against typhoid fever.

We shall see a great many of those natives before we reach the shores of New Guinea, and no use to disillusion the reader right now, but the specimens of the natives one saw (rather sketchily, I confess) along the shores of Limon Bay failed miserably to come up to the beautiful specifications of those who are continually comparing the Brown Man's noble status before the arrival of the white despoiler and afterwards. Most of them looked as if they thought the business of existing much too much of a burden for their slender shoulders. The gift of life had been bestowed upon them without they themselves having been in any way consulted. There was nothing therefore they could do about their miserable and unhappy existence, just as there was nothing their hideous, mangy and flea-bitten dogs could do about being hideous, mangy and flea-bitten.

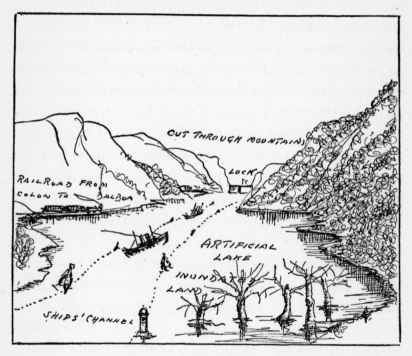

CUT THROUGH MOUNTAINS

LOCK

RAILROAD FROM COLON TO BALBOA

ARTIFICIAL LAKE

INUNDATED LAND

SHIPS' CHANNEL

MOST OF THE CANAL IS REALLY A LAKE

However, there had been one completely and perfectly happy day in their miserable lives. It had come to them almost a generation before, as they counted time, for old age was not a very common luxury among these poor natives. One fine morning an emissary had come to them from the absurd White Men who now seemed to be in control of their country and he had told them that they would

have to move, as their villages were in the way of Progress
(whatever that might mean) and that they would be paid
a handful of pesos for what really was not worth more than
a couple of centavos. Of course, they had taken the money—
none too gratefully, for the whole transaction had seemed
too preposterous to them to be real—and they had spent it
on cockfights and tickets in the government lottery and on
cheap jewelry for their women and indigestible sweets for
their children and of course they had lost every penny of
it again in less than a week and had moved to a cluster
of ramshackle shanties in some nearby valley, praying
ardently to their favorite saints that some day soon the
foolish government in Washington would decide to dig still
another canal and find it necessary to flood a few hundred
more square miles, right where they were now living.

I am making all this up as I go along. I may be entirely
wrong. They may have felt just as unhappy as the Pilgrims
leaving Scrooby but I doubt it, for few natives are of the
Puritan breed. If they were, they would be digging their
own canals and they would be traveling in solid comfort
on the steamers that sail from New York to San Francisco.
Instead of which, they live horrible lives, full of that constant irritation which is the result of never being quite well
and of dying much too young and of being forever filled
with a dread of the unknown, for although most of them
are now supposed to have been converted to Christianity,
their poor souls dwell in a constant twilight zone of horror
and to the fear of Hell has now been added those dreadful

instruments of torture with which the White Man pricks them in the arm to make them immune from typhoid and all those other plagues, which used to settle their problem of over-population without the interference of any systematic effort at birth control.

Come to think of it, this whole outburst is really due to the sight of those ghastly trees which still lift their whitened arms to high Heaven, for there are few things quite as sad to behold as the death throes of a tree. From my mountaineering days (long, long ago) I retain a deep admiration for the courage of the members of the arboreal tribe. Their will to live makes them overcome difficulties which even the bravest of men would hesitate to face. They will catch a feeble hold upon a mere handful of earth in some little slit between two rocks and there they will establish and maintain themselves in spite of blizzards, gales and hurricanes and in an atmosphere so rarefied that except for a few members of the insect family (who, if they must, will make themselves comfortable in a barrel of gasoline) no other living being is able to share their exile. Provided they survive the first ten years, they are apt to do fairly well and to reach a proud manhood, but with the first signs of advancing age, they are doomed. For the merciless winds know that these lonely intruders are now at their mercy and they will attack them with the fury of so many howling maniacs.

First they will make them sway and quiver and shake until they are bent like a gladiator beset by too many enemies. Next, with shrewd cunning, they will deprive them of their arms and fingers and finally they will twist their backs and break their legs, but the trees, like the heroes in some long-forgotten Carolingian saga, will continue to fight back, resting on the stumps of their strong old limbs, and when those too are worn away, a few defiant sprouts each spring will tell the world that even then the hopeless struggle has not yet been given up.

✦

I had better move on or I will get stuck right here in the Canal. Bridges, canals and tunnels have always had a special fascination for me. They seem to be one of man's most successful attempts at beating Nature within her own domain. Nature makes herself a beautiful landscape and digs a dozen deep rivers across the surface of the land and says, "There, my good children, now go and live among these lovely fields but remember, each one of you must stay on his own little lot, for that is the way I have arranged things and that is the way I want them to be run."

In the beginning, of course, Man is obedient enough, for what else can he do? But as soon as he has learned to fill a goatskin with air or cover a basket with clay, he will propel himself and his insatiable curiosity across that current to find out what secrets may lie hidden along the other shore. A little later he will discard his makeshift rafts for a boat and finally he will bid farewell to all these undependable modes of conveyance and build himself a bridge; after which, that river ceases to exist as a further impediment to progress.

It is the same with the tunnels which treat a mountain as if it were non-existent and unite countries which Nature for thousands of years had tried to keep separated from each other. And then there are the canals, the sort of canals like those of Suez and Panama, and these I like best of all. For they boldly thumb their noses at all of Nature's best-laid plans.

Nature constructed a granite barrier which was intended to divide the eastern and western parts of the American continent for all time and when our ancestors wanted to move from the coast of the Atlantic to that of the Pacific, they had to board a ship and make a detour of several thousand miles and often were obliged to spend several months trying to get round the Horn. And for one century —two centuries—three centuries—these little men on their little ships patiently obeyed Nature's dictates and even the riches from the Orient must first of all be taken from Manila to Panama, must thereupon be loaded on the backs of mules and Indians (I give preference to the mules as they were the more expensive of the two and therefore the more valuable), and must then be carried painfully across the mountain ridges of the isthmus, to be dumped into other galleons and sailed across another ocean to the storehouses of Seville.

The steamer and the increasing safety of the route by way of the Cape of Good Hope greatly reduced the distance between China and Europe, but the desert of Sinai and the peaks of Darien still made direct communications impossible. Then in the sixties of the last century, the Rockies were pierced by the iron tracks of the railway companies and on the fifteenth of August of the year 1914, the ships of all the world were invited to come and avail themselves of an aquatic short cut which allowed them to bid a definite and grateful farewell to the horrors of all Patagonian blizzards and which today allows the whole of the United States battle fleet to move from the Atlantic into the Pacific and vice versa in less than a day and a half.

By the way, the idea of connecting the two oceans with each other by means of a canal at this particular spot is almost as old as the first trail the White Man blazed across the Isthmus. Most of those early plans were of course considered completely fantastic. But many years ago, in looking for something quite different in the Dutch archives, I came across a carefully worked-out plan for a canal in this part of the world. It was made by a commission of Dutch engineers during the early quarter of the nineteenth century. I am sorry but I have forgotten the details of this project. But I mention it because prospective Ph.D.'s are always looking for suitable subjects to display their industry and erudition and this would be a most suitable subject. For the thing might have worked, the Dutch being fairly good at this business of digging canals, and it would have completely changed the course of history in the Pacific.

Unfortunately, there was the problem of yellow fever and

malaria—the same difficulty which contributed so distressingly to the collapse of de Lesseps' grandiose project in the year 1888. In the case of poor de Lesseps, the microbes of the Paris Exchange proved even more fatal than little *Anopheles.* With old King William, there would have been little danger of such an inside attack, for His Majesty was one of the cleverest financiers of the House of Orange, and that is no small praise. But even he, apparently, was baffled by the difficulties of so gigantic an enterprise and so nothing came of the idea except perhaps a footnote in one of the preliminary studies of one of our own numerous Canal commissions. And it really does not matter very much. A thousand years from now, when the flying machine shall have completely superseded the steam-propelled vessel, Theodore Roosevelt, who gave us the present "ditch," will also have been relegated to a footnote together with Goethals and Gorgas and all his other mighty contributors. For that is the way it goes in this world and perhaps it is the only sensible way. We live and we die and that seems about all that is of any importance.

# 2. SILENT ON A BENCH IN DARIEN

THERE is a pleasant promenade along the Pacific ocean-front of Panama City. It is usually referred to as the Sea Wall, for it follows the course of the old granite wall which once upon a time defended this city against its enemies from the west. Most likely, three centuries from now, someone will be sitting on a bench in a park on Governors Island and he will talk patronizingly about the New York of our own day, the ruins of which he can see just across the waters of the river, for everybody loves to play the role of the old Preacher in Ecclesiastes and mumble, "Vanity of vanities—all is vanity" down his beard and ponder upon the transitoriness of all human endeavor. For surely there are few sights which so clearly expose the futility of man's attempt to build for the ages as a visit to a dust-covered rubbish pile which once upon a time was the centre of a power or an empire.

This little town of Panama was no Palmyra, Troy or Babylon, but for several centuries it could claim to be the most important commercial centre in the whole of the New World. Its very smallness, even in the days of its greatest glory, shows on what a modest scale the European White Man began his experiments in plundering his American neighbors. The guide books inform us that the old city of Panama was "richly endowed with buildings and churches." The ruins of some of those churches still stand and from their size, one would put the population of the city during the early half of the seventeenth century at two or three thousand at the very most and the majority of those must have been soldiers or government employees, for under the monopolistic system of ancient Spain, there was no room for any sort of private initiative.

As for the natives, they existed on sufferance except once a year when they were needed as pack mules and were forced to carry the cargoes of the Manila treasure vessels across the mountains of the isthmus to be reloaded on the Atlantic side into still other ships of His Most Catholic Majesty's mighty armada.

To the modern travel bureaux, the old city of Panama is a veritable gift from Heaven—chock-full of glamour and picturesque bedevilment. In reality it must have been a terribly dull hole, one of those jumping-off places which one still finds along the northern coast of Australia—unhealthy, filled with a sort of brooding boredom, inhabited by the shabby-genteel servants of that extraordinary Spanish crown which dominated half of the known world and yet was in a state of perpetual bankruptcy, financing itself as it went along with disastrous loans from those same Jews which it delighted in torturing on those off days when it did not need their financial assistance.

One of the greatest mysteries of all times is the secret by

which Spain was able to maintain her position as a world empire and for quite such a long period of time in spite of her completely preposterous approach towards all colonial problems. To begin with, the system of government in her overseas possessions was slow, awkward and cumbersome to an almost unbelievable degree. Reports about the most important discoveries, events which could have completely changed the course of history, were either mislaid in the wrong pigeonhole or were left apparently unread for centuries at a time, and nobody seemed to care. In spite of the millions of dollars' worth of loot that flowed ceaselessly into the storehouses of Seville, His Majesty's sailors and soldiers were never paid on time. Indeed, they were often not paid at all. They were badly fed, they enjoyed no medical benefits and were no more mercifully treated than the Negroes on one of their own slave ships. And while the crews starved or rotted away from all sorts of most unpleasant afflictions, the officers grew lean and rich (Spanish politicians, in contrast to our own, grow lean the richer they get) and the slightest murmur of discontent was answered by repressive measures which make even the severity of Nelson's navy look mild and pale by comparison. Yet somehow or other, crews were always found, for life at home was even more miserable than on the quarter-deck of His Majesty's navy.

Yet somehow or other, this bizarre empire of grandees and paupers existed almost as long as most other empires that were and are infinitely better run and managed. Indeed, its cultural and religious and social framework sur-

vives to this very day, whereas, should the English leave
India tomorrow, nothing would remain to reveal their prolonged presence in that sun-scorched peninsula but a few
thousand miles of rusty rails, a number of decaying docks
and endless rows of empty buildings, left to the mercies of
Omar Khayyám's lion and jackal.

I am supposed to be writing about the Pacific and, properly speaking, the problem of Spain's colonial empire be-
longs to the Atlantic. I can therefore be very brief about
it and I am grateful, for I really have no idea where to look
for an answer. That whole world is much too Catholic to
be understood (or for that matter, appreciated) by a man
whose Calvinistic ancestors drowned their own country
rather than see it contaminated by the henchmen of a
Torquemada. I therefore can only guess. But I have a suspicion that it may have been the absolute formality of Spanish life which gave it the strength that allowed it to endure
long after it had ceased to be more than an empty shell of
its former self.

In our own Republic we are rather apt to dismiss all this
"formal nonsense" as something unworthy of the attention
of real he-men and sound believers in democracy. Since
contempt for the outer forms has by most people been
accepted as part of our national credo, I shall not waste
time arguing against it. But academically speaking, there
is something to be said in favor of a rather rigid code of
manners for the ordinary run of people. It may at times
make them look rather silly but it makes it possible for

them to play their little roles with a certain amount of dignity and that is an asset of incalculable value. Just as a man endowed with native intelligence can get along quite nicely without any formal education, whereas those not so fortunately placed will find it necessary to grab all the education they can, so a person of genius may make his own rules as he goes along, whereas the others had better stick to their Emily Post. That, at least, is what the example of Spain seems to show us. And the truth of this statement is borne out by a great many other organizations and institutions based upon a rigid code of manners. For there is a terrific strength in such canons of deportment. Not infrequently it was the only thing that kept whole countries and dynasties going, hundreds of years after they had lost everything else. The Roman emperors and afterwards their Byzantine successors somehow or other managed to maintain themselves for centuries by sheer strength of their rigid system of etiquette. Barbarian chieftains might swagger through the streets of their capital, loudly boasting of their intention to proceed to the Imperial Palace and throw the sacred occupant of that ancient edifice out on his holy ear, but once inside the Imperial Precincts and made part of the thousand year old ritual until brought into the actual Presence, their braggadocio and bluster evaporated like the dew of the fields before the sun of early morning and these wild brigands were quickly tamed by the awesome sight of embodied Tradition.

History is full of such examples. Like all good Protestants, brought up on the stern doctrines of John Calvin, I can theoretically prove that the Church of Rome has become a mere historical curiosity and will collapse the moment the Catholics take the trouble to ask questions and to think for themselves. But once inside St. Peter's, with the Pope himself slowly proceeding among the faithful, the old Egyptian fans (emblem of authority of the earliest of the Pharaohs) waving slowly and methodically over the head of one who is the direct successor of St. Peter, I begin to suspect that this branch of the Christian faith will still be a living issue to hundreds of millions of people long after the Protestants have destroyed their own cause through lack of just such a rigid ritual.

And what has enabled so many European and Asiatic dynasties to survive in spite of all revolutionary pressure from the outside? Nothing, I feel certain, but the need of most people for a definite form of ceremonial. Surely the English, the Swedes, the Dutch, the Danes, could, if they should so feel inclined, change their forms of government from a monarchy into that of a republic without the firing of a single gun. The men and women who rule over them would, if they were asked, most willingly give up a job which to most of them, most of the time, must be an almost unbearable burden. But they were trained to a high sense of duty. They realize that in their person they happen to embody a tradition which to the vast majority of their so-called subjects is almost as necessary as their daily ration of bread and butter. And so they stick and they deserve more credit than we are usually willing to give them.

Imagine a world without Gustaf of Sweden, Wilhelmina of the Netherlands, Christian of Denmark, Haakon of Norway—a world full of Hitlers and Mussolinis. God forbid! Democracy may find something irresistibly funny in tradition, but there is where Democracy might learn a lesson.

This little town of Panama, the ruins of which invited this soliloquy, was founded in the year 1519. That was two years before Magellan discovered the Philippines and more than half a century before the city of Manila became the capital of all the Spanish possessions in eastern Asia. Until then it therefore had existed merely as a starting point for the marauding expeditions which the Conquistadores (the lovely Spanish equivalent for our brutal word "gangsters") undertook against the unfortunate natives of the south. But once the Spaniards had definitely established themselves among the Philippine Islands, Panama became a most important link in that curious commercial chain which reached all the way from Asia to Spain by way of the Isthmus of Panama. There was no canal but that difficulty could easily and cheaply be overcome, as long as there was a sufficient supply of human beasts of burden. And so, twice a year, this part of the coast swarmed with thousands of miserable little men and women, for when it came to their native charges, the Spanish authorities believed in a complete equality of the sexes and they would just as soon beat a woman to death as a man.

Herded together like cattle, these miserable wretches waited out in the open, living God knows how and dying the same way. Finally the Spanish galleons would be sighted rounding Cape Mala and making for the Pearl Islands. They were an extraordinary looking craft, slow and cumbersome, the sixteenth century prototype of our own useless dreadnaughts. For long after the other maritime nations had changed over to the smaller and infinitely faster type of vessel, the Spaniards stuck to their galleons.

This unwillingness to change their ideas, in spite of all information to the contrary, was probably the main cause of Spain's downfall as a naval power. Those heavy ships, veritable floating fortresses, had been a great success in the comparatively quiet waters of the Mediterranean, but on the stormy seas of the Atlantic and the Pacific, where it was impossible to open their portholes and use their heavy guns, they became mere helpless targets. It is true that one successful volley from their hundred big guns would be fatal to the much smaller English or Dutch pirates who used to hunt these Spanish treasure carriers, but the fast-sailing heretics had learned the trick of maneuvering their vessels so rapidly through the danger zone where they might be hurt that in less than no time they would have reached a spot where the Spanish bullets would fly right over the tops of their masts while they themselves were sure that every one of their bullets was sure to be a hit.

It was a risky business, that final quarter of an hour which the Englishman or Dutchman needed to zigzag his craft

through that intervening half mile when he was at the
mercy of the Spanish ten-pounders. For they knew that any
moment might be their last, as the survivors of such encounters were only rescued from the waters of the ocean
to be hung from the yardarms of the ships flying the flag
of His Most Catholic Majesty, who had little use for heretics,
especially when they tried to interfere with his revenues.
But if the attacking party happened to be lucky and escaped
that initial shower of redhot iron, he knew that the rest was
merely a matter of time.

He would first concentrate his power upon the Spaniard's
steering gear and having destroyed her rudder, so that she
was no longer able to maneuver, he would attach himself
to his prey like a dog, harassing a wild boar, and would follow her, often for days at a time, until some fortunate shot
hit her in a vital spot and there was nothing left for the
poor Dons but to surrender or to drown.

Some of the naval encounters fought in this lonely part of
the Pacific must have had a touch of Homeric greatness.
For the tiny English and Dutch vessels, which occasionally
found their way to these uncharted seas, were from six
to twelve thousand miles away from home. All the harbors
along both sides of the American continents were closed to
them. Whenever they needed fresh water or were obliged
to beach their ships and scrape off the barnacles, they must
find some deserted cove where they ran the risk of being
murdered by the natives (to whom all White Men looked

alike) or discovered by a Spanish coast guard with the subsequent final chapter on the gallows.

The chances of victory were infinitesimally small. The percentage of failure was extraordinarily high. All the same and in spite of these handicaps, there had been enough of such foolhardy expeditions to make the Spaniards feel very uncomfortable and to proceed with great caution. And so, year after year, their treasure ships were made larger and more impregnable and provided with more and heavier guns, and after the middle of the eighteenth century, they were also protected by a few smaller vessels of the scouting type which preceded them to warn of the presence of "suspected sails" and to prepare for action.

But even that was no absolute safeguard, for a single one of these floating treasure chests might net its captors between a million and two million guilders and that meant a nice little house and a nice little garden and a life of ease and comfort for every member of the crew. Incidentally, that cheerful lust for plunder was the reason the British and Dutch ships were apt to keep the number of their officers and sailors just about as low as was compatible with at least a certain degree of safety. And this arrangement in turn forced the Dutch and English naval architects of the sixteenth and seventeenth centuries to invent all sorts of labor-saving devices, so that ten men might henceforth do what it had taken fifty in the bad old days when every one of those fifty would have claimed his share of the Spanish ducats.

I wish we knew a little more about these old naval architects than we do. But details about their lives are almost as scarce as those about the careers of their scientific and artistic contemporaries. Such a thing seems incredible to us who live in an age when, come depression, come good times, the publicity mills keep grinding twenty-four hours a day and when the private life of the Singing Mouse is considered quite as important as that of Kirsten Flagstad and when the sayings of any half-literate ward heeler are as carefully preserved as those of Albert Einstein. But when it comes to the great men of the Middle Ages and even those of the seventeenth and eighteenth centuries, we rarely have more than a bare outline of their existence, a few dates that had been incorporated into the acts of the notaries public who drew up their wills and witnessed their marriage ceremonies.

Even glamour seems to have made much less of an impression upon our ancestors than it does upon us, so that the facts about even as flamboyant a figure as Joan of Arc have to be dug out of the local archives of a few obscure villages before we can reconstruct them and re-create them in terms that are comprehensible to the modern reader.

But this may to a certain extent explain the success they achieved. They were able to take themselves and their work for granted. They were content to be good craftsmen and did not perform their tasks with one eye on the possible reaction from the side of those, who, lacking the skill to become first-rate artists under their own steam, undertook to tell the others "how it should be done." They were not obliged to waste valuable hours on trivial details with which to satisfy the ravenous appetite of the social scavengers who today hover forever around the Towers of Fame, and when they talked shop (and what artist can live without that agreeable pastime?) they exchanged ideas with their equals, with members of their guild, and not with amateurs.

There is no more fascinating story than that of the growth and development of the sailing vessel, from the clumsy square box of the Middle Ages to the clipper ship which could outsail all the earlier steamboats. But about the men who with an axe and a pair of callipers and a working model (the early naval architects never used blueprints but worked from models) launched the vessels which gave us our modern world, we know nothing.

Rembrandt happened to have painted one of those old shipbuilders and we probably can accept him as a true representative of his craft—a solid and completely reliable citizen who spent his days among his workmen and whose wife looked after the household. Common, everyday people, but they knew their job, and at the same moment the *Titanic* went down, the century and a half old wooden ship, the *Success,* crossed the ocean without a mishap. We don't know who built that old hulk, whereas we know who drew up the plans for the *Titanic,* and perhaps it is not quite fair to try and draw a moral from this unfortunate incident. But a bench along the sea wall of Darien is apt to make one think of a great many things.

I wonder what ideas came to poor old Balboa when he sat on his little peak and looked at this same ocean? Perhaps he was only worrying how he could get safely down again. As a matter of fact, it would have been much better for him if he had stayed where he was. Having your head

BALBOA

chopped off in the public square of Acla in return for a lifetime of hardships and privations must have been very disappointing, not to say provoking! But again, that is the way it goes and after all, I don't make history. I only write about it.

✦

Let me see! Where was I when I dozed off? I was trying to imagine what this spot must have looked like in the days when the accumulated plunder from the East used to be brought here after having successfully crossed from Manila to the isthmus. Once safely inside the Gulf of Panama, the galleons were thereupon unloaded, the boxes and bales were hoisted on the backs of the natives and the ghastly procession started northward across the isthmus.

The trip seems to have taken about a month. The number of those who fell by the wayside was enormous but in the end, the boxes and bales and barrels reached the Atlantic seaboard. Then they were once more moved from the backs of the Indians into the holds of a dozen Spanish galleons, for from that moment on, the perils of the voyage greatly increased, as the Leeward Islands and the Antilles offered excellent opportunities for surprise attacks from the side of the English and the Dutch, who had established themselves on these rocky islets, like the robber barons who during the Middle Ages used to infest the banks of the Rhine and for the same sort of economic purposes.

It was all very slow and cumbersome, this method of carrying treasure from one end of the world to the other, but somehow or other, it worked and for two centuries and a half, the gold and silver of Asia and America kept steadily flowing eastward.

Many historians have guessed at the total amount of treasure which Asia and the New World contributed to the well-being of Europe, but it is very difficult to get at any sort of reliable figures. But we are very well informed about the immediate effect of this unexpected deluge of gold and silver upon the economic life of the old continent. It was a disaster. The sudden appearance of so much actual cash among a people who for the last ten centuries had lived almost exclusively on barter, completely upset all previous notions about "a fair price." It ruined the carefully estab-lished balance of power between the different classes. It destroyed the power of the feudal squirearchy and it directly contributed towards the outburst of that spiritual revolu-tion which became known as the Reformation.

At first, of course, it meant a lot of "easy money" for a few lucky ones and for the less scrupulous members of the com-munity. God knows, the French, the English and the Dutch have produced a large number of navigators and colonial pioneers, of whom they had very little reason to feel proud and every reason to feel ashamed. But never, even in their most unfortunate moments of cruelty and greed, could they quite measure up to a Cortez or a Pizarro. For first and last and all the time, they were traders and their lust for gain was therefore always tempered by the consideration that a dead customer is no longer any sort of customer at all and that as long as a man is willing to sell his wares, it is none of your business to sell him your own ideas about life as it should be lived.

The Spaniards, driven to an almost incredible frenzy of intolerance and bigotry by half a thousand years of warfare with the Infidels, saw in every Indian another Moslem, either to be converted or slain. The people from the North realized that only a fairly contented goose could be expected to lay the much desired and highly profitable golden eggs. The Spaniards expected the eggs, regardless of the feelings of the goose. Just now it is perhaps not the happiest moment to say all this. We have gone in for loving our fellow-democrats of the southern continent in a big way and as "good neighbors" we should praise the marvelous achievements of our brethren below the Rio Grande. Perhaps our common dislike of Herr Hitler will make us overlook the fundamental differences that exist between the two Americas.

But once "Handsome Adolf" shall have gone to his eternal reward (and will *that* be a party!), we shall probably be as many million miles removed from each other as we always have been. Not because as a people they are less intelligent than we or less brave or less anything else, but by and large, they are followers of a different philosophy of life from that which is part of our own creed. They are followers of a totalitarian school of thought. Their ancestors changed from the totalitarianism of the Roman Empire to the totalitarianism of the Church of Rome, combined with the totalitarianism of the Habsburg dynasties.

Politically, they are now supposed to be their own masters, but emotionally and spiritually, they have never been able to cut themselves loose from the totalitarian ideology of their own past. In less highfalutin' language, they are Catholic-minded. Whereas we, who are descended from a people who were exposed to the Roman ideas for only a comparatively short space of time and who have always retained something of that primitive urge for personal freedom which has made us perennial heretics and rebels, are still "protesting" when it comes to the true essentials of life and are still unreconstructed rebels and uncompromising individualists. That does not mean that we fail to understand the value of teamwork in business and science and politics, whereas, especially within these fields, our South American friends are infinitely more individualistic than we can ever hope to be.

Nowadays, with everybody lustily shouting for tolerance (for himself) and for the brotherhood of all nations, it is not perhaps in the best of good form to bring this up. But a quiet bench along the water front of Darien invites honesty and clarity of thinking.

I have just spent a day in the Canal Zone and another day in the capital of the Republic of Panama, free and independent by the grace of Theodore I of the House of Roosevelt. I shall not reward their hospitality by indulging in any gratuitous comparisons. Only these two conflicting ideals about the Good and Desirable Life will never quite understand each other, no matter how often they may meet. They will, of course, come more and more in contact with each other as our physical world continues to grow smaller and smaller. But when they come together, it seems much wiser that they should openly recognize the fundamental differences which separate them from each other, rather than try to pretend to a common basis of thought and feeling which does not exist and never can exist as long as each side remains faithful to its own spiritual loyalties.

This does not mean that I am advocating a return to the medieval system of treating each other like implacable enemies. Perish the thought! I want us to be much better friends than ever and that is why I am so thoroughly opposed to all this futile talk about "loving each other," to which we are now being exposed whenever some South American Presidente descends upon our shore and we waste $3.98 of good gunpowder on himself and his charming lady, who wonders when she can escape from all this silly fuss and go shopping on Fifth Avenue.

I believe much more strongly in "mutual respect" between the different nations than in love, for this business of loving someone is always rather difficult and often quite risky. I may never again visit South America, for I confess that there is little there to interest me, and it may be my last chance to say all this. I am sitting here on a bench amidst the ruins of an old empire which died from two causes. One of these was a complete misunderstanding of even the most primitive workings of the most elementary laws of applied political economy. The other was its all-dominating conception of its duties as the Defender of the Faith.

Still conscious of those duties, the sons and daughters of the old Spain continue to defend that Faith and to defend it with a courage and a zeal which deserve our most profound admiration. But just now, still somewhat dazed by the conflicts between these two worlds—the world of the North, as expressed by a tiny strip of territory known as the Canal Zone, and the world of the South, as it reveals itself in the Sovereign Republic of Panama—I feel that we will all of us be much better off if we practice a little "realism" in our relations with our neighbors of the other half of our continent.

For almost four centuries, that vast expanse of water that lies before me was really an extension of the Mediterranean. Culturally speaking, it was part of the Latin heritage. Today, the Pacific Ocean is at the crossroads, so to speak. For it is rapidly becoming a sea dominated by the Stars and Stripes and our American civilization (unless we completely forget our antecedents) is one of the North Sea and the Baltic.

The next item on the program will probably be a conflict for the mastery of this most profitable stretch of water between the civilizations of the North Sea and the Baltic and that of the Sea of Japan. At least, that is the way it looks to this historically minded observer, who realizes that man does not really change a great deal in his reactions towards his fellow-man except in the methods by which he tries to impose his will upon his opponents. For in spite of all the well-meaning efforts on the part of lots of well-meaning people to tame the creature, *homo sapiens* is still a predatory animal, only different from the other beasts of the jungle in that he will also attack and destroy the members of his own species, something which no self-respecting wolf or hyena would ever do except in an absolute emergency.

POLYNESIAN EMIGRANTS

As I am merely writing a history of the discovery of this vast expanse of water, this side of the picture will not be touched upon in the present volume, and therefore, rather than waste time and show my ignorance of the political aspects of the case, I will at once proceed to one of the most fascinating and one of the least known chapters in the history of human courage and perseverance. I mean the discovery of the Pacific by the original explorers. I do not mean Magellan or Tasman or Cook, for the White Man did not appear upon the scene until much later, when all the pioneering had been done and when every inhabitable island had its cocoanut trees and its handful of inhabitants. But who exactly did the pioneering? and where did these people hail from and how had they been able to overcome those difficulties of space which had so completely baffled the Europeans that even in the days of George Washington they knew much more about Greenland and Spitzbergen and all the Arctic regions than they did about Australia and the Hawaiian Islands?

It is a most fascinating subject. It is still shrouded in a haze of romance and of mystery. The romance, upon closer investigation, did not prove to have been quite as attractive as we used to believe in the days of our youth. But the mystery remains. How could a few handfuls of people in small open boats and without any maps, compasses or modern instruments of navigation find their way across almost 70,000,-000 square miles of uncharted waters? The voyages of heavily laden Spanish treasure ships from Manila to Panama were interesting in a way, but we understand how they could be made in comparative safety and with a fair average of success. But to travel in an open canoe, even if it were a double one, from New Guinea to Easter Island, a distance of approximately eight thousand miles—that is something else again. Yet such trips must have been made and with great regularity, for once all the islands from New Zealand to Honolulu had been settled, their people never quite lost touch with each other. They sometimes failed to visit each other for years at a time, but they always remembered each other's existence and were conscious of a common origin.

The few survivors are now watching the twilight of their own race. There probably never was a lovelier world than that of the Pacific Islands, uncontaminated by the White Man. Not that the dwellers in this paradise were exactly angelic in their treatment of their neighbors or addicted to any of the major virtues of the Christian Decalogue. But even if they were wicked sinners, there at least was nothing miserable about them. For it is one thing to be a hungry savage in Tahiti, but quite a different thing to be a hungry bum on New York's Bowery. The former goes to the nearest tree and gets himself something to eat and even if he has to sleep out in the open at night, it is not going to make him catch his death of cold. Whereas the latter must either starve to death or humbly beg a free meal from the Salvation Army. The Army will give it to him, but only after it has reminded him of his deplorable lack of grace and that does not make the meal taste any better.

But why go on? For more than a century now, the White Man has been rampant among the benighted Polynesians. Small wonder that as a race, they preferred to die out. If I myself had to choose between the river (however cold or muddy) and a cup of coffee and a doughnut in a flophouse, swallowed to the accompaniment of the songs of Messrs. Moody and Sankey, I would know what to do and do it right away.

But these are hardly suitable thoughts for a quiet bench along the water front of Panama. And so I shall leave the thorny land of Darien and wade into that ocean which Magellan called the South Sea and which his followers, looking desperately for a gust of wind to lead them to a fresh supply of water and food, called the *Mare Pacifico,* the all-too-quiet Pacific Ocean.

Judging from present prospects, we may soon have to re-baptize it the Sea of Conflict—the *Mare Bellicoso.*

# 3. THE PREHISTORIC PACIFIC

*A chapter which makes our own western explorers look like rather clumsy amateurs*

THE ERRORS in this part of my book are of my own making. The truth it contains I borrowed from others, more familiar with the subject than I am. And to no one am I more deeply indebted for my borrowed plumage of erudition than to Dr. Peter H. Buck, whose book, *Vikings of the Sunrise,* is a book which every visitor to the Pacific Ocean should have somewhere in his luggage and which he should read before he starts upon the bundle of detective stories which loving relatives have bestowed upon him to wish him (or her) a *bon voyage.*

This distinguished doctor and ethnologist was a lucky fellow. He had a European father but his mother was a Maori and he was brought up in New Zealand among his mother's people so that he knows his Maoris as well as I know my Dutch and he was able to become one of our few ethnologists who are not obliged to look at strange races from the outside, but who are able to do so from the inside. And what that means, few people can understand quite as well as the present author. For he too leads a double life. He is completely at home in his adopted American world, but let him go back to his Zeeland village and for all his neighbors can tell, he has never been away at all. He still has the "feel" of his former environment and that is the only way in which one can ever hope to understand another race.

The eminent Peter Buck told me that he fully agrees with this statement and that it is nowhere as true as among the Polynesians. All over the Pacific, one has to be a native (or one must at least be fully accepted as a native) before it is possible to get into real contact with the original population. Wherever Dr. Buck went, his maternal antecedents made him a member of the clan. He was not considered an outsider and consequently could learn things which would forever remain hidden from even the best-intentioned and best-equipped field workers who were of European stock. At the same time, his European training made it possible for him to sift and classify all this information which he obtained by the family approach and to know how much must be deducted on account of racial pride, faulty memory or the desire to please the stranger. For these poor Polynesians, until exposed to the influence of the whaler, the trader and the missionary, were a people endowed with a most delicate sense of courtesy. They did not consider it good form to contradict a stranger. If the visitor from afar said, "Oh, that beautiful statue must be at least a thousand years old!" one bowed politely from the waist down and answered, "Your venerable worship, it is exactly a thousand years old." It made no difference that one had been present as a child when the village sculptor hacked this deity out of a piece of local sandstone. The foreign visitor believed it to be a thousand years and so it was a thousand years old.

There was only one way in which one could arrive at an approximation of the truth. Collect all the available evidence, collate and compare the different items and then by carefully gauging the local sense of civility, reach a final conclusion that seemed to make sense. No ordinary White Man could ever hope to do this. He would soon be exasperated by all the conflicting statements he heard and would denounce the poor heathen as incorrigible liars. The heathen would resent this reflection upon their surely praiseworthy "desire to please" and thereafter would never again open their mouths, except to tell the stupid foreigner some cock-and-bull story which they were sure he would swallow if only they made it preposterous enough. Hence such delightful yarns as that one about the famous calabash which the Hawaiian navigators were said to have used as some sort of primitive sextant while finding their way across the Pacific. There was not a word of truth in it, but an Oahuan chieftain, who knew his White Men and who saw a marvelous opportunity to put something over on one of his cocksure guests, invented it on the spur of the moment, and ever since, that calabash with its holes and its watery contents has made its appearance in every handbook on the Pacific and no matter how often contradicted, it will undoubtedly be repeated until the end of time.

I fully appreciate the attitude of this beautifully browned

THE WORLD OF THE POLYNESIANS

brother, for I have often been guilty of that sort of thing myself. Whenever, in the days of my youth, the inevitable ladies of uncertain age and good intentions but doubtful brain power used to descend upon my unfortunate native land in search of "local color" for still another book on "picturesque little Holland," and when all attempts to tell them the truth had failed, then I took a malicious delight in filling them with a staggering collection of assorted nonsense. And as the natives, noticing what was going on, would invariably join me in this delightful auto-da-fé, the results were apt to be almost as startling as those revealed by that famous Dutch classic known as *Hans Brinker; or the Silver Skates*. Ever since that book appeared, well-meaning Hollanders have sweated blood trying to convince the American public that it comes about as close to the truth as a story about America in which befeathered Indian warriors should race up and down Broadway while the President of the United States, in a buckskin coat, was amusing himself by shooting at buffaloes from the windows of the White House. But all to no avail. *Hans Brinker* for four successive generations has taught our people all they will probably ever know about "Life in the Low Countries." And when a better-informed critic dares to raise certain modest objections, he is told to hold his peace, or he is suspected of envy because he himself was never able to write a best-seller of such astounding vitality.

And so we poor natives have ceased to bother and long may they live—the Hans Brinkers of the North Sea and the

Hans Brinkers of the Coral Sea. For no person on earth can hope to defeat our female colleagues, once they are in search of local color and glamour. And so here is luck to them and to the dear lady of New Guinea who has made quite a reputation on "man-eating flowers." She at least had the delicacy to leave for the interior when she heard of the approach of a few real botanists.

✦

The learned Indian Swamis, whenever they accept a new pupil, ask him to begin by forgetting everything he has ever learned. It is one of the hardest things to do. Nevertheless, I too shall hereby request that you try and forget everything you ever knew about the early history of the Pacific. Forget what little you were taught at school. Forget such names as Magellan and Tasman and Captain Cook and all the other famous European navigators who fill so many pages of our histories of navigation. For they were mere miserable amateurs, mere beginners. Even such a highly competent skipper as James Cook, probably the most intelligent and undoubtedly the most humane of all the men who ever sailed the Seven Seas, dwindles down to very modest proportions when we compare him to those unknown Polynesian explorers who a thousand years before the arrival of the White Man had found their way from Tahiti to Hawaii and New Zealand, and every other part of this vast ocean.

In the first place, there was the matter of equipment. The

Europeans had regular ships. Not very luxurious from our own modern point of view but ships with decks and cabins and storage rooms and water kegs and masts and sails and pulleys and compasses and places where you could sleep and dry your clothes. Whereas the earliest Polynesian mariners had been obliged to find their way across thousands of miles of an uncharted sea in open boats with only the most primitive sort of sails, without any real shelter in case of bad weather, no compasses or any other sort of nautical instruments and nothing but a few calabashes in which to carry the necessary water. And yet they not only were able to reach such remote spots as Easter Island (which may have been just a piece of dumb luck), but once they had established themselves on a rock, about as conspicuous as a needle in a haystack, they were able to keep in touch with the islands they had come from. Often such communications were interrupted for half a century or so, but once discovered, these islands remained discovered and were not lost again, as was the case with the Canaries and Madeira and with Greenland and America, which were so completely forgotten by the men of the latter half of the Middle Ages that they had to be discovered all over again when Europe finally braved the displeasure of the learned doctors of theology who had declared that a belief in the existence of the Antipodes was a gross case of heresy.

About the earliest boats and the methods of navigation used by their Polynesian skippers, we of course know nothing. Theirs was a civilization of wood and of stone. They did not discover the use of metal until after they had come in contact with the White Man.

Stone implements, except in the form of weapons, of axes and spear points, were much too heavy to be carried on board such frail wooden craft. Therefore, everything connected with the old Polynesian boats was of either wood or hemp. It had been either hammered or woven. Even fire did not play any part, for whereas it is possible to burn a narrow groove into the trunk of a tree (a method employed by our own ancestors along the shores of the North Sea and the Baltic) the canoes these navigators needed for their trans-Pacific trips had to be much longer and wider than those that could be made out of a single tree trunk. The tree-trunk canoe still survives in New Guinea and in some of the smaller islands, but as a rule, it is now only used as a toy to teach very small children how to paddle and it is about as seaworthy as the rubber horses which we give to our own infants when we want them to get familiar with salt water.

Of course in one respect, the Polynesian was not different from the natives in every other part of the world. After he had come in contact with the White Man, he began to despise the work of his own hands. I shall have to come back to this a little later. It is a phenomenon one can observe in every part of the world. Primitive man is invariably struck by a most devastating sense of his own inferiority the moment he comes face to face with the White Man. The

**LONELINESS**

White Man is a god who can do everything better than
the brown man or the yellow one or the copper-colored one
can ever hope to do. Suddenly the native feels deeply
ashamed of his own accomplishments. Whatever his ancestors have bequeathed to him is either destroyed, hidden
or allowed to go to ruin. The most marvelous pieces of
sculpture are left to molder away in the jungle. Boats that
are museum pieces, so cleverly have they been constructed,
are pulled on shore and allowed to rot away. One tenth-rate
blunderbuss of modern construction is a treasure, but a
spearhead, carved with infinite care from a piece of flint, is
thrown among the kitchen rubbish. No longer will anyone
wear those woven garments which were as beautiful as they
were practical and which are now replaced by hideous cotton Mother Hubbards, which are fatal to the health and
make the women look like scarecrows.

One could continue this dreary list until one had mentioned practically every article of wear or ornament. And
this pathetic sense of humiliation does not stop inside the
tangibles of life, but also penetrates into the realm of the
spirit. Gods that have shaped the destinies of the tribe for
thousands of years are denounced as impostors and the
desert deity of Moses takes their place, together with his
Son-who-died-on-the-Cross and whom the Christians regard
as the founder of their own faith. The desert god is at least
more or less familiar to the Polynesians, for he is quite as
bloodthirsty, as vindictive and as ruthless as any of their
own heavenly potentates and the Old Testament speaks a

THE OUTRIGGER CANOE

language which all primitive peoples have understood—the language of hatred and intolerance and of arrogant contempt for everything foreign.

But what, so one asks oneself, can these poor heathen have found to attract them in that New Testament with its gospel of love and kindness and forbearance? The answer is that the first Whites who reached these regions were as orthodox in their beliefs as the skipper of Charles Darwin's vessel of exploration and that most of the earlier missionaries too were followers of Jehovah rather than disciples of Christ and that therefore the Polynesians were not really forced to make as abrupt a change as it might seem. And then there is that other fact which we should keep in mind while studying this highly interesting subject of the early interrelationship between the White Man and the native: the White Man's magic worked. Indeed, it worked infinitely better than that of the benighted heathen.

The magic of the White Man allowed him to build faster ships and stronger ones than those made by the Black Man. His guns were more deadly than the arrows and slingshots of the natives. His medicine really saved the lives of all those who were brave enough to swallow it. Indeed, everything that the White Man had created for himself was more efficient than that which was at the disposal of the colored man. Including his god, who always gave him the victory (usually a very easy one) over all his enemies.

And then, one day, he woke up. The White Man had not only brought him all the accursed camp followers of the great army of Progress, carrying misery, death and destruction among these poor creatures who had never been able to work up any sort of resistance against the ailments of the Old World, but now the White Man appeared in a new role. He came no longer as the trader or the missionary but as the conqueror and the explorer. He brazenly planted his own flag amidst the lands which since time immemorial had belonged to the descendants of the earliest settlers, as a record of their foolhardy bravery. He surrounded his flagpole with walls of masonry. Along the top of his parapets he planted heavy bronze cannon, and these destructive monsters were served by the lowest dregs of the White Man's slums—great big strong creatures who came to those islands without wives of their own and who helped themselves to the daughters of the natives with the same unconcern with which their masters had helped themselves to the natives' lands. And quite often other ships, flying a different flag from that which was limply hanging from the flagpole of the now familiar fort, would appear in the harbors of those islands and during the ensuing battle, the natives had to run for shelter or take a risk with those high explosives upon which the White Man depended for his ultimate success as a "colonizer."

Then there arose among the older and brighter of the natives a faint suspicion that they had committed a grave error when they had so eagerly discarded their own gods for those of the pale-skinned miracle-makers who had come to them during the days of their grandfathers. And here and there they had made a feeble effort to save themselves by a return to the standards and the traditions of a bygone age. But the hands of the clock of time cannot be set back and the attempt only resulted in further humiliation and defeat.

WHERE THE OLD GODS LIVE

There was no way out. One either had to accept the inevitable or die.

Be it said to the everlasting honor of most of the natives that they seem to prefer death to surrender. And those about to depart this world, with a sense of such utter futility as then descended upon most of the Polynesians, no longer care about a past that has lost all meaning. As a result, what little we know about the early history of the Polynesian discoverers of the Pacific has come down to us in the form of circumstantial oral evidence. For these islanders had not yet devised a method of preserving speech by means of the written sign or word when they came in contact with the members of our own race. And when they accepted the White Man's alphabet, it was the alphabet of the Bible and the hymnbook, for the white teacher (with a few notable exceptions) was not interested in the early chronicles of these sea wanderers who fitted so badly into his own scheme of cheap labor and easy profits. And so we have nothing but the endlessly repeated stanzas of the Samoan and Tahitian and Maori sagas to give us a clue to the terrific drama of their great age of exploration and conquest. These have now been collected, classified and studied by a few of the descendants of the men who wrote these chapters with their own flesh and blood. And so, while we still know very little, we can at least do a little guessing without the risk of wandering too far away from the narrow path of historical accuracy. But it is pitifully little, what has been preserved. The rest lies somewhere—God knows where—or it was drowned in the White Man's gin and rum.

## 4. MORE GUESSWORK

*By what route did these people from the Asiatic mainland penetrate as far as the coast of America?*

WHERE did the original Polynesians come from? We don't know.

We are fairly certain however that they are not of Malayan stock and that there is only a very small strain of Papuan among them, except in the case of the Fiji Islanders, whose bushy hair indicates a close relationship to the people of New Guinea.

As for Australia the Polynesians, although they eventually reached New Zealand, seem to have been as ignorant about the existence of the Great Southern Continent as our own ancestors were until a little over a century ago. They may have been occasionally blown out of their way and then may have set foot on the soil of the *Terra Australis Incognita,* but they probably felt the same aversion towards the Australian aborigines we ourselves do, as something that may possibly be human but only by a mighty stretch of our imagination. And being a race proud of its origin and conscious of its fine physique and with a lusty love for battle, they probably avoided all contaminating contact

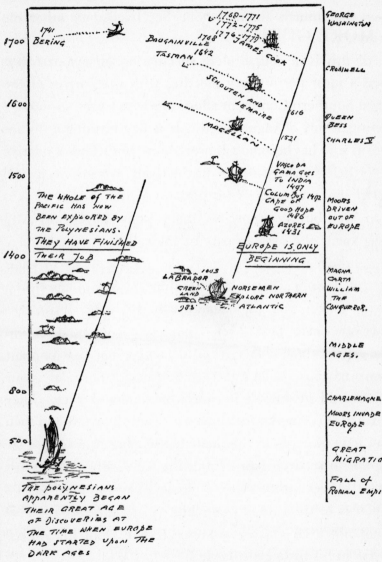

1741
BERING

1700

BOUGAINVILLE
TASMAN 1642

1768-1771
1772-1775
1776-1779
1768 JAMES COOK

GEORGE
WASHINGTON

CROMWELL

SCHOUTEN AND
LEMAIRE 1616

1600

QUEEN
BESS

MAGELLAN 1521

CHARLES V

1500

VASCO DA
GAMA GOES
TO INDIA
1497
COLUMBUS 1492
CAPE OF
GOOD HOPE
1486
AZORES
1431

THE WHOLE OF THE
PACIFIC HAS NOW
BEEN EXPLORED BY
THE POLYNESIANS.
THEY HAVE FINISHED
THEIR JOB

MOORS
DRIVEN
OUT OF
EUROPE

1400

EUROPE IS ONLY
BEGINNING

MAGNA
CARTA
WILLIAM
THE
CONQUEROR.

LABRADOR 1003
GREEN
LAND
983

NORSEMEN
EXPLORE NORTHERN
ATLANTIC

MIDDLE
AGES.

800

CHARLEMAGNE
MOORS INVADE
EUROPE

500

GREAT
MIGRATIONS

FALL of
ROMAN EMPIRE

THE POLYNESIANS
APPARENTLY BEGAN
THEIR GREAT AGE
OF DISCOVERIES AT
THE TIME WHEN EUROPE
HAD STARTED UPON THE
DARK AGES

with these creatures who were only a few steps removed from the animals among whom they lived their miserable existence.

All this is of course mere speculation on my part, but even a most perfunctory meeting with the natives of the Great Southern Continent affects one with a very unpleasant feeling, a sort of vague disgust. It is like meeting a distant cousin who has become a Bowery bum, but who is a relative nevertheless—whereas one instinctively recognizes in the Polynesian an equal. He is perhaps a little darker of skin than we, but no more so than many Europeans who have spent the greater part of their lives in the tropics, while their women, especially during the years of their youth, have a charm and a dignity and a loveliness which makes one understand why so many Europeans and Americans have been completely contented to bid farewell to their own civilization and adopt that of their native wives.

It would be foolish to deny that many of these dusky ladies gain perhaps a little more in size at a certain age than is exactly pleasing to the modern eye. But even then, they are apt to retain a pair of eyes that can still make a great many canoes proceed to a great many strange places. Whereas in the case of our white "stout forties," the eyes could not even make a goldfish deviate from his aimless course in his little glass bowl.

✦

And now I shall have to take to the maps, for geography should be seen and not heard. I shall avoid all reference to the mystic origin of the Pacific Ocean, for it will take a great many more years before we shall have enough reliable data to venture a few guesses.

The Pacific, as all the world knows, is a very large body of water. It covers 68,634,000 square miles, which is considerably more than the Atlantic, which is only 41,321,000 square miles. Also (in spots, at least), it shows a much greater depth than the Atlantic, for between the Philippines and Japan, the explorer's lead has gone down to 34,210 feet, whereas the Atlantic (near Porto Rico) can show no greater depression than a mere 27,972 feet. To give you an idea of what 34,000 feet mean, just remember that if you should stick Mount Everest, the highest of all our mountains, into that hole, the top would still be 5,000 feet below the surface of the sea.

As for its size, North and South America put together cover almost 15,000,000 square miles and the Pacific is therefore more than four times as large as the two continents, four times as large as Asia and almost twenty times as large as poor old Europe.

Where did that hole come from? Why is it there? Why did it happen? We have not the slightest idea. There exists of course that famous theory (devised by, I believe, a German scientist) which regards the moon as a chunk of terrestrial real estate which at an unfortunate moment, millions of years ago, was cast off by our earth and which there-

THE POLYNESIANS WERE SAILING EASTWARD TOWARD AMERICA

AT THE SAME TIME THE NORSEMEN WERE SAILING WESTWARD
TO LABRADOR

upon set up for itself in the lunar business. It may be true. It may be false. I don't know and I am contented to leave the problem to the editors of our popular Sunday supplements. It is a godsend to them when "The Tragedy of Mayerling" or "Sex Among the Insects" is beginning to pall upon their patient readers.

Meanwhile, there is another guess about that big pond which seems to have a much sounder scientific foundation. When Alfred Wegener's book on the origin of continents and oceans first appeared, it was received with that skepticism which the professors invariably bestow upon one of their colleagues who is guilty of heresy and who hints that there still are a few things to be discovered about our planet and its occupants. But Wegener could not be laughed out of court with a few learned sneers, for he was not only a geologist of note but a polar explorer with a great deal of practical experience. Wegener's brilliant idea is generally known as the theory about the continental drift.

According to this amendment to the first chapter of Genesis, in the beginning the earth consisted of just one ocean and on top of this vast expanse of water there floated a solid chunk of dry land, very much like the skin of cream in your morning cup of coffee. As you will remember from your experiments at your own breakfast table, when you take your spoon and stir your coffee you will notice that that bit of skin begins to change its shape. Cracks will be found where the skin is not as thick as in other places, and finally these cracks widen and little bits of the skin float away from the centre. That, as far as I can follow it, is the general idea underlying the continental drift theory of Professor Wegener.

If you happen to have an old atlas lying around which is no longer of any particular use to anyone, I suggest that you tear one of the maps of the world out of it and with a pair of sharp scissors cut out all the continents. Then when, after jigsaw-puzzle fashion, you fit them together, you will be most agreeably surprised to notice that they fit snugly into each other, like the pieces of a broken dinner plate.

Wegener felt convinced that the continents are still drifting and are moving further and further away from their original central point, which was somewhere near the polar regions. The people who five thousand years from now are supposed to fish Professor Wheeler's famous Time Capsule out of the Flushing garbage fields may know more about all this than we do. But even now, with insufficient data, we have begun to suspect that Alfred Wegener had something there, as the very suspicious man in the street would express it, and all of us should keep it in mind in case Adolf Hitler and Joe Stalin succeed in turning Europe into a Bolshevist hinterland. We can then move to that remote corner of Patagonia that promises to float furthest away from the homelands of these two great political philosophers and live happy ever after.

✦

And now, will you please look at your map. From the coast of eastern Asia to the coast of western America there reaches an endless series of islands. Some of those, like Australia and Borneo and New Guinea, are as big as a small continent. Others are mere rocks. I have forgotten their exact number but it runs into something almost incredible. In the Philippines alone there are more than seven thousand islands and islets. But it is not of those big ones that we think when we talk of the Pacific proper, for those western islands are usually identified with the Asiatic continent of which, once upon a time, they formed an integral part. No, the islands of the Pacific proper, the "blessed islands" of Captain Cook and the other early discoverers—these are in the heart of the Pacific and they are grouped together under the name of Polynesia, a combination of the Greek *poloi* or many and *nesos* or island.

Polynesia, on most atlases, does not include the Hawaiian Ridge, which is too far towards the north and which therefore was the last group to be discovered. But it is composed of the Sporades in the north, of the Phoenix, Ellice, Union, Manihiki and Marquesas in the centre, the Cook, Tubuai, Society and Tuamotu groups in the east and finally, one small rock 1,100 miles from Pitcairn which is the advance post of Polynesia towards the coast of America and which is known as Easter Island. It gets its curious name from the fact that the Dutch skipper, Captain Roggeveen, with a ship full of scurvy-infected sailors, discovered it on Easter Sunday of the year 1722. It is also known to all the world because it was here that the White Man came across one of the most extraordinary products of Polynesian civilization —the gigantic images of creatures that may have been men or gods (we don't know), done in a style which stands absolutely unique in the history of sculpture. For these stone giants with their blind eyes staring across the empty spaces of the Pacific seem the incarnation of doom. Even in a museum they will frighten you, for Dante, in all his infernal travels, never saw anything like that concentrated form of despair.

Nowadays, ships rarely visit Easter Island. There is nothing there for the average tourist and the island is chiefly interesting as an example of what was apt to happen to all these Polynesian settlements, once they had had the misfortune to come in contact with the White Man.

The Easter Islanders know nothing about their own past but they seem to have been a race of Polynesians with a considerable admixture of Malayan blood. They also must have reached quite a high degree of civilization, for without the help of horses or oxen and depending entirely upon their own mechanical contrivances, they had been able to move statues weighing more than fifty tons from the quarries to the place where they wanted to erect them. And furthermore, and without any assistance from elsewhere, they had devised some sort of written language of their own. Their pictograms are still to be found on the rocks, but we shall probably never learn what they mean, for the natives have as completely lost touch with their own earlier history as

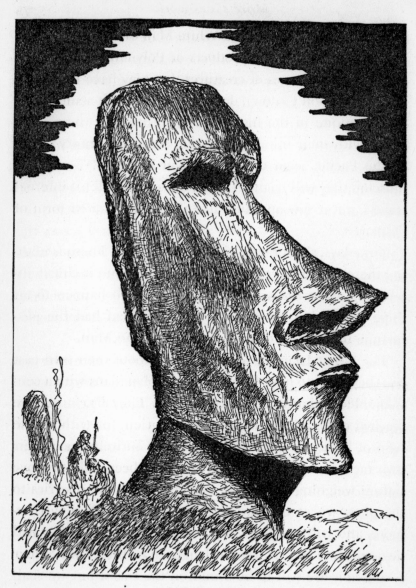

EASTER ISLAND
STATUES STARING WITH UNSEEING EYES INTO A FUTURE THAT NO
LONGER MAKES SENSE

the inhabitants of the valley of the Nile of the eighteenth century had done with the Egypt of the classical era. Only in the case of the Egyptians there had been a Rosetta Stone, which gave us a key to their mysteries by telling the same story both in hieroglyphics and in Greek. Whereas on Easter Island there is nothing left today but a mere handful of miserable people who do not even understand why those large statues are there. Yet among them there must be descendants of those Polynesian chieftains who during the fourteenth century of our era had ventured to cross the 1,400 miles of open sea which separated their new estates from the Tuamotu group and who, in the heyday of their power, appear to have ruled over as many as 6,000 subjects, which is quite a large number for that part of the world. Of those 6,000 there are less than 250 left.

The others were killed off during the first half of the last century. It happened during the days of the great guano boom. The islands along the coast of Chile and Peru, which since time immemorial had been the breeding place of myriads of birds, were thickly covered with bird manure. The Peruvians had used this fertilizer for hundreds of years before the arrival of the White Man, but it was not until the beginning of the nineteenth century that Europe, with its rapidly increasing need for richer crops, began to pay any attention to these treasures which the little birds had so gratuitously bestowed upon the western shores of the great American continent. Unfortunately, the actual operations necessary to remove these excremental deposits were of such an unpleasant nature that even the Chinese coolies (whose olfactory organs are not too nicely developed) drew the line at offering their services for this kind of a job. Whereupon the padrones from the Chilean mainland hired a few ships and a few troops, raided Easter Island and stole every able-bodied male for their own nefarious purposes. But somehow or other, the story leaked out. Today the survivors of the old Easter Island kingdom sit and quietly degenerate. Once in a long while a schooner brings a small group of anthropologists to their shores. But they have been preceded by so many others of this craft that there is nothing now for them to learn. And so, after having duly examined the only stone houses that were ever built anywhere within the Polynesian groups, they leave again by the next trading sloop and the islanders can once more sit and wait for the end.

This is not exactly the sort of South Sea story which you will find in the pamphlets of the travel agencies. But in a general way, it is the story of all Polynesians. Once a race of mighty warriors and lusty seafarers, they have now become part of the tourist trade of Messrs. Thomas Cook & Son and the other travel bureaux. Contented schoolma'ams from Kansas and fluttery ladies of uncertain age and an equally uncertain domicile in southern California pay their pennies to watch the creatures dive or dance for their "exclusive entertainment." And the poor fellows have sunk so low that they never pick up grandpapa's stone battle-axe to cleave the dumb skulls of their tormentors and thereupon consume their limbs, according to grandma's best recipe for tough meat. They take their pennies, beg for a cigarette and then go to sleep, or they die of boredom. And after all, why not? For what else is there left?

✦

The Polynesian group is connected with the Asiatic mainland by two island bridges. The northern one is called Micronesia because the islands are often microscopically small, a fact well known to all aviators who have tried to follow this route on their first flights across the Pacific. The Micronesian bridge starts just south of Guam, which in turn is the most southern of the group known as the Ladrones or Marianas.

There is something fascinating about the names of most of those Pacific Islands. No matter how terrible they may be to the eye, they appear upon our maps under all sorts of glamorous disguises. Take the Ladrones or Marianas. They tell whole volumes. When the sailors of Magellan first visited these little specks of land (in the year 1521) they noticed that the inhabitants (like a certain type of American tourists) would carry off anything not actually nailed to the deck of the ships. Wherefore they called this whole group the Islands of the Thieves. To our Anglo-Saxon ears, *los ladrones* sounds almost as charming as our "cellar door" does to a Spaniard. But the Spanish cartographers seem to have felt differently, for a century and a half later, they gratefully dropped all allusions to thievery and rebaptized

those islands the Marianas, in honor of Her Most Catholic
Majesty, Maria Anna of Austria, widow of King Philip IV
of Spain. After that, they remained the Marianas and under
that name they were sold by Spain to Germany in 1899,
immediately after the war with America. In 1914 they were
occupied by the Japanese and in 1918, they were made a
Japanese mandate.

The island of Guam is one of the smallest of the group
(210 square miles and 18,000 inhabitants) and was not included in this mandate, for we had taken possession of it
at the beginning of the Spanish-American War because we
expected to use it as a convenient naval station, in a possible
conflict for the mastery of the Pacific. For the same reason,
we acquired the mysterious isle of Yap which, strictly
speaking, does not belong to the Marianas but is part of
the Caroline group of Micronesia.

That island is apt to bob up in the news at all sorts of
unexpected moments. In the year 1919 it led to considerable
difficulties between ourselves and the Imperial Japanese
Government. For the Japanese, after the great grab of 1919,
had acquired the Carolines as well as the Ladrones and they
therefore claimed that Yap belonged to them. Washington
protested. Washington had every interest in doing so, as
Yap is the meeting place of the cables from America to
China and from America to the Dutch East Indies. Since
however the United States had not ratified the treaty of
Versailles and had persistently refused to have anything to
do with it, our government could pretend that all these

arrangements were something that did not in any way affect
us and put up a fine pretense at indignation at being even
asked to do such a thing as surrender one of our proudest
possessions—the island of Yap.

In the end, the matter was negotiated and after a solemn
conference held in the city of Washington (the agreement
was signed on December 12, 1921) it was decided that while
America recognized Japan's mandate over all these islands,
Japan agreed to give America free access to the islands "on
a footing of complete equality," which means one of those
joint directorates which either of the high-contending
parties (whenever it happens to suit his convenience) can
use to start an argument and then throw the other party
out with an indignant "How dare you!"

The development of wireless has of course greatly dimin-
ished the importance of both Yap and Guam as cable stations but trans-Pacific fliers now need these tiny spots of
dry land for their flights between America and China, and
we shall undoubtedly hear a great deal more about them
when the moment has come to decide for once and all (read
"fifty years") which nation is to be recognized as the supreme master of the Pacific.

In that case, the 7,155 Yapers or Yaponese or whatever
the natives call themselves will probably fare as badly as
the Brown Man has always done whenever his white masters
fell out among themselves and used the Brown Man's territory to engage in a free-for-all at the expense of his unwilling but helpless hosts.

But we must get back to the Micronesian island bridge. It starts on or about longitude 140° east of Greenwich among the islands known as the Carolines. These were first sighted in the year 1527 by a Spaniard who, for reasons best known to himself, called them the Sequeira Islands. A century and a half later, they became the Carolines in honor of King Charles II of Spain. The Spanish government however remained indifferent about their existence until the year 1875. Then it sent a few officials who accomplished nothing, except that they were on the premises when the men-of-war of other nations dropped anchor in their ports. In the year 1899 at the remnant sale of her colonial empire, Spain sold the Carolines to the Germans. They in turn held them until the World War, after which (by grace of Versailles) they too were turned into a Japanese mandate.

Traveling eastward, we first of all reach the Marshall Islands. They had been discovered in the year 1529 but they were not really explored until the year 1788 when they were visited by two British captains, Gilbert and Marshall. Today the Marshall Islands are a Japanese mandate, while the Gilbert Islands have remained under British control.

The Micronesian bridge then turns slightly southward towards the group of the Lagoons or Ellice Islands. Most of those, like the Gilbert Islands, are atolls, low coral islets which rise only a few feet above the surface of the sea and therefore are of no particular interest to western nations, for it is difficult to defend them. At this point, the Micro-

THOSE WHO HAD MISSED THEIR ISLAND

nesian bridge joins the great Pacific ridge, which runs from
south to north and which is known as Polynesia.

This brings us to the second one of our two island
bridges, the one that is situated further towards the south.
It is called Melanesia because the inhabitants show evidence
of having become slightly mixed with the races of New
Guinea and therefore have the darker skin (you will remember that *melas* is the Greek word for "black") which
is so typical of all Papuans. Whether New Guinea is part of
the real Melanesia or not is a question which has been much
debated but which I prefer to leave to the professors who
read papers upon the subject when they meet each other
for luncheon in Washington or Buffalo during their Christmas conclave.

Going eastward across the Melanesian bridge, we first
reach the Louisiade Archipelago. These islands were
brought to the attention of the White Man in the year 1606
by one Luis Vaes de Torres, the same Spaniard who was
the first European to navigate the strait which separates
New Guinea from Australia and whom we therefore shall
meet again a few pages further on. In the year 1768, the
famous French navigator, de Bougainville (the godfather
of the lovely bougainvillea vine) happened upon this group
while traveling westward from Tahiti and Samoa. Being a
faithful servant of the Crown, he rebaptized the islands
after the patron of his expedition, King Louis XV of
France, and the name has stuck ever since.

From there the bridge turns slightly towards the north and then reaches the Solomon Islands. Once upon a time these were feared as the grizzly headquarters of the head-hunting industry of the Pacific, but today they are the home of a rapidly dwindling race of rather dejected Christians. As for the name they bear, the Solomon Islands, they were actually called after that great Hebrew king who built the temple of Jerusalem and who established such cordial relations with Abyssinia that the world still talks about them. This is the way it happened.

The Spaniard, Alvaro Mendaña, who got official credit for having discovered them (though other White Men most likely had been there before him), was so delighted with the rich aspect of his newly found territory that he hopefully baptized them after the richest monarch of antiquity, the Islas de Salomon. Alas, the poor man must have been greatly afflicted by thirst or scurvy when he identified the Solomon Islands with the old Ophir! For when subsequent visitors tried to land there, they found the natives so ferocious and the country so miserably poor that it was not until the year 1838 that the coast line could at last be placed on the map with some degree of accuracy.

An attempt to bring the natives within the sphere of European civilization was fatally ended in the year 1845, when the first vicar-apostolic of Melanesia was murdered (and probably eaten) by the aborigines. In the middle of the last century, they were still so far from safe that an Englishman, visiting them on his yacht about 1856, was captured by a band of natives and disappeared without leaving a trace—not even his skull.

But then the planters on those islands that lie slightly further towards the southeast, the Fijis, and those of the

FIJI

mainland in the west began to feel the need of "free labor" to work their plantations. These gentlemen meant business and soon their well-armed schooners succeeded in breaking the resistance of the poor Solomoners, who still fought with the stone axes of their primitive ancestors and who were thereupon packed off to Queensland and the Fijis, as the

Easter Islanders had been taken to the guano fields of Chile.

In order to put an end to this scandalous state of affairs, Great Britain officially annexed the Solomons in the year 1893. During the Great War, a few of the islands belonging to Germany (which in the meantime had also established itself in the Bismarck Archipelago, further towards the west) were taken over by the Australians. In 1920, by a special mandate from the League of Nations, the islands were handed over to the Commonwealth of Australia. But I regret to say that in the matter of administrating colonies, democracies as a rule fall far behind those countries where such matters are handled by the Crown. For as recently as 1927, there was such a serious outbreak of revolt among the woolly-haired Solomonians and so many missionaries were killed that the whole group had to be placed under martial law. Since then, the natives seem to have become resigned to their fate, and they are now dying off at a high rate of speed, for when you deprive a Papuan of his main interest in life—the highly gruesome but exciting sport of head-hunting—he loses all initiative and is ready to die.

What use building the fastest war canoes and polishing the sharpest stone knives and keeping yourself in perfect physical trim, when the White Man decides that you can only use your boat to go fishing and that that stone knife, on which you worked for so many years to get that razor-like edge, may never again touch human flesh?

Better cease living altogether than become the laughingstock of all the girls who (properly brought up) would never consider marrying a weakling without a single human skull to his credit!

This may strike you as an altogether reprehensible and repulsive point of view. But as you may remember, no Spanish government, no matter how liberal and enlightened, ever dared to deprive the populace of its accustomed bullfights.

In England, even the sport of killing Germans has never been allowed to interfere with the happy chase of the unhappy fox. And right here at home, while all college presidents may inveigh against certain forms of sport which often prove harmful or even fatal, they find themselves completely helpless against that mysterious inner impulse which makes every small American boy turn to the nearest vacant lot to prove his skill and courage, just as every male child of the western part of the Pacific felt compelled to venture forth into the jungle to show that he had the makings of a real he-man.

I realize of course that there is a vast difference between kicking a leather ball around and playing with human heads. But whether we like the game or not, all of us know that without football, our colleges would soon degenerate into Marxian debating societies and something else even less desirable. And those who know their New Guinea or who for a long time have lived among the original inhabitants of the Solomon Islands, realize that it is the abolition of the native sort of football which has done more to bring ruin and degeneration among these poor heathen than anything else, including the obligation to wear clothes and to

NEW GUINEA CANOES

trade for cash with the visiting representatives of the White Race.

After leaving the Solomon Islands, the Melanesian bridge turns sharply southward towards the Santa Cruz group, the New Hebrides and New Caledonia. Santa Cruz, like the

Solomon Islands, was first sighted by the Spanish captain, Alvaro Mendaña. Today it is a British protectorate.

The New Hebrides (some 90 in all) were discovered by that strange Portuguese adventurer, Pedro Fernandez de Quiros, whom we shall meet again a little later. He visited them in the year 1606 and, firmly convinced that they were part of the long-suspected Southern Continent, he bestowed upon them the high-sounding name of Austrialia del Espiritu Santo. It looks well on the maps, but the reality is far from imposing.

After a long period of wrangling between the French and the English during the first three-quarters of the nineteenth century, the islands are now a condominium administered jointly by High Commissioners of France and Great Britain. The original name was changed for that of the New Hebrides, after the visit which Captain Cook paid to this part of the world in the year 1774, but you may still find it on a few of our modern maps, for such names are as persistent as certain kinds of French perfumery. No matter how hard you may try, you cannot get rid of them!

Due south of the New Hebrides lies the small Loyalty group. These were not discovered until early in the nineteenth century and they now belong to France, together with the much more important island of New Caledonia. New Caledonia is 250 miles long and from 25 to 35 miles wide, quite a big piece of dry land for that part of the world and made very difficult of access by a series of dangerous coral reefs.

Captain Cook discovered New Caledonia in 1774, hence its English name. The English were not interested in it and this gave the traders in sandalwood a most welcome opportunity to abuse the natives in the usual outrageous fashion until the year 1853, when France took possession of New Caledonia and turned it into a penal colony. The less said about this establishment, the better. The people of France have many admirable qualities. A gift for colonizing is, I am afraid, not among these. On the other hand, they somehow manage, even in the most remote parts of the world, to provide the hungry pilgrim with a dinner that makes him forget the endless procession of badly cooked cabbage dishes (believe it or not, but the stuff is specially imported in tin cans) to which British officials, in the full glory of their European accoutrements, will sit down with apparent relish and satisfaction. For this relief I am willing to overlook many rather painful shortcomings in such details as the Romans would have grouped together under the heading of "law and order." But what will you? I have so far discovered only one race which has struck a happy medium between East and West and a sense of modesty forbids me from mentioning it. So I had better drop the matter here and now.

After leaving the New Hebrides group we once more turn sharply eastward until we reach the Fijis. The name Fiji calls up visions of bushy hair and indeed, the bushy hair is still there, but the old reputation of the natives as terribly dangerous, cruel and cunning cannibals no longer

WE TALK ABOUT PACIFIC ISLANDS FORGETTING THAT THEY RUN
ALL THE WAY FROM THIS

TO THIS

holds true. They have lost all their former spirit and are
as meek as sheep. The "Men of God" have been making
up for lost time among these benighted heathen. They have
forced their women into hideous Mother Hubbards. The
children ditto. The sorrowful God of the Jews has killed
the old lusty love of battle. And like people lost in a dream,
these former warriors now wander through the Main Street
of their capital city which the English have succeeded in
making look exactly like one of the less attractive thorough-
fares of Bridgeport, Connecticut.

The Fijis (at least, the northern part of them) were discovered by Abel Tasman, the Dutch navigator who was the
first white man to sail around Australia, although he had
not the slightest idea of what he was doing, since he mistook the only part of the continent he saw for a part of
New Guinea.

All the same, Tasman did some very valuable work as an
explorer, for he not only put the island of Tasmania on the
map but he also was the first man to catch a few glimpses
of New Zealand, which he called by that name after the
old Zeeland in the Dutch Republic.

From New Zealand he went northward and eastward
as far as the Tonga or Friendly Islands. Quite naturally in
doing so he passed along the coast of the Fijis, which he
called the Prince William Islands. However, after his disastrous meeting with the natives of New Zealand, who had
killed several of his sailors, he was careful not to set foot
on land unless he was certain of his welcome, and the Fijis

therefore remained a hazy outline on a sketch map tucked away in a ship's journal.

The southernmost group, which Tasman failed to sight, was discovered by Captain Cook in the year 1773. But the Fijians remained a most inhospitable race, for when Lieutenant Bligh of *Bounty* and Hollywood fame tried to replenish his water supply on the Fijian shores, he too met with such a menacing reception that he fled for his life.

From the point of view of the great Polynesian migrations, the Fijis are very important because it is here that the Melanesian bridge joins the real Polynesian ridge and it is also here among the 250 islands of this group that we bid farewell to the Papuan characteristics, the fuzzy hair and the flattened out noses which make the poor Fijians in their hideous cotton garments so very unattractive to most Europeans. But our great-grandchildren won't be bothered by this problem of Fijian pulchritude. For the original stock— already a pretty bad mixture—is now rapidly being changed by an influx of some 70,000 East Indians. The majority of these were coolies—work-animals brought to the islands by the white plantation owners, looking for cheap labor and finding the Fijians unwilling to become the sort of beast of burden which at practically no expense could be imported from the scorching plains of southern India.

But why go on? That story of the deliberate ruination of a whole race is the story of the White Man in his relationship to the people of the Pacific Ocean. There are those who claim that it is not yet too late—that something can still be done about it. I doubt it. If it were merely a matter of all the vile physical ailments the White Man carried to these islands, the famous Dr. Lambert of Suva might in due course of time have saved them from their aches and pains and with Mr. Rockefeller's millions behind him, he could undoubtedly have cast out the quintillions of quintillions of microbes which are the Brown Man's chief inheritance from his white benefactors. But no physician can cure the patient whose soul has been killed.

I shall never see these islands again. I don't want to. The final recollection was enough to cure me of any desire to retrace my steps in the footpath of Abel Tasman. Our ship was about to leave. Toasts of queer vintage were being drunk to the gangplank. Bushy-haired natives were dragging white men up the gangplank. Those white men and an occasional white woman were too drunk to stand on their own feet.

The next day was to be a Sunday and the patient Fijian would put on a clean Mother Hubbard and go to his little chapel to be told of the perfections of that civilization which on the previous night he had had to fish out of the gutter. A hundred years ago, he would not have been so charitable. He would have crushed the creature's skull with his heavy truncheon. Which, by and large, would have been a much better solution!

# 5. THE EARLIEST HISTORY OF POLYNESIA

POLYNESIA?" said the charming lady with the lovely smile and the satisfied air of someone who was going to show the Man-who-had-written-a-Geography that she too knew her little world. "Why of course! Polynesia is the island where they have the bay of Waikiki, where you go riding in those funny canoes."

It would have been ungracious to correct that rather vague statement. The bay of Waikiki is undoubtedly part of Polynesia. And after all, what does it matter? The movies and the song-writers now provide that part of the world which really counts (the shopgirls and their gentlemen friends) with all the information that particular part of the world needs. The professors know where Polynesia is but they will never have the money to go there. Those who have the money to go there know what sort of bathing suit should be worn on the beach of Waikiki when you let those handsome native boys take you surf-riding in one of those funny canoes. And no great harm is done—until you sit alone on some rock along the southern shore of Oahu, far away from that up-and-coming metropolis on the other side of the island, and stare out over that ocean which for

some queer reason looks vaster and lonelier than any ocean
you had ever imagined and lose yourself for a moment in
a dream of the past. Then the mere word Polynesia assumes

THE OTHER SIDE OF OAHU

proportions of such tragic magnificence that they almost
overwhelm you by their grandeur.

I use the term "magnificence" in its original meaning as
something "great in deed" and "characterized by admirable
or splendid achievements," for nothing else can describe
these voyages which the earliest pioneers of the Pacific
undertook more than a thousand years before the arrival of
their white-skinned competitors. And I would also like to
apply it to the people who manned these crazy little cata-

marans, for even today they (or what little there is left of them) stand apart from the rest of the world by reason of their splendid physique and by a bearing which gives them an air of quiet dignity, even in this, their season of dire adversity.

Nobody knows whence they came, and as they did not learn the art of writing, their own traditions are entirely oral and the human ear is not a very trustworthy instrument when it comes to dates and years. But here, as far as we have been able to reconstruct their adventures, is a guess at their earliest history.

Of one thing we are certain: the Polynesians are not related to the dark-skinned and bushy-haired natives of Melanesia nor to those of New Guinea or Australia. They are on the contrary not very far removed from the White Man of central Europe and it is possible that we had some sort of common ancestors who hailed from India, who were obliged to leave that teeming peninsula on account of overpopulation, and who thereupon decided to try their luck elsewhere, part of them going westward by land while the others proceeded eastward by way of the sea.

As to the exact date of their departure, we know nothing. But that exodus must have taken place before the introduction of Brahmanism throughout the Indian peninsula, as their own religion shows no influences whatsoever of that highly complicated faith and as none of the curious rituals connected with the Brahman ideal of culture have ever been found among the true Polynesians.

However, there is one item which pleads strongly in favor of the theory that originally these Polynesians had hailed from India and that is their knowledge of a great many crafts which were practiced in that part of the world, thousands of years before the Greeks had ever learned how to make a crude stone wall or how to forge a steel sword. Boat building, too, had been an Indian specialty and the first of these Polynesian pioneers seem to have been expert marine engineers. Quite naturally, as they got more and more separated from their homeland (both in time and in space), their hand began to lose its cunning and their technical skill had begun to dwindle more and more until in the end, they had forgotten a great many things they had known in the old home country.

Even then, they must occasionally have remembered something from the past, for otherwise we would never have come across such curious constructions as those stone villages which have been discovered on Easter Island, way at the other end of the Pacific. But our own history is there to show us how such things will come about.

The earliest settlers along the Atlantic seaboard had, with their own eyes, seen many of the cathedrals and churches of Europe and when they came to the New World, they brought with them not only a recollection of how such buildings should be constructed but they were still part of the architectural traditions of their old guilds, and those traditions lived on in the American wilderness and they crossed mountains and plains and swamps and they under-

went all sorts of modifications, but even so, the Gothic outlines of a medieval cathedral or the simpler silhouette of
a Roman basilica will suddenly face you in a landscape that
is as far removed from Milan or Chartres as Samoa is from
Benares. And those places of worship were not the work
of a bright young man who had studied at the Beaux Arts
in Paris but they were the product of the imagination of a
simple carpenter who had inherited his father's and grand-
father's skill and their traditions.

Of course, in our own case, only a few hundred years
separate us from our former homes and we have books and
blueprints to guide us. Whereas the eastward progress of
the Polynesians must have begun at a much earlier date
and they developed nothing in a pictorial way to assist their
memories except those grass maps which helped them find
their way across their island empire.

But let me remind you once more that when I use such
expressions as "they must have begun," I am indulging in
a mere generality to cover my ignorance. For even the experts are still completely lost when it comes to any definite
dates. This may be a blessing in disguise to the Polynesians.
Some say that the great voyages started in the year 600 of
our era and others claim that they did not really begin
until four centuries later. Even if the followers of the latter
school of chronology are right, it is still a very respectable
date when we consider that at that moment no Norman
had as yet set foot on English soil. And four more centuries were to go by before Columbus performed the much

simpler feat of sailing across the Atlantic Ocean. But unless we find some really concrete evidence upon the subject (which is most unlikely) we shall always be obliged to guess and within the realm of the historical surmise, a short chapter is as good as a long one. Better even!

Now another deep and dark puzzle. By what route did the ancestors of the Polynesians reach their Melanesian and Micronesian island bridges and when and in what fashion did they cross these bridges to reach their ultimate homes in the east?

The Polynesians, like all other peoples, cherished a tradition about an ancestral paradise. In their case, it was called Hawaiki and that name has since then been associated with the island of Java which the early geographers called Jawi. We know that Java was considered one of the richest and most desirable parts of the world long before the northern and western parts of Europe had become fit for human habitation. We also know of the establishment of a Hindu colony on Java about the same time that Augustus made himself the head of the Roman state. We have a large number of monuments to show us the existence of a flourishing Buddhist culture in Java in the days of Charlemagne, long before William the Conqueror founded his Norman kingdom in England. But at what precise date the advance guard of these Indian emigrants reached the shores of those islands which today are part of the Netherlands East Indies, we shall probably never find out. The marvelous sculpture of the Borobudur in eastern Java shows us that the people who had built this Buddhist shrine were already familiar with a sort of vessel which was not to be built in Europe until hundreds of years later. But when the Borobudur was erected, the Polynesian wanderers had long since left, and their voyages must therefore have been made in those rather primitive double canoes which have now apparently completely disappeared from use, but which were still the chief mode of aquatic conveyance when Captain Cook explored the Pacific only a century and a half ago.

This double canoe was just that, no more and no less. Two large seagoing canoes were connected with each other by means of wooden beams. A sort of deck was thereupon placed on top of those beams. This wooden deck held the light mast and a straw hut was also added for the protection of the women and children who were to accompany their menfolk. Under those conditions, the sailors could dispense with all outrigging apparatus, for the two canoes acted as each other's outrigger and the craft could not possibly be upset except by a very severe storm, in which case it would have been sunk in spite of all outriggers.

Just to hear it described or even to see a picture of such a vessel cannot possibly give you a very good idea of the seaworthiness of these ships. They must have been much safer however than the clumsy wooden boxes in which the Greeks crossed the Aegean and in which the Romans sailed along the coast of Africa. For the skippers of the old Mediterranean rarely ventured out of sight of land, whereas the Polynesians eventually found their way from one end of the Pacific to the other and were able to maintain regular communications between such islands as Hawaii and Tahiti and New Zealand, which are more than a thousand miles removed from each other.

As for the instruments of navigation which were at the disposal of these early mariners, there were not any! The famous story about the calabash with the holes in it, which could be used as a primitive sort of sextant, we now know was part of an elaborate practical joke, played by a native chieftain upon a too inquisitive European visitor. And the maps made out of reeds were so primitive that they can only have been of use to people who were already completely familiar with the lay of the land (or rather, the lay of the water) and who probably could have done just about as well without them.

But for one thing. Having from earliest childhood been brought up on board a ship, the Polynesians of the Polynesian Middle Ages, quite like our own ancestors of the Christian Middle Ages, must have been able to read the stars as today we read the signs along one of our automobile highways.

There remains the question of how they were able to carry sufficient provisions for voyages that often must have covered several thousand miles. Unlike the contemporaries of Columbus and Vasco da Gama, there was no hold on board their ships in which to stow away barrels of pork and hardtack. Neither was there any extra space for water. The water could be transported in gourds but most likely the

Polynesians waited for the rainy season before they started upon a lengthy voyage and in that case, they could depend upon a plentiful supply easily caught and preserved (for a few days at least) in their watertight mats.

As for the food they needed, in the first place they were an extremely sober race who could subsist upon about one fifth of what a European sailor would need and in the second place, they were probably much cleverer at smelling out a piece of dry land than poor Magellan, who managed to sail all the way from Tierra del Fuego to the Philippines without ever seeing anything that resembled a respectable island and who, in the end, was obliged to boil and serve up the skins that protected the base of his masts to still the hunger of his scurvy-infected crew. But then, Magellan, being still a faithful son of the Middle Ages, still depended for his guidance upon his patron saint rather than upon his knowledge of navigation.

The Polynesians, being heathen, had no saints to come to their rescue and had to rely upon their own ingenuity. They gave evidence of being extremely resourceful by the introduction of a method of navigation which never seemed to have dawned upon even those Vikings with whom they had so much in common. For one thing, unlike their European colleagues, the Polynesians were never in a hurry. They could take their time. And so, whenever over-population of their old home forced them to pull up stakes and try their luck elsewhere, they apparently spent years getting ready for their next trek, and when they started, they moved *en masse*—ten, fifteen or twenty large canoes with hundreds of women and children and with all those animals which were not large enough to prove a nuisance nor too danger-ous to be tolerated as fellow-passengers.

Once away from land and out at sea, these fifteen or twenty canoes did not sail in a group, as the European mer-chantmen of the Middle Ages used to do for the sake of greater safety. The question of safety hardly entered into their calculations, for they were much better fighters than the natives of either the Melanesian or Micronesian islands and so they need not have any worries on that account and they could devote themselves primarily to the business of navigation.

But how were they to find a new group of islands which were even less conspicuous amidst these watery wastes than the proverbial needle in the haystack? The old theory was ingenious but a little too simple. It presumed that they sailed in a long line, the ships being as far removed from each other as possible without actually losing sight. Therefore, when one of these squadrons consisted of—let us say—fifteen canoes and all of them kept a mile away from each other, they were really in visible control of fifteen miles of sea. The moment the lookout man at either end of the line saw land, they would communicate their observa-tions to their neighbors and so all along the line, until the entire fleet had been able to change its course and make for the point that had been indicated.

But that idea has now been discarded by Peter Buck

THEY TOO SAILED BY THE STARS AS OUR OWN ANCESTORS DID

and the other experts upon this mysterious subject. And they insist (and rightly so, it seems to me) that the Polynesians found their way across the ocean in just the same manner as our European ancestors did—by knowing the map of the heavens and by following the stars. It seems much more plausible than the old theory about lineal sailing, wherefore it will have a hard time making itself accepted.

And so these hardy fellows set sail for the rising sun, thereby following a course exactly opposite to that of our own ancestors who always kept moving in the wake of the setting sun. And they merrily departed for the unknown in canoes in which you and I would hesitate to cross Long Island Sound, let alone the Great Lakes, and provided with weapons and tools made mostly of stone, for the few pieces of metal they had been able to bring with them from the mainland were soon lost and none of the islands of Polynesia could provide them with substitutes for their swords and spear points. But in spite of these handicaps they pushed ever further into that unknown region where some day— somewhere—they might find what all people, ever since the beginning of time, have craved most of all—a home of their own!

They found that home after hundreds of years of incessant searching. Then they were able to establish themselves among a number of islands that were completely sufficient for their very simple needs. After that, for more than seven centuries, they were left to themselves, to live and die as they pleased, to enjoy the excitement of battle, to go forth upon voyages infinitely more memorable than those ever undertaken by a Columbus or a Hudson. And then came the day of doom, the day on which the first of the White Man's vessels dropped anchor outside of the reef that protected their villages and when they went blithely forth in their canoes to bid the stranger welcome and offer him the hospitality of their own land.

The White Man eagerly accepted the hospitality and he is still there. But his host is gone—or survives on sufferance, patiently and resignedly awaiting the hour when he shall pass entirely out of the picture and become a memory of something that was probably too good to last.

But let us stick to the facts. The Polynesian paradise existed only in the imagination of the writers who came upon these islands before their people had been soiled by the touch of the whaler, the trader and the missionary. Judging merely by what they were able to see on the surface, they failed to notice the dangerous indications of moral and spiritual degeneracy that had set in, the moment those people had no longer been obliged to endure the hardships of the old seafaring life, but had been allowed to dwell in a state of such absolute ease and comfort that existence had become a dull burden rather than an exciting adventure.

For the land was exceedingly generous and so was the sea. The climate was temperate and the absence of ferocious animals deprived them of the necessity of building themselves houses of stone. A few simple huts were enough to protect them against the fury of the heavens and as for clothes, they could practically pluck them from the trees.

Meanwhile, society had become so completely satisfied that all personal initiative had long since been killed. Why try to better yourself when what you had was good enough for anyone and when you knew that no matter what you might accomplish, you would never be able to rise into a higher class than that into which you had been born? Cannibalism and head-hunting, the two tremendous incentives to the development of personal prowess, had long since been discarded as unworthy of a truly civilized people. These unpleasant vices still survived in New Zealand and among the Marquesas, but everywhere else the meat of the scavenging pig had long since replaced the stew made out of your enemy's flesh.

And so, what had been left except a sleepy and leisurely existence in a world in which all the days resembled each other except for an occasional bit of fishing and fighting? The coming of the White Man was the last bit of excitement in the lives of these dwellers in paradise. But the White Man had not come alone. He had brought his two inevitable companions—alcohol and disease. The Polynesians, inclined to obesity both by nature and by their sedentary habits, had already lost most of their former vigor. Now comparatively harmless ailments like measles and influenza and all sorts of pulmonary afflictions killed them by the tens of thousands and venereal diseases did the rest, for the women were comely and that curious and almost

FIRST CAME THE TREES—THEN CAME MAN

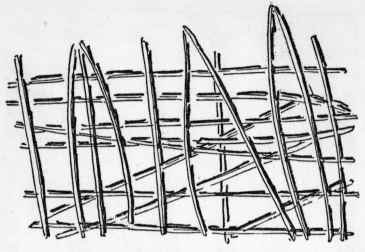

A STRAW OR REED MAP OF THE POLYNESIANS

holy respect for the White Man's skin (which somehow identified him in the popular mind with the ancient gods) made
them more than willing to console the poor sufferer and
make him forget the absence of his loved ones—those loved
ones who consisted of a drab wife and some scrawny children in a London slum.

But the noble White Man, in his pride of race, had no
use for the sons and daughters that were born out of wedlock and they remained behind when their fathers departed
—a race of unwelcome infants, handsome like their mothers,
vicious and useless like their fathers, despised by their white
neighbors, but considering themselves too good for their
native relatives—complete misfits therefore in the community in which they had to spend their days.

As always happens under such circumstances, some of

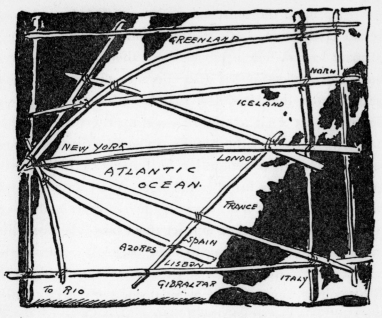

AND HERE IS HOW SUCH A MAP WORKED

the islands fell into decay sooner than the others. Tahiti, the centre of the Society group and perhaps the loveliest of them all, has sunk pretty low, aided and abetted by a slovenly French bureaucracy, but doomed to perish, no matter which European nation should have bothered to annex it in the great scramble for Pacific possessions. The Tonga group, on the other hand, together with nearby Samoa, has fared comparatively well.

Those islands seem to have been one of the main centres of distribution for the great Polynesian migrations of the eleventh and twelfth centuries of our era. Even today, this part of the Pacific gives the traveler a feeling that here he

has come upon the only healthy remnant of the old Polynesian civilization. Both the men and the women have a
pleasant look of independence about them. They practiced
the art of navigation for many decades after it had disappeared from the Hawaiian Islands and from Tahiti. In
order to get the right kind of wood for their canoes, they
had to cross over to the heavily timbered Fijis. And those
same Fijians, whose reputation for ferocious cruelty was so
great that even the European skippers rarely dared to land
on their shores, had a holy fear of the highly trained tribes-
men from nearby Samoa and let them take whatever they
wanted without bothering to fight back. As a result, the
Samoans have not only managed to survive, but they have
also retained some of their original sense of independence,
but God only knows what will happen to them when Japan,
in its need of further expansion, decides to attack this part
of the world, now that England seems to be ready to withdraw as a first-rate power.

As for the islands belonging to the French, they are
doomed beyond hope of recovery and those which have
been administered by the Dominions of Australia and New
Zealand for the last twenty years—they too seem to be in a
very poor way. For Republics are very apt to allow local
politics to enter the field of colonial administration and the
moment that happens, the natives are lost. They have no
vote, so who cares?

But that is only one part of the story. Greed and politics,
imported from Europe, played their part in dragging these

islands down, but the religion of the White Man was to prove itself almost as disastrous to the poor natives as his cannon and his cheap gin.

I hate to say this, for there will be an immediate hurricane of indignation from perfectly well-meaning but badly informed men and women all over the Union, but the gospel of love, which the Christian missionaries brought unto these contented heathen, was completely unsuited to their spiritual and material needs. It deprived them of their old gods, but what did it give them in their place? I don't know and I have never met anybody who seemed to know. Once in a while I have come across some old priest of the Catholic faith who, after a lifetime spent on some Godforsaken island, way off the main route (for not all of these Pacific islets are as beautiful as the picture postal-card version of Tahiti), had been sent to the regional capital to place himself under the care of the local doctor to await the end. Realizing that the curtain was about to descend upon his own little tragedy, such a pious and kindly soul was apt to become contemplative and occasionally he would even listen when you asked him the question, "Was it worth while? Did the final results you achieved make up for all the endless years of stark loneliness? Didn't you merely waste your own time and that of those you forced to listen to your mysterious message?"

Of course, it would be against his professional code for him to confess that it would have been much better if he had stayed at home to cultivate his father's olive trees, or

RAIN

preach unto his neighbors of Provence. No, never! For how can the Church Militant hope to survive unless it constantly keeps before the eyes of the faithful the ideal of the Church Triumphant? And so one usually hears that it had all been very much worth while, for even if only one single soul had been saved from everlasting damnation during the thirty years the good Father had spent in his village, then he would have been more than repaid for his loneliness and his doubts and the tortures of the flesh which were now carrying him to an early grave.

After a time, I came to know those answers by heart, as I do the amiable little alibis of my own grandchildren. Yet I could never quite make up my mind. Had the sacrifices of those humble apostles been commensurate with the results they obtained? Even today, I don't know. How could I have done so without spending years in those distant regions instead of a few short weeks? But fortunately, there are a great many others, reasonable people, unbiased people, or let me say people who at least try very hard to be fair and unbiased, and who were sometimes willing to talk to me.

I do not of course refer to the barbarians who had come out to one of these islands to make their fortune and who, intent solely upon quick and easy gains, bristled with indignation every time they heard the word church and who, over their fifth gin fizz, would wave their pipes at you and who thereupon, but in strict secrecy (for the Mission has long ears), would tell you:

"My dear Sir, these islands would be all right—sure! they would be fine—if it were not for those damn fellows with their collars the wrong way around. Why, I could tell you tales—did you ever see *Rain* by that fellow—what is his name?" and so on and so forth, until they came to the real point of their story, which had to do with a shady but highly profitable deal they could undoubtedly have put over on the natives if it had not been for the interference of some honorable man of God.

Of course, we all of us have seen *Rain* or we have read it and we realize as well as Mr. Maugham that that poor simpleton he depicted was an exception. And it is quite as futile to listen to anybody who tries to attack the missionaries from that particular angle as to bother about those eager enthusiasts who will undertake to inform you about the secret life of Herr Hitler. In the case of Herr Hitler, there is no secret life, so why waste your time listening to the scandal stories of those who think that they can get rid of the unpleasant little fellow by telling you a couple of nasty stories? It is the same with the missionaries and whatever you do, if ever you visit that part of the world, please don't waste your time listening to the endless lamentations that arise from the bungalows of the commercial settlements. But should you have a chance to get at the point of view of those who have no axes to grind, who love the natives, although they clearly realize their weak points and who respect the good qualities of some of the missionaries, although constantly annoyed by the irritating habits of the majority of these salesmen of Heaven, then listen carefully for then you will probably learn why the greater part of the more intelligent Europeans in these distant regions consider the missions with such profound irritation. I could give you my own answer but I would much rather that you found out for yourself.

But speaking of missions, here is another problem. What was the religion of the Polynesians before the arrival of the White Man? It was the religion of all primitive people all over the world at that particular and primitive state of their development. From their distant home in India they seem to have brought with them some vague conception about one original deity, a Great God over-shadowing all the others, a sort of Zeus or Jupiter, a dictator whose word was law unto the entire universe. Gradually as they began to lose all recollections of their earlier surroundings, their conceptions about this chief Divine Being became hazier and hazier and living as they did in close and intimate touch with Nature, they began to identify the forces of Nature with actual personalities, just as the Greeks had identified their rivers and lakes and mountains with certain definite deities, half god, half human, who were as familiar to them as the old fellows who used to fish along the shores of the sea or the shepherds they used to meet coming down the mountainside.

In the case of the Greeks, we know that gradually they had gone one step further and had begun to see abstract matters, such as music or acting or writing history, as fields of human endeavor administered by a special Head of the Department, as we would probably call him today. It sounds all very complicated to the modern scientific mind, but apparently it was as simple and understandable to the people who grew up in that sort of an atmosphere as the hierarchy of the saints is to a good Catholic.

As far as I can make out, in the Polynesian world these minor gods played very much the same role as the less important saints of the Catholic faith play in the life of a Spanish or Italian peasant and as the *dei minores* did in the lives of the Greeks and Romans of twenty centuries ago. They were potential intermediaries between man and the All Highest, who if properly approached could perform very useful services in presenting one's cause to the higher-ups on the ladder of sanctity.

It is always extremely difficult for a complete outsider to enter into the emotional life of someone else, but the Polynesians seem to have taken this arrangement quite as much for granted as an American banker or manufacturer who wants to get certain things done in Washington. He feels that if he is able to assure himself of the right kind of lobbyist, he will eventually gain the ear of one of the departmental heads who in turn can put his case before the Secretary of State or the Secretary of the Treasury or the Attorney General or the Postmaster General, who thereupon, if he is convinced that the matter is of real importance, can bring it to the attention of the Great White Father himself.

The subject has always fascinated me, for having been brought up in an atmosphere of a very strict sort of Calvinism, it took me years to rid myself of all my soberer notions about the relations existing between the individual and the Supreme Being and even today I do not think that I have got quite hold of the essential principles of a scheme so far removed from my own way of thinking. But I learned a lot during the happy interval we spent on the island of Walcheren in the province of Zeeland, whence the Romans used to sail for the British Isles.

Quite often (especially at low tide) we would find small votive statues which the ancient Romans had offered to the local heathenish gods whenever they had safely crossed the turbulent North Sea, which seems to have frightened them almost as much as the harmless Gulf of Naples scares the modern Neapolitans when they have to go all the way to Capri. Somehow they had apparently associated the waves and the winds with a Head of Department of the North Sea, and they had hoped that by promising this dignitary a nice little statue if he were not too hard on them and saved them from the worst miseries of seasickness, they would gain his good will, and therefore, the moment they had set foot on land, they used to hasten to the nearest idol shop, buy themselves a stone image of the deity and present it to his temple with a small donation in cash for the upkeep of the building and the officiating priests.

They could of course have indulged in a little cheating and they could have forgotten all about their promise the moment they set foot on dry land. But this they dared not do, for some time in the future they might be obliged to take that dreadful trip once more and then the North Sea god, remembering how shabbily he had been treated, would get even with them and perhaps he would be so angry as to make them perish in the waves. For the whole transaction was apparently highly personal, just like that strange incident I witnessed many years ago in a small Italian village.

There had been a prolonged drought. A few more days and the crops everywhere would be entirely destroyed and all the cattle die of thirst. Only rain—abundant rain—a deluge—could bring salvation and only God, of course, could make it rain. Therefore the Lord must be approached but this must be done discreetly and the local saint must act as the intermediary and must present the sad case of this small village to the ruler over Heaven and earth.

The only way in which to please the saint, as everybody knew, would be by means of a solemn procession. That procession was therefore held, but it took place at high noon and in a broiling sun. At the stroke of twelve, every man, woman and child of the neighborhood stood ready to follow the holy image. But when the wooden statue of the saint made its appearance, I noticed that the mouth of the holy man had been filled with salt. That, so the populace felt, would teach him a lesson. Let him spend four hours in this scorching heat with his mouth full of salt and not a drop to drink and he would know for himself how the people and the cattle fared with all the wells completely dried up!

Europeans who have spent much time among the Polynesians inform me that one may still come across such incidents, identical in every detail, among the inhabitants of the more remote islands. But the poor heathen have been exposed to so many odds and ends of the Christian faith during these last hundred years that today they hardly know what to do or where to turn for relief. They want to please their white masters but at the same time they hesitate to offend their old gods who may still be lurking somewhere among the mountains.

On the whole, they seem to have found it easier to accept the teachings of Rome than those of Geneva and Heidelberg. For Rome allows them to change their own complicated pantheon of gods and demigods for the saints of the Catholic faith. Such a system they can understand, having since time immemorial lived under a well-regulated social system in which each person from the hereditary chieftain down to the poorest fisherman knew exactly where he stood, what his duties were supposed to be and also his rights. But they seem to have experienced much greater difficulties when brought in contact with the catechisms of Martin Luther and John Calvin.

Their own relations with their nebulous God-in-Chief had always been of a very practical nature, for the Polynesian All Highest realized that if he failed to give satisfaction he might be deserted for a rival who promised to be a little more reasonable. The old desert God of Moses, the frowning tyrant who brooked no opposition to His will, an im-

placable tyrant, a vengeful despot, the dictator of a totalitarian universe, was quite a different personage and much
harder to deal with than the benevolent God who lived in
that little wooden chapel where it smelled so pleasantly of
incense and where the walls were covered with pictures of
the old chieftain himself and of his mighty warriors for
the True Faith.

I may of course be putting ideas into their minds which
were never there. One can never be quite sure about such
matters which one has not experienced for himself. But my
opinion seems to be shared by most of the people with
whom I talked upon this subject, but who, of course, did
not belong to the missionary class.

These skeptics did not take much stock in the stories of
wholesale conversion of those cheerful heathen which were
published in the missionary annuals. It looked very fine on
paper but how about the actual facts? And then they would
tell me curious yarns about the hopeless hodgepodge of the
old and the new which filled the souls of these Polynesian
Christians.

There was one famous legend hailing, if I am not mistaken, from the Tuamotu Islands, familiar to all. On one
small island of that group, a well-intentioned priest had
diligently tried to imbue his dark-skinned children with a
decent respect for the holy sacrament of marriage. There
must be no more loose unions between men and women.
The couples who wished to take each other until death
should them part must proceed to the church and must

there be united in holy wedlock by a duly anointed servant of the Christian God.

Thereafter these couples came regularly once a year to be
married. But each time they presented themselves, they consisted of a different man or woman. It showed that these
heathen had understood that part of the Holy Man's ex-
hortations which dealt with the sinfulness of living with a
partner to whom one had not been united by due process
of canonical law, but that it should always be the same man
or woman whom one took as husband or wife, that was
something else again and something that had apparently
never dawned upon them.

Anybody who has ever visited the Pacific must have heard
similar stories. I am only repeating this one because it is
so typical of what will happen when we undertake to give
a people a new set of ready-made beliefs which are totally
unsuited to their own needs and which they accept under
compulsion or out of curiosity or politeness or a desire for
a novel experience, but which have not grown out of the
same soil and out of the same historical background as the
converts themselves.

In the matter of the Protestant missionaries, there is still
another angle which is rarely mentioned but which is really
at the bottom of that almost universal dislike which the visitor will encounter whenever he is so rash as to mention the
word "missionary." It is perhaps easier to explain this to a
European than to an American, for the European almost instinctively recognizes the existence of different classes of

society, whereas the American, faithful to his democratic antecedents, feels that he must stoutly protest whenever anybody suggests that all men are not born equal, unless of course he should hail from Alabama or North Carolina, when he will make certain reservations in regard to the Negroes or unless he should come from Boston and has his doubts about the Irish, or from Lake Placid where he has been taught to draw the line at the Jews.

Well then, to speak in the vernacular of the Old World, the missionary, especially today, is apt to be decidedly middle class. That is only to be expected, for the church of the year 1940 does not particularly flourish among either the very high or the very low. In the case of the very high, that is to say, among those who are economically independent, they feel that it does not matter very much what they do or think. They are safe. No one can touch them. The same of course holds true among the very poor. They too are safe, for what have they got to lose since they have never had anything?

If they were born into the Catholic faith, the case is a little different. They have been so thoroughly trained in the fear of the Hereafter that they will always keep on the safe side, lest their insurance against everlasting perdition should unexpectedly lapse and leave them to the mercies of a big black devil with a red-hot pitchfork.

The Protestants, having eliminated the idea of eternal punishment in quite such a dramatic form and not being able to attract the more intelligent elements of society in

**STORM**

some other manner, have to recruit their missionaries almost exclusively from among the middle strata of the
middle classes. The men and women they can persuade to
go forth among the heathen and bring them the blessings
of the Christian faith are no doubt most deserving of our
admiration. They are excellent people, entirely sincere in
their beliefs and completely unselfish in their desire to save
their less fortunate fellow-men. But they are also very
sound in their doctrine and rather set in their prejudices
and it is very much to be doubted whether that doctrine
and those prejudices are best suited to the needs of the natives whom they have set out to make happy and save from
perdition. For after all, if your religion does not make you
happier than you were before, then why bother about it
at all?

I am of course not giving you my own view, which is
neither here nor there, but that of those neutral observers
who during a great many years have come in daily contact
with this problem as it happens to exist in the islands of
the Pacific Ocean. And they very seriously doubt whether
any form of evangelical Christianity can ever really contribute seriously to the well-being and contentment of the
natives. For although all of them agree that too many centuries of a life of absolute security and the absence of all
incentives towards physical and mental exertions had already caused great havoc among the Polynesians even before the White Man came upon the scene, they also feel
that with intelligent supervision the process of degeneration

might have been stopped long ago and they accuse the missionaries of having shown more zeal than intelligence in their dealings with the indigenous population and to be more interested in a favorable balance of souls in their annual report home than in giving their charges what they really need, medical supervision and better agricultural methods and a new purpose in life.

Lest these remarks be misunderstood and I be accused of rank ingratitude to some of my kindest friends (whom by an accident of travel I met long before I had seen a single American and who happened to belong to the missionary dynasties of Honolulu), I want to state emphatically that the Hawaiian Islands offered that specific exception without which no rule ever seems to hold true. The New England Congregationalists who during the twenties of the last century bade farewell (and often a farewell forever) to their ancient homesteads to sail around the Horn and spend the rest of their days among the natives of the Hawaiian archipelago—they were of the same breed as the men and women who stayed behind and bestowed upon us the most interesting cultural development our country has thus far seen—the America of Emerson and Thoreau— the America of Harvard College and the Abolitionists.

They also were a great deal more than mere preachers of a new religious creed. They were people of taste and cultivation, so that the Hawaiian chieftains could recognize in them a kindred spirit of dignity and graceful manners and treat them as their equals. Being full of the zeal of learning and hating ignorance almost as much as sin, they accomplished what few other missionaries have ever done—they were able to blend the civilization of America into that of Polynesia and to introduce new habits of thought and conduct without destroying the old ones.

It was my early privilege to know some of the last sur- vivors of this advance guard of America at its best and here I gladly bear tribute to that Grand Old Lady who so well remembered the days of the old royal court of the Kame- hamehas and who could talk about it with such delightful simplicity. But she, more than anyone else, showed me how completely the modern type of missionary is out of place among those rather sensitive and aristocratic races of Poly- nesia because he—the missionary—is apt to come from a class of society which is still so naive in its outlook upon life that it fails to recognize that what is sauce for the goose in Kansas, U.S.A., may be poison for the gander in Manga- reva, in the Tuamotu Archipelago. Furthermore the mis- sionary undertakes to bring a desert god to an island popu- lation. He preaches a code of behavior which suited the needs of a tribe of wandering shepherds who were ever on the verge of thirst and hunger to a group of people who live in the homeland of manna and who only have to open their mouths to let the refreshing liquid from a hundred water- falls pour down their throats. He is forced to explain the workings of a rigid totalitarian state, dominated by a class of professional priests, to a people whose relations towards their gods and their medicine men have always been of a very loose and happy-go-lucky nature.

Having first of all explained in great detail the rigid laws and by-laws of the Old Testament, the missionary must then suddenly switch over from the God of Hate of the Israelites to the God of Love of the Christians and ask the natives to follow him in a jump which is too much for even a great many white people. Next, in order to explain the details of the New Testament, the missionary must endeavor to make his bewildered charges understand such simple little details as the exact relationship between the Father, the Son and the Holy Ghost, who are one yet remain three individual units, and finally, while denouncing these sanguinary heathen for their human sacrifices, he must make them feel that he himself is performing an act of ultimate sanctity when he swallows the flesh and blood of his own God.

I know the answer—that all Protestants must accept Holy Communion as something entirely symbolical. But the Polynesians who are urged to assist at this ceremony are not Protestants. Only a few years ago they were still cannibals and the question arises whether those people, separated from us by tens of thousands of years of an entirely different historical development, benefited in the slightest degree from having dropped Maui in favor of Jehovah? I shall leave it to the observant reader, while I proceed to still another point: What effect has the Church had upon the moral and social life of these island people?

There the picture becomes even more complicated. For within that field the missionary is not only the representative of the code of ethics and manners that prevailed in his

own class at home—the class of the small merchants, of the
well-to-do farmers and schoolteachers—honorable people
all but rather inclined by their economic and intellectual
limitations to observe a set of very strict rules of behavior
about which none of the other classes of society seem to
bother very greatly and the willing slaves of a large number
of outworn taboos which are undoubtedly different from
the taboos of the Polynesians but which, to the unpreju-
diced observer, make just as much or as little sense as those
which Captain Cook found in these remote parts of the
world when he first visited them.

And it is this rigid and very class-conscious code of ethics
on the part of the missionaries and all these ancient Hebrew
taboos which they drag around with them wherever they go
which seem to have caused most of the havoc among the
Polynesians. For not only has his new religion made the
native conscious of "sin" (a word which in its terrifying
Christian meaning had never existed in his own vocabu-
lary), but he was also made aware of his body and he has
now been taught to consider that perfectly adjusted and
beautifully balanced physical instrument as something of
which he really ought to feel ashamed.

Desire and passion, which came as natural to him as song
comes to the birds of the fields, he is now taught to regard
as inventions of the Devil, another new and strange personage to whom he was introduced when the earliest of the
missionaries set foot on his shores and repaid his hospitality
by taking a hammer and destroying the images of his ancient gods.

We are apt to pass over such incidents as mere trifles. But what would we do if a shipload of Maoris should land at the Battery and after having been nobly entertained by a committee of prominent citizens, headed by Grover Whalen, should defiantly march up Fifth Avenue, demolishing all the statues in all of the Christian churches they encountered on the way to St. Patrick's, which they would thereupon burn down to the ground?

It would be easy to continue this list of grievances for a great many pages more but I am afraid that it would take up a great deal of space and besides, those who see the world the way we do would agree without being told and the others would bitterly disagree, no matter what proof we should be able to offer in support of our contentions.

And so I shall be as brief as possible and merely state that wherever one goes in the Pacific one comes across evidence of the damage done to the native character by the introduction of a code of manners and morals which come quite naturally to the sort of people at home from among whom the missionaries are recruited but which was and is so completely unsuited to the needs of these islanders that by submitting to it they were in reality writing their own sentence of death.

The Polynesians, as long as they were left to themselves, seem to have been one of the few people who knew the meaning of the expression, "the joy of life." The mere business of being alive had been a pleasurable experience. They had loved to laugh. They had derived intense satisfaction from the contemplation of beautiful flowers. They

had been skillful weavers of cloth, expert engravers in stone
and wood, highly original in the way they devised ornamental patterns to adorn their houses, their ships and every
article of daily use. And today? They were told that it was
unpleasant in the sight of their new god to waste so much
of their precious time upon such worldly matters as out-
ward adornment and physical perfection and to care so
much for things which in no way contributed towards the
well-being of their immortal souls. As a result, their innate
feeling for the arts has been destroyed and artistically they
have now come down to the level of their teachers, whose
houses (even in these remote regions) are fine examples of
the worst degradations of the taste which has become associated with the name of the great Queen Victoria.

Fortunately the more farseeing elements among the governments which have control over these islands seem at last
to have come to a realization of what they had been doing
when they gave the missionaries too much of a free hand.
They have at last reached the point where they are beginning to see that by depriving the natives of their sense of
beauty and their joy of living, the Christian missionaries
also deprived them of all further desire to live. And since
colonies without a population are not much of an asset, the
missionary ladies and gentlemen are now encouraged to
restrict their activities to the realm of the spirit and to put
a check upon their own hatred for everything that might
make this present world such a pleasant paradise that the
inhabitants might feel a little less inclined to worry about
the next one.

There is of course one exception to this universal criticism and this exception will be most eagerly stressed by even the most embittered enemies of the missionary movement. They will agree that there can be no possible objection to the so-called medical missionaries and to those who came out to teach the natives more scientific methods of agriculture. And furthermore, everyone seems always to know of at least one exceptional case and then will tell you of a few men or women who have really devoted themselves wholeheartedly to the purpose of showing the natives by their own example that one could be a good Christian and at the same time a kind and cheerful neighbor, who was willing to put the command of "Love ye your neighbor as yourself" ahead of everything else. But having paid their respects to these exceptional individuals, the bill of indictment will be continued until the Southern Cross has long since disappeared below the distant horizon and it is time to go back to your hotel.

It was not exactly pleasant to say all this but I was only doing what almost everyone with whom I came in contact had asked me to do. "We can't speak out," they used to complain. "We have jobs which we can't afford to lose and the missionaries are so strongly entrenched economically that they could easily destroy us, were we known to be openly opposed to them. They suspect us, of course, of not being very friendly but they have no proofs and therefore they have got to leave us alone. At the same time, if you feel any sympathy for these natives, whom many of us have come to love very dearly, then please speak out if ever you should write anything about this part of the world."

I have now spoken out as per request. For this is the tragedy of the Pacific, which soon begins to haunt anyone who is able to look a little further than the printed circular of the travel agency and who realizes that all these picturesque "native dances" and "native village feasts" and "war canoe races" with which he is pursued during his voyage are nothing but a deliberately prearranged fraud, as they no longer bear any sort of actual relationship to the real native life.

Indeed, the more elaborate these phony feasts happen to be, the greater the feeling of despair which they inspire in the spectator. It was bad enough during the last twenty years to watch Russian generals, disguised as Cossacks, dance what were supposed to be Polish polkas in some dreary Parisian cabaret. But, believe me, to see a noble-looking Samoan chieftain, who may have been an intimate friend of Robert Louis Stevenson, swing a sword (made in Germany), which he has never used, in a death-defying dance, which he only performs when there is a tourist vessel in port—that too is an event which one does not easily forget.

I, at least, found it very difficult to assist at those macabre gaieties, for all the time I was supposed to be watching this marvelous native display of ancestral prowess, I saw myself (who never wore a wooden shoe nor donned a pair of Volendam pantaloons), I saw myself doing a "dance of the Island of Marken" (which I have visited for just three minutes during the whole of my lifetime) for the benefit of a shipload of Samoan females of indefinite age who had come to look at my "quaint country" with its "quaint and picturesque customs."

I don't think that there is anything quite as dreadful in this world as to come face to face with fallen grandeur. One can visit the ruins of the Acropolis, because everybody connected with the glory that was Greece has been dead for at least twenty-three centuries and their modern descendants don't count. But I wonder how a Roman of the third century B.C. felt, who had come to Athens and was thereupon obliged to throw a handful of coppers at some shabby philosopher in a dirty old tunic, who undertook to recite verses from Homer against the background of the Acropolis on some lovely moonlit night? He must have shuddered as I did whenever the image of some early Polynesian traveler was momentarily called back to life to chant songs of conquest and love to a tune that bore every evidence of having been inspired by *Bei mir bist du schön.*

If those Polynesians had been docile little Javanese, whose people had never moved an inch from their own villages for at least a thousand years, I probably would not have cared quite so much. But while crossing on a modern steamer, amidst all the comforts of modern existence, from one island to the next, often going for days and days without seeing any signs of land and crossing eight hundred or a thousand or twelve hundred miles of water and more

THIS WAS THE WAY THE NATIVE LIVED BEFORE HE GOT CIVILIZED

AND THEN HE MOVED TO THE STREET OF PROGRESS

water and then still more water until at last there was a
tiny speck on the horizon, one was constantly being reminded of the fact that only a few centuries before the
ancestors of these postcard-selling natives had been fine,
upstanding fellows, roaming the sea at will, proudly conscious of their own strength and courage and as nearly
masters of their own fate as it has ever been given to mortal
man to be.

Yes, it is a sad story and the Western world has not even
begun to suspect what a drama has been enacted in that
part of the world. Nor are we in America at all aware of
the glorious history that lies buried there, almost within
stone's throw of our own shores. At school, our children
learn all about brave Magellan and about the good and
kind Captain Cook and Tasman and de Bougainville. But
of the exploits of these early Polynesian skippers, who performed feats of daring and skill which the Europeans, even
at a much later date, never could have repeated, we are completely ignorant. Of those incredible voyages which led the
Polynesians from Tahiti to Hawaii and to New Zealand
and from Tubuai to Easter Island, our children have never
heard a word and none of our authors guilty of *Histories
of the World* (the present one included) have ever bothered
to devote as much as a single page to the most magnificent
chapter in the whole history of navigation—the discovery
of the Pacific by the Polynesians.

# 6. THE SECOND DISCOVERY OF THE PACIFIC

*The White Man at last appears upon the scene*

VASCO NUÑEZ DE BALBOA is usually relegated to a footnote in those textbooks which inform a not particularly
interested juvenile world that he is the man who discovered
the Pacific Ocean. "1513: Balboa finds the Pacific," and
that is that.

I am very fond of reading the lives of those whom we
might call the minor discoverers and navigators. They are
apt to have been men of much greater calibre than the
Pizarros, the Cortezes and the Magellans and the other
headliners whose praises are forever being sung in beautifully illustrated special biographies. In my mind, their lack
of success means nothing at all, for often their obscurity
was due to their superior virtues and to that lack of ruth-
lessness, cruelty and brutality which was so characteristic
of their more famous rivals.

Our modern world, however, dominated by the idea of
"success," is not apt to pay much attention to a poor devil
who, it is true, may have discovered the Pacific and may
have been appointed Great Admiral of the South Sea, but

who had his head chopped off before he could cash in on his achievements. All the same, he was a fellow of parts, this shabby gentleman from Jerez de los Caballeros in the province of Estremadura, whose name, like those of so many of the other distinguished heroes of the age of the Conquistadores, makes one think of the postage stamps issued by the republics now located in the territory he had chosen for his own explorations. The more hopelessly bankrupt the treasuries of these sovereign nations, the more resplendent the stamps they print on all possible and impossible occasions.

During the first half of the era of the Spanish conquests, we run continually across these noble Dons with their high-sounding surnames, patronyms and eponyms (no one less than Julius Caesar would ever do as the founder of their families!) but with their toes showing through the tips of their shoes—provided they had any.

Their pretensions were as enormous as their ambitions. During the day they strutted around like peacocks, but at night they disappeared into some dark attic and dined on a crust of bread they had scavenged out of somebody else's ash can. A motley crew without even the rudiments of a conscience, a complete disregard for the sufferings of others, but absolutely convinced that some day their luck would turn and that they would then be able to return to their ancestral castle (now unfortunately converted into a cow stable) accompanied by a fine retinue of retainers,

SAMOA

private chaplains and dusky mistresses and a thousand mules carrying sacks full of ducats.

Vasco Nuñez de Balboa (it is a joy to repeat that name!) was an exception to the rule that all these grotesque bravos must invariably be so many scoundrels. He was, so it would seem, a fellow of considerable ability. What ill wind had blown him to the island of Hispaniola (the bit of land in the Caribbean now shared by the Republics of Haiti and San Domingo) nobody knows. But since all bankrupt Spanish noblemen of that era would sooner or later find their way to that fortunate island, as today they are bound to come to the island of Manhattan and for the selfsame purpose (to get rich both easily and quickly), we need not be surprised at finding him there. As to the manner of his leaving the colonial capital hidden in a barrel of salt pork, it meant a pleasant piece of gossip along the Spanish Main, but unfortunately, Balboa is only a minor character in my little story and I have got to leave the interesting details of his unhappy life and his lamentable death (murdered by a jealous rival) to some other time and occasion.

The point of interest in the career of Balboa is this: it stresses the fact that the Spaniards were not in the least interested in the scientific aspects of the business of navigation but were inspired by only one feature of the problem of exploration—where could they find that gold of which they had seen samples but in such small quantities as to be useless? Somewhere there must be an inexhaustible supply of that mysterious metal, which ever since the beginning of organized society had given man such terrific power over his fellow-men. But where? It was not to be found among the islands which Columbus had discovered. It was not to be found on the mainland. Where was it? That was the problem which occupied all the best and all the worst minds of Spain during the first twenty-five years after the death of Columbus.

And Balboa too, when he crossed the Isthmus of Panama, was not looking for a new ocean but was trying very hard to find a short cut to the still unidentified land of Coyba, where everything, as all the natives had told him, was made out of gold.

What this island of Coyba really was supposed to have been, we do not know. But that there was a lot of gold to be found in the general direction of the southwest, way beyond the mountains of the mainland, that was a fact known to all the Spaniards then residing in the New World, and each one of them, in his own way, had his pet theory of how to get there.

Balboa realized that it was not going to be an easy trip and that only a well-equipped expedition could have a reasonable hope of success. He diligently lobbied for his plans at the Spanish Court and afterwards at the court of the Viceroy in Hispaniola, until in a sudden panic that someone else might try to get there ahead of him he started on his western trek with less than two hundred men.

He had to find his way through a dense jungle, but he was full of hope, for the natives whom he encountered told him that a few days further towards the setting sun he would come upon a large expanse of water. Suppose they were right, then that vast expanse of water might be the sea which separated the real gold-land of Zipangu (for which Columbus had been looking and which he had failed to find) from the shores of that useless wilderness which was all the absurd Genoese mountebank had added to the domains of their Most Catholic Majesties of Spain. Suppose he, Vasco Nuñez de Balboa, were thereupon to achieve what none of the others had been able to do! With renewed vigor and fresh courage, the noble Don loaded his baggage on the backs of those Indians whom he had forced to serve him as pack mules and pressed further into the woods which stretched endlessly up towards the tops of the ragged mountain chains.

Among his contemporaries, Balboa seems to have enjoyed the reputation of someone who perhaps was a little too lenient and too soft-hearted in dealing with the natives. That gives us an idea of his colleagues, for we know from his own reports to the authorities in Seville that, much to his regret, he was obliged to exterminate all the aborigines who fell into his hands as he had too few soldiers at his disposal to keep them as prisoners. Since a Spanish nobleman could not defile his sword with the blood of a mere Indian, these poor creatures were usually left to the mercies of the dogs who accompanied those modern crusaders on their travels. Apparently they were rather proud of this method of solving the native problem, for many of the

SUNSHINE
THE HILL WHERE R. L. S. LIES BURIED

books dealing with the marvels of the New World show us pictures of Indians being torn to pieces by very savage-looking canines. And I regret to say that I am not a sufficiently good dog-fancier to be able to identify the breeds that were used for the purpose of "destroying the rats," as the old chronicles put it in their quaint and amusing fashion. But the pictures show two varieties—a sort of whippet with pointed ears and a longer-eared variety of hound. As neither of those two breeds are particularly ferocious nowadays (least of all the ferocious-looking hound, who whenever you let him will sit down in your lap and lick your face), it may have been some specially bred kind of dog which since then has gone out of existence.

But even in the time of Lord Amherst, the memory of those happy days survived, for His Lordship in several letters expressed regret that the newly risen fad of humanitarianism did not allow him to follow the example of the Spanish Conquistadores. And so, for lack of that more direct method, he used to present the heathen with the clothes recently worn by the victims of smallpox. It took a little longer, but in the end, the results were just the same. The noble Lord died in the year 1797. Perhaps, after all, the world doth make some progress!

✦

On September 25 of the year 1513 Balboa reached the highest point of the isthmus. Way in the distance and far below him he could see the glittering waves of the great sea of the south, or the Pacific Ocean, as it came to be known after the days of Magellan. And so he returned, after all sorts of uncomfortable adventures, to report proudly to his royal master that he had found a new ocean and also that he had returned with a considerable amount of gold. The news about the gold was most enthusiastically received but the existence of a second ocean was immediately and bitterly refuted by the learned clerics of His Majesty's court. These good fathers argued that since God had created this earth for man's special benefit and convenience, it was absolutely blasphemous to maintain that more than half of the globe was covered with water, of no use to anyone except fishes and whales.

✦

The rest of Balboa's story is known to everyone. It was the curse of the New World that it had been discovered by a mystic who was completely lacking in the gift for leadership. But we should not judge Columbus too severely on account of this very serious defect. He shared it with many of the greatest navigators of all times. Hudson and Bligh, to give you only a few examples, performed veritable miracles within the realm of their own craft. They could take their vessels anywhere at any time and under the most adverse of circumstances. But when it came to handling men instead of ships, they were hopeless failures and their careers were sadly marred by an unceasing series of mutinies and rebellions. Perhaps they were too self-

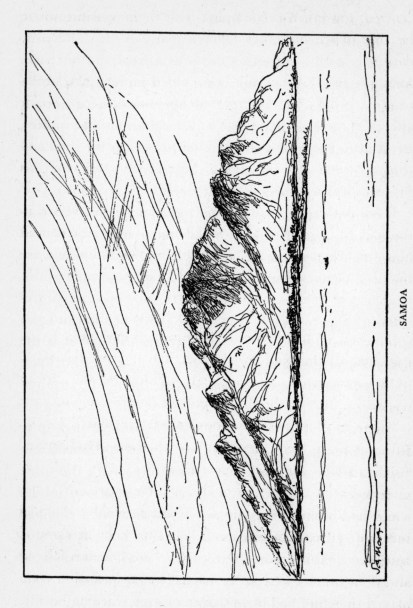

SAMOA

centred, too much preoccupied with their own dreams to
be able to see the other fellow's point of view. I hardly
dare to put this suggestion down as a hard and fast rule,
for there was James Cook, who added more square miles
of new territory to our maps than any man either before or
after him, and he never had any trouble with his sailors,
never even had to flog them unless for their own good and
to make them eat those fresh vegetables which were to
protect them against scurvy.

It is a problem I recommend to someone better versed in
the science of psychology than I happen to be. He should
however begin his studies with Christopher Columbus, for
the poor Genoese was the most deplorable example of this
tendency of truly great mariners to be hopeless failures
when it came to the more practical affairs of life. And as a
rule, within the field of colonial administration, it is the
first man on the spot who will put his own imprint upon
the whole subsequent development of the newly acquired
territory.

The rule of Columbus in the New World had led up to
all sorts of scandals and even after he himself had been sent
back to Spain in chains (like a common felon), the spirit
of jealousy and distrust and that absolute lack of loyalty
which had been so characteristic of his short-lived rule had
survived. Hispaniola remained a plague hole of intrigue
and greed. The home office was far away. Letters could
always be intercepted or be made to disappear and com-
plaints therefore had little chance of ever reaching Seville.

And if perchance they should be brought to the attention of the authorities in Spain, it was always possible to claim that one had failed to receive the proper instructions. If that did not work, a valuable present, discreetly offered to the right person, would usually bring the desired results.

Under those circumstances, it was very easy for an unscrupulous man to establish himself as a local dictator. During Balboa's absence, such a little potentate had established himself in Hispaniola. His name was Pedro Arias de Avila (usually known as Pedrarias) and he hated and feared Balboa, for the discoverer of the Pacific knew too much.

When Balboa thereupon crossed the isthmus for a second time, he built himself several small vessels on the Pacific side, by means of which, if it had not been for a sudden storm, he might even have reached the gold-land of Peru.

Pedrarias decided to rid himself quickly of a subordinate who was much too energetic and too independent to suit his own taste. He sent word to Balboa, inviting him to report at the Governor's headquarters in Darien (the old name for the whole of the isthmus). Balboa, expecting a reward for his labors, accepted the invitation. He was at once arrested, accused of high treason, brought before a special tribunal which, acting upon the Governor's orders, condemned him to be decapitated. Such was the end of the man who discovered the Pacific.

It was also the end of certain plans which Balboa seems to have had in regard to the further exploration of his pet

ocean. About these plans we know only through certain
letters he had apparently sent to Spain before his fate over-
took him. But as the blundering Pedrarias had every reason
to want the memory of his dangerous rival to be forgotten
as quickly as possible, the home office never received these
documents until it was too late. In the meantime, in order
that the Spanish crown might be impressed by his own zeal,
Pedrarias in the year 1519 founded a city on the Pacific
side of the isthmus. It was that same city of Panama which
is now the capital of the republic created by the grace of the
late Teodoro di Campo Rosso, twenty-sixth President of the
United States and, according to the latest information from
Naziland, the descendant of an Italian Jew who settled in
the Low Countries in the middle of the sixteenth century
and thereupon Dutchified his name into Roosevelt.

And here we reach the end of the sad story of Don Vasco
Nuñez de Balboa. The four ships which he had started to
build on the Pacific side were never finished and it was not
until the year 1525 that Pizarro, in search of the gold-land
Peru, followed in the tracks of his unfortunate predecessor
and actually found what everybody had been looking for—
a country full of gold.

In the meantime, the problem of the Pacific had been
attacked from quite a different angle and it had been definitely shown that in spite of the objections of the learned
Spanish monks, who had rejected Balboa's theory as an un-
pardonable heresy, that ocean was a very large piece of
water indeed. The final proof that the Pacific existed was

due to a Portuguese nobleman by the name of Fernão de Magalhães, but known to the Anglo-Saxon world as plain Ferdinand Magellan.

The reason for this most ambitious project—a deliberate attempt to reach the Indies by way of the back door and via the west instead of through the front door and via the east—was a curious one. It was the direct result of an old legal squabble between Spain and Portugal as to who should be the "rightful owners of what."

This feeling that no matter what issues were at stake, everything must always be done in a "legal" and "legitimate" manner was typical of the mentality of the Middle Ages. Here were Spain and Portugal. For the last hundred years they had been discovering, exploring and plundering every nook and corner of Africa, Asia and America. In the end, they were of course bound to get into each other's hair and whiskers and start fighting about the spoils. But when this point had been reached, the cooler heads among the two governments managed to make their influence felt. "Let us arbitrate this matter," they suggested, "and in this way let us avoid bloodshed and a loss of revenue."

The Pope had been asked to act as intermediary and between the years 1452 and 1455, just when Portugal was on the verge of discovering the sea route to the Indies, the learned Pope Nicholas V (the great benefactor of the Vatican library) had given the Portuguese the exclusive right of exploring the Indies and of administering the territories they might want to occupy along the road that led from

**HEAT**
PORT MORESBY, NEW GUINEA

Lisbon to Calcutta. This allowed the Spaniards to take possession of everything in the west, but as the world was a small, flat square which came to an abrupt end a few miles west of the Azores, it did them very little good.

Well, in the year 1486, Bartholomew Diaz had rounded the southernmost point of Africa (Cape Agulhas, and not the Cape of Good Hope, which is ninety miles further towards the north) and twelve years later, Vasco da Gama had at last reached India. But in the meantime and while the Portuguese were still looking eastward for their route to the spice-lands of the Indies, an unknown Italian, sailing in the service of the Spanish crown, had claimed that he had reached the Indies by following a westward course that led straight across the Atlantic.

At that time, in the year 1492, nobody of course knew or could even guess what it was that Columbus had really discovered. Hence there arose a terrific confusion. All the professors and geographers and cartographers got busy and God only knows where the conflict might have ended, had not the Pope, grieving to see two Christian nations go to war with each other, decided to intervene. He did this by the simple expedient of taking a ruler and dividing the map of the world into two equal halves. His line of demarcation ran from north to south, three hundred miles west from the Azores and Cape Verde Islands. Upon the Portuguese he bestowed everything eastward of this line. The Spaniards could help themselves to everything that lay on the west of the same line. The whole thing seemed fair enough, but the Portuguese did not feel that they had got all they deserved.

In consequence of their violent protests, a meeting was thereupon held in the Spanish city of Tordesillas, where a new agreement was to be drawn up. By this famous treaty of Tordesillas of the year 1494, the line of demarcation was pushed further towards the west and now ran from north to south 370 leagues (1110 miles) west of the Cape Verde Islands. If you care to look it up on a map, you will find it between the 45th and 50th degrees of longitude west of Greenwich. It cuts off most of the tummy of Brazil (which therefore fell within the sphere of influence of the Portuguese) but left everything else in America to the Spaniards.

Meanwhile the world had continued to move and even those who insisted that the Old Testament must be regarded as the only reliable handbook on geography were now no longer able to insist upon the complete flatness of the earth. After that twenty-four thousand mile voyage of Vasco da Gama, they were forced to admit that, in spots at least, it might be slightly curved. But if this were true, it followed that the line of demarcation of Tordesillas must run all the way around a globe and was not just a straight line running from north to south on a flat map. And in that case, parts of the Indies (the real Indies, not the so-called Indies of Columbus) might be found to be situated within that part of the world which the Pope had bestowed upon His Majesty of Spain.

The geographical theorists of that day—and who was not dabbling in geography during the last half of the fifteenth and the first half of the sixteenth centuries?—indulged in all sorts of wild speculations, but nobody as yet knew anything about the actual lay of the land. It was then that Fernão de Magalhães made his bid for immortality.

The noble Dom was quite true to type. History has ranked him high among the great navigators of the past, but today we would have considered him a promoter, rather than a mariner, and we would have hired half a dozen of the best known corporation lawyers to examine his plans most carefully before we would have dared to invest a penny in one of his schemes.

By birth, Magellan was a Portuguese, but this did not prevent him from offering his services to the King of Spain, the sworn enemy of his native country. And why, indeed, should he have had any scruples? Was not Columbus an Italian who worked for a Spaniard? Was not Cabot another Italian who had offered his services to the King of England? Did not, a few years later, Henry Hudson, the Englishman, discover the New Netherlands for the benefit of a Dutch trading company?

Such acts of divided allegiance were quite in keeping with the internationalism of the late Middle Ages and nobody took any offense at them. To equip ships and sail to the other end of the earth, you needed a backer with a lot of money. If you were fortunate enough to find him at home, so much the better. If not, what was the difference?

Your idea remained just as sound, whether financed by Spanish ducats or Dutch guilders or English sovereigns.

In the case of Magellan, certain alleged irregularities in connection with supplies for the troops in Morocco seem to have been instrumental in making this Portuguese patriot decide that he had better try his luck elsewhere. And so Magellan and his idea had bidden farewell to their native land, had crossed over into Spain and had gone to see what could be done with that country's young king, Charles I (better known as the Emperor Charles V), then only eighteen years old but said to be a bright boy and very hard pressed for ready cash.

As for the plan which the Portuguese mariner hoped to sell His Majesty, it was as follows: Magellan wanted to be given command of a small squadron to try and discover a new entrance into the sea which separated the West Indies from the real Indies. These West Indies were now beginning to be known as America, the name under which they had first appeared on the map which Martin Waldseemüller (Ilacomilus to the learned world) had published in the year 1507. To the man in the street however they continued to be known as the West Indies and as a result, there was a great deal of confusion and when a sailor merely asked permission to explore the Indies, who was to tell whether he meant the East Indies or the West Indies?

Magellan intended to give the West Indies a wide berth, make for the south and then endeavor to find some sort of opening somewhere along that endless coast, through which he would be able to slip quietly into Don Balboa's newly discovered sea. If he were able to do this, so he reasoned, then Spain would be able to trade directly with the East Indies without in any way interfering with the stipulations of the treaty of Tordesillas.

True to type, Magellan was most careful to safeguard his own interests while drawing up his contract with his Spanish employer. He was to be given five ships and with these he was to discover and explore all the spice-bearing islands of the East Indies which lay outside of the sphere of official influence of the Portuguese. In return for his services, he and his partner, a certain Ruy Faleiro, were to receive five percent of the gross revenue, a knighthood and high rank at His Majesty's court.

At the last moment, Ruy Faleiro decided to remain at home because his horoscope warned him that he might never return, and on August 10 of the year 1519 Magellan left the Spanish mainland, confidently expecting that he would spend the rest of his days as governor-general of the Moluccas or some other island empire which he was to conquer for the benefit of the crown of Castile.

Three years later, thirty-one of his sailors returned to the harbor of San Lucar. Magellan himself was dead. Four of his ships had been lost. Only one, the little *Vittoria*, returned to tell that tale of suffering and misfortune which will ever remain associated with the White Man's first attempt to sail a vessel of his own making across the broad expanse of the Pacific Ocean.

Here, in some detail, is the story of Magellan's adventures, as they were afterwards told by one of the survivors, the Italian Antonio Pigafetta, to a certain Ramusio, who just then was publishing a collection of exciting travel stories, not for the purpose of contributing to the serious literature of the world but in the hope of being a "best seller."

Like almost all other voyages of discovery, the expedition of Magellan started with a violent quarrel between the commander-in-chief and his subordinates. Each one of these had his own pet theory about the course that should be followed, but as they sailed without the slightest idea of where they were going or what they should look for, they could indulge in all sorts of fine fantasies without ever reaching any definite conclusions.

However, in the beginning, Magellan, still basking in the glory so recently bestowed upon him by royal favor, could insist upon a certain amount of discipline. The fleet therefore sailed the way he wanted it to go. First of all, towards the south until it reached the coast of Guinea. Then the ships turned sharply westward and made for Brazil, sticking to the route which today is favored by the airplanes which ply between Africa and South America.

Once in the New World, Magellan was really in forbidden territory, for the Tordesillas line of demarcation had given all that part of the world to the Portuguese. Hence Magellan's careful observance of all the amenities of international intercourse. For example, when his ships

**BECALMED**

entered a wide bay known as the Rio de Janeiro (because it had been discovered in the month of January), he did not allow his sailors to swap steel knives for slaves, as the simple-minded natives wanted them to do. For such "engaging in trade" might have given offense to the Portuguese authorities.

From the River of January, which they left two days after Christmas of the year 1519, they sailed south until they reached the mouth of that muddy stream which for some curious reason had been given the name of the Silver River —the Rio de la Plata.

Three years before, Captain de Solis, the first explorer of these regions, had been killed there in a quarrel with the Indians and since then few European ships had come to visit this neighborhood.

At the mouth of this river a serious quarrel broke out. Several of Magellan's captains and pilots argued that this river, which is as big as a lake near its mouth, might well be the long-sought entrance to the sea that must lie at the other side of the continent of Columbus.

Magellan suggested a compromise. He sent several of his ships westward, to explore the bay. But they got lost in the Uruguay River and finding it grew narrower and narrower, they decided that they had been mistaken and returned to the main squadron, satisfied that the Plate was merely a river. Magellan hoisted anchor and the trip southward was continued.

Every bay, every estuary and river was carefully explored

to make sure that it was not that long-desired "short cut" which had been the dream of all the great explorers ever since the days of Columbus. But nothing was found except a few inconsequential bays and in the meantime it was steadily growing colder. For the summer of the southern hemispheres is really its winter, a fact known to all modern travel agencies, but not to the contemporaries of Magellan.

Finally it grew so unbearably frigid that these good Castilians decided to mutiny rather than to run the risk of being frozen to death in their own bunks. Again Magellan tried to save the situation by promising the men that he would let them spend the winter on shore in one of the bays they had discovered which was full of fish and clams and oysters. But when he noticed that pleasant words accomplished nothing and that the crews of two of his ships were going to mutiny, no matter what he said, he decided to follow another course and show them who was the master!

He gave orders that the captain of the *Vittoria* be killed, while that unsuspecting gentleman was peacefully reading a letter which the admiral had just sent him. As soon as that had been done, the loyal ships attacked those which had shown signs of rebellion. The captain of the *San Antonio* was quartered and the four pieces of his body were shown to the mutineers as an example that awaited them if they continued to show disobedience.

The captain of the *Concepcion* was merely put into irons for the rest of the voyage. A similar fate befell a priest who had made common cause with the rebels, and that was the end of the first of Magellan's labor troubles.

His relations with the natives were on the whole more amicable than those with his own sailors. These hardy sons of nature did not seem to share the Spaniards' dislike of the cold, for they went about practically naked, even in the worst blizzards. They were men of large stature with enormous feet. Hence their name of the *Patagones,* or Big Feeters, which the people of Patagonia have borne until this day.

On August 24, Magellan finally left his safe harbor and continued his trip southwards. And behold! after several weeks, the coast on his right at last began to recede and a wide opening showed itself. A fierce current ran through it and the waters were subject to a great difference in tides. Otherwise they were perfectly safe and Magellan felt certain that there at last must be the entrance into the sea that separated the East from the West Indies.

Magellan delightedly imparted this good piece of news to his sailors, but these quite reasonably answered that, as long as the road to the South Sea had now been found, why not call it a day, return to Spain and tell the folks at home about their wonderful discovery?

Magellan settled the argument by promising to hang all those who should ever again speak to him about turning back, and this threat was effective except with one of his captains. That was the commander of the *San Antonio,* who conveniently used an opportunity to "lose himself" while exploring a distant part of the coast and who, as soon as he was out of sight of the main squadron, hastened north-ward and with such speed that he was back in Spain within three months. Needless to say, his sailors did not fail to depict their admiral as an ogre of cruelty, who instead of

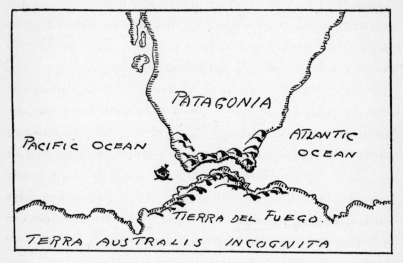

WHAT MAGELLAN THOUGHT HE HAD FOUND

obeying his instructions to proceed directly to the Moluccas, had wasted most of his time doing nothing in particular along the coast of Brazil.

This however was hardly true, for just then Magellan was far from wasting his time. He was trying to navigate the strait that lay between Patagonia in the north and the land of the south, which he had called Tierra del Fuego on account of the fires which he had noticed there at night when the natives, who had never yet learned to build themselves houses, were trying to keep warm. For, as Magellan then found out, this was by far the most inhospitable part of the world. It was given to sudden violent outbursts of snow, hail and sleet and the wind blew from all the quarters of the compass at the same time.

But finally after twenty days of misery, the straits widened out into a sea—a sea with blue skies and flat calms —which ever since has been known as the Peaceful Ocean, and as the Pacific it still appears on our maps.

So far, so good, but here Magellan entered upon the most difficult part of his voyage. For he now must find the Moluccas, which according to all the best geographers and mathematicians of his day lay within the Spanish half of the world. These Moluccas were the home of those spices in search of which the Europeans of the pre-icebox days had wasted all their best efforts, ever since the conquest of Constantinople by the Turks (almost three generations before) had cut them off from the old overland trade route to the Indies. These Moluccas, since they were able to grow spices, must lie directly on or very near to the Equator. Magellan figured it out and decided that he must sail in a northwestern direction if he wanted to reach the Moluccas in the shortest possible space of time. He did so, but what a trip it proved to be!

While in the strait which still bears his name he had not dared to go on land in search of fresh provisions. To do so might have cost him some of his men and executions and sickness had already lessened their number very considerably. There was only one thing for him to do—he must sail westward and trust to luck. But Magellan, alas, was not born under a lucky star, as you will notice for yourself by following his course on the map. Not only did the winds persist in blowing consistently in the wrong direction, but in a sea as full of islands as the Pacific, he managed to sail for several months without ever catching sight of anything resembling a mountaintop or a cluster of cocoanut trees!

Finally nothing remained of the supplies he had taken on board in Europe except a little rice. For lack of fresh water, this rice had to be boiled in sea water and as a result of this unsavory diet, twenty sailors died. When the rice gave out, the ox hides that were strapped along the base of the masts (to prevent the cutting in of the ropes) were cooked and eaten, mixed with some sawdust and salt—not a very healthy diet, but anyway, it killed the worst pangs of hunger.

At last two small islands were sighted. They proved to be uninhabited but nothing was found that could be eaten by these starving sailors.

This torture, during which the last rat on board was caught and duly turned into a stew, lasted for ninety-eight days, or a little over three months. Then at last the ships reached a group of islands where there was both food and water, but the natives proved to be so light-fingered that the Spaniards called the islands the Ladrones, or Islands of the Thieves. For all we know, Guam may have been the first of the Ladrones on which Magellan set foot.

And now if you will once more look at the map, you will notice that on the way from the island of Cabo Deseado at the western end of the Straits of Magellan to the Ladrones, the expedition must have been almost constantly within one or two days' sailing from dry land. But instead of holding a little further towards the west or to the east, Magellan, who was in a hurry to reach the Equator, stuck to a course almost due north and thereby traversed that part of the Pacific which is nearest devoid of human habitation.

Finally, on March 16, he once more sighted land. Magellan called the first place where he dropped anchor the Island of St. Lazarus. The name was afterwards given to the entire group but when all this territory was definitely occupied by the Spaniards, the whole of this vast group was rebaptized the Philippines, in honor of the Spanish king.

Here Magellan was at last able to make himself understood by the natives. The navigators of that day, whenever they could do so, tried to get hold of some native who somehow or other had found his way to a European port. That dusky citizen was thereupon supposed to speak all the tongues of all the heathen of his own part of the world and they fared very badly when they had to confess that they were not familiar with the dialects of some of their supposed brethren. They soon learned what was expected of them and faked the conversations they held with the occupants of the canoes that came out to inspect the White

MAGELLAN

Man's vessel, a fact which quite often seems to have contributed to the outbreaks of hostilities which led to the
disgraceful incidents which were an almost integral part
of all early voyages of discovery.

Somewhere or other, Magellan had actually picked up a
native boy from one of these islands, who after many wanderings throughout the Indies had finally found his way to
Europe on a Portuguese ship. This young man was more
than willing to join this new expedition, for this gave him
a chance to return to his native land. We are not quite sure
what sort of a native he was. It is usually accepted that he
was a Filipino and in that case the honor of having been
the first person to circumnavigate the world would go to a
Filipino and not to one of the survivors of Magellan's expedition, who did not accomplish this feat until several years
later.

Anyway, this interpreter, like all the people of that part
of the world, seems to have had a little smattering of the
Malayan language. From a linguistic point of view, the
people of that part of the world which is situated between
Sumatra and the Moluccas are far ahead of their white
brethren of Europe. For they have developed a sort of international jargon which, based upon the Malayan of the true
Malays, has gradually become a practical method of com-
munication between all the inhabitants of this vast island
empire.

In Europe, during the Middle Ages, the floating population of the different ports of the Mediterranean had done

something very much like this. They had developed a vernacular of their own which, known as the lingua franca,
consisted of Italian, Spanish, French, Greek and a considerable admixture of Arabic. In the fifteenth century, Malayan
had become the lingua franca of the whole of the Indian
archipelago and it therefore is quite possible that Magellan,
through his interpreter, now learned that he was very close
to the island of Borneo, which was known to lie south of
the islands of St. Lazarus (the Philippines to us) and due
west of the Moluccas. Magellan therefore had reason to feel
that at last his luck had turned and that a few more weeks
would allow him to hoist the flag of Spain over the rich
spice-islands of the Indies, well outside of the territories
which the Pope had bestowed upon the Portuguese.

And all would now have gone well if Magellan had been
just a little more practical. But like so many of these lonely
sea wanderers of the late Middle Ages, he was a strange
hodgepodge of the greedy adventurer and the religious
fanatic. Columbus, whose mind, all his livelong days, had
been filled with dreams of gold and glory, had died a few
years before in the garb of a simple monk. Magellan, who
belonged to the same breed and believing that his task as
an explorer had come to an end, suddenly felt the urge to
do something for his faith. As a result, instead of preparing
his ships for a hasty departure, he set out to convert the
local chieftain to Christianity.

This potentate, a treacherous scoundrel, showed great
eagerness to let himself be baptized. He had his reasons to

do so. For years he had been at loggerheads with all of his neighbors and he had carefully observed what the White Man's cannon could do against native canoes. The White Man's god, who could speak so loudly and eloquently

ISLANDS EVERYWHERE—HOW DID MAGELLAN MANAGE TO AVOID THEM?

through the mouth of a gun, would undoubtedly be most useful as an ally in His Majesty's long-planned attack on some of his nearby rivals. And so the King of Cebu was duly baptized and the delighted Christian commander, being as good as his word, now placed himself at the head of an expedition against the rival King of Mactan, right in the heart of the Philippines, to bring this unruly monarch to reason.

But Magellan, as I have already said, had not been born

under a lucky star and with everything he had worked for so hard and so long at last within his grasp, the poor fellow got himself killed in an insignificant brawl between the natives of Mactan and those of Cebu.

The King of Cebu pretended to be deeply touched by the untimely departure of his newly found friend and invited his successor, Juan Serrano, and the captains of the other ships to a conference. Apparently they had learned nothing from the experiences of the past few days, for they came willingly enough to this meeting and all of them were promptly murdered.

This disaster left the expedition so sadly deprived of man power that the survivors decided to burn one of the three remaining ships and to embark the remaining sailors on the *Trinidad* and the *Vittoria*.

The *Trinidad*, however, was in such a deplorable condition that the captain refused to risk the lengthy trip home by way of Africa and decided to try his luck in an eastern direction. Perhaps he could reach the Isthmus of Panama and from there send a report of the voyage and of Magellan's death to the authorities at home. The *Trinidad* actually set sail for Panama, but after four months of storm and hunger, the vessel was forced to return to the Moluccas. It took only a month and a half to cover the same distance which it had taken four months to navigate while going eastward. Finally, and by sheer luck, the *Trinidad* found its way to Ternate. The Portuguese, who for the last two years and a half had lived in constant dread of the "tremendous fleet" of the traitor Magellan, breathed a sigh of deep relief when they beheld the crew that manned this spook ship—all that apparently remained of the famous armada that was going to conquer the Spice Islands. They treated the survivors decently but they kept the *Trinidad* (which was not much of a gain) and then sent the crew to Java as prisoners of war.

From Java, these unfortunate creatures were thereupon despatched to Cochin in India where they had to wait a whole year until the Viceroy, off on some expedition, had returned to decide what should be done with them. They apparently used their leisure to study the habits and customs of those elephants who had been trained to do the work that was too heavy for human beings and who were said to be so intelligent that if only they could have spoken, "they would have been much brighter than most men."

When the Governor finally returned, he was too busy welcoming his successor, Vasco da Gama, to bother about his Spanish prisoners and afterwards, da Gama refused to let them depart. However, soon afterwards he died and thereupon the few remaining survivors were allowed to sign up on a Portuguese ship which brought them safely back to Spain, where they arrived more than five years after they had left.

✦

As for the *Vittoria,* it was a little more fortunate. All alone, it reached the Moluccas. There it filled its holds with all sorts of spices and under the command of a certain Juan

Sebastian del Cano it began to grope its way homeward. The island of Tidor was left on December 21, 1521, two years after the expedition had set sail from Europe, and from there on, the ship was in enemy territory.

The fear of encountering any Portuguese was so great that the tiny craft gave the Cape of Good Hope a wide berth and kept several hundred miles to the south. The sudden cold, after so long a time in the tropics, caused many of the sailors to die of pulmonary troubles. Others fell victim to scurvy. Still others merely starved to death. Finally, in July of the year 1522, in a state of complete exhaustion, forty-four men reached the Cape Verde Islands. A sloop was sent to shore to beg for water and fresh supplies, but the Portuguese, now beginning to sense what Magellan's expedition might mean to their own Indian monopoly if any of the survivors should reach Spain, promptly jailed the thirteen members of the crew and demanded that the *Vittoria* surrender on pain of being sunk. Del Cano, however, seems to have been a man of parts. He immediately hoisted sail and with his exhausted and starving men he made for the safety of the open sea.

Two months later, thirty-one out of the two hundred and seventy-five, who three years before had so confidently taken service with Magellan, returned to the harbor of San Lucar to tell the tale of their disaster and their triumph.

Ever since, the world has been debating upon the merits or lack of merits of Dom Fernando Magellan. He was undoubtedly a man of great personal courage and on occasions he could be as brutal as a skipper had to be in those days if one ever hoped to get anywhere at all with the hoodlums and jailbirds who, having been offered a choice between the gallows and the navy, had chosen the latter. But his voyage added very little to the sum total of the world's geographical knowledge. The existence of the Pacific Ocean had already been proved by Balboa, though it had remained for Magellan to give that new sea its name. The Moluccas had long before been explored by the Portuguese. So had the road from India to Europe by way of the Cape of Good Hope. The main achievement therefore of Magellan lay in the fact that from the year 1522 on it was no longer possible for the theologians to insist that the world was as flat as a pancake. They were now forced to concede that it was as round as a cannon ball.

To console themselves, the good clerics thereupon found great pleasure in accusing Magellan's comrades of having eaten meat on Fridays and of having celebrated Easter on a Monday instead of a Sunday. And in this charge of impiety the Church was undoubtedly right, though we can hardly say that the sailors had committed a willful offense. On their trip, the White Man had for the first time come in contact with the perplexing problem of that extra day which is either lost or gained when one passes the international date line of 180° longitude. In the year 1521, the strange behavior of the calendar at this point had not yet been noticed and the sailors of Magellan therefore had been one day behind in all their reckoning, once they had passed the Fiji Islands. From the contemporary theological point of view, this was quite a serious matter, but the only good that came out of their agitation was a more thoroughgoing study of the date line, which ever after was most carefully observed by the sailors who had to cross this part of the ocean.

All in all, therefore, Magellan's voyage had been a waste of money and energy for his employers but without quite realizing what he had done, he had rendered a tremendous service to their rivals who lived along the shores of the North Sea. He had conclusively demonstrated that the new continent, discovered by Columbus, did not continue all the way to the South Pole but that there was an opening a few hundred miles south of the Silver River, through which one could pass from the ocean of the east into the ocean of the west without encountering any opposition on the part of the Spaniards, and during the first half century after Magellan's death, a large number of English and Dutch pirates and patriots actually availed themselves of this convenient back door to raid the Spanish settlements along the west coast of America. But gradually they came to the conclusion that Portugal had grown so weak that there was no reason why one should go all the way to the southernmost point of South America when the much easier route by way of South Africa was open to all comers. After which, the Strait of Magellan lost its popularity and remained in stormy obscurity until the discovery of the California goldfields, during the last century, caused a sudden boom in traffic.

Then came the Panama Canal and now very few ships ever take the trouble to visit this lonely spot, called after the unfortunate Dom Fernando, who was a man of considerable ability but who had not been born under a lucky star, and that—as Herr Goethe so wisely observed only a century and a half ago—that does make all the difference in the world.

As for the legal aspects of the case, which had seemed so very important to most people when Magellan had first approached King Charles with his clever idea of claiming the Moluccas for Spain (since they lay within that half of the world which the treaty of Tordesillas had given to the Spanish crown), nothing was definitely decided by this very costly expedition. For the Portuguese denied the correctness of Magellan's calculations and they insisted that the Moluccas lay well within their own sphere. In the end, both parties agreed to leave the final decision to three different committees of experts: one composed of lawyers and theologians, one composed of geographers and one composed of professional sailors. These committees actually came together a few times but they lost themselves in such acrimonious forms of debate that they only confused the issue and finally reached a point where nobody any longer knew what anybody else was talking about.

The King of Spain and the King of Portugal thereupon did the sensible thing. They took the matter out of the

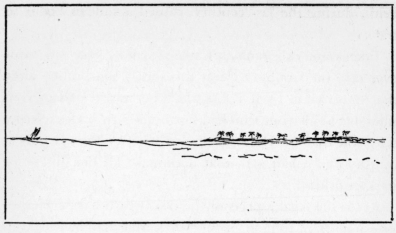

THE ATOLL SEEN FROM A DISTANCE

hands of their experts and left the settlement to a couple of well-seasoned diplomats. In the year 1529 these gentlemen drew up a treaty whereby the Spaniards, for a consideration of 350,000 golden ducats, promised to recognize Portugal's exclusive rights to the Moluccas. Portugal, from its side, closed its eyes to the Spanish occupancy of the Philippines. This was not a matter of generosity for the Portuguese had already completely exhausted their forces by over-expansion and did not really want them. But they found them a convenient "talking point" in their negotiations about the Moluccas and in this way they forced the Spaniards to give them more than they had any right to expect.

✦

Two years before Magellan set sail, a German monk, a certain Dr. Martinus Luther, in an obscure town of north-

THE ATOLL SEEN FROM ABOVE

ern Germany, had nailed ninety-five theses to the door of the court church at Wittenberg. Those ninety-five theses had contained very serious accusations against certain abuses within the bosom of the Church about which this honest Teuton wanted the Holy Father to "do something." As the Pope just then was either unable or unwilling to do much about anything, the controversy was allowed to drag on and this conflict, which looked harmless enough in the beginning, led up to a schism which ever after was to divide the whole of Europe into two mutually hostile groups, which came to be known as Catholics and Protestants.

During the struggle that followed, both sides needed large sums of money for warlike purposes and it was then that the Protestants began to consider the possibilities of depriving their Catholic opponents of their main source of revenue— the profits they derived from their monopoly in colonial

products. Today, it is curious to reflect that the descendants
of these religious rebels are in full possession of every piece
of land ever owned by the Portuguese and the Spaniards in
both the Indies and the Pacific Ocean. But it is very much
to be doubted whether the buccaneers of the North Sea
would ever have dared to rise in open rebellion against
both Rome and Spain if Magellan's voyage had not convinced them of the weakness of the whole of that colonial
fabric which the people of the Mediterranean had tried to
build up—a bit too hastily—among those islands that lie
just west of the Pacific Ocean.

# 7. THE QUEST OF THE GREAT UNKNOWN CONTINENT OF THE SOUTH

O NE OF the most fascinating problems in the history of geography is this one: how much did the people of the past "suspect" before they actually "knew"? For now that we have at last explored every nook and corner of the planet, we are beginning to realize that these dumb medieval folk, who in our opinion were so sadly lacking in concrete information about the world in which they lived, were perhaps not quite as ignorant as we have always taken for granted. In some mysterious way all sorts of queer details about distant lands and continents that still remained undiscovered had apparently found their way to the waterside taverns of the different European harbors. Together these curious odds and ends of information and misinformation had become incorporated into a regular mariner's folklore. This nautical mythology was full of nonsense and exaggerations, yet it contained bits of the truth that could not just be dismissed as the tall yarns of a skipper with a particularly active sense of imagination and the hope of a plentiful supply of schnapps on the house.

There was, for example, that very persistent legend about Prester John, who was said to be a Christian potentate on an African throne. This story was for a long time disregarded by all intelligent geographers as merely another piece of medieval fiction, until the rediscovery of the Negus of Abyssinia revealed that such a dark-skinned African potentate, who was also the head of a Christian church, did exist. There were the tales about people in the polar regions who had no necks and who carried their heads on their chests. The ancient world knew about them but it was not until the explorations of Greenland were resumed in the sixteenth century that we recognized these strange old monsters in the fur-clad Eskimos of Baffin's Bay.

There was, above all things! that persistent rumor about a vast continent at the other side of the Atlantic, which practically all the geographical experts ever since the days of the Greeks had mentioned as an actual fact. They even knew the name. It was called Ultima Thule. Where had the rumor come from? Had it found its way to Europe from Vinland by way of Greenland and Iceland and the Faeroes? Or had it been carried to Europe by those French fishermen who seem to have visited the Banks of Newfoundland centuries before Columbus was born?

Then there were the everlasting tales about golden cities situated in the heart of Asia and many of those stories definitely antedated the explorations of the Polo family. A great deal of all this common hearsay was of course pure fiction. But upon a closer examination of these picturesque fables, we are bound to come to the conclusion that most of them had been based upon something more than mere hearsay.

The difficulty was to decide who had been responsible for bringing these scraps of information to the Old World. But when we tried to do so, we ran up against almost unsurmountable difficulties. For in our own age of endless pub-

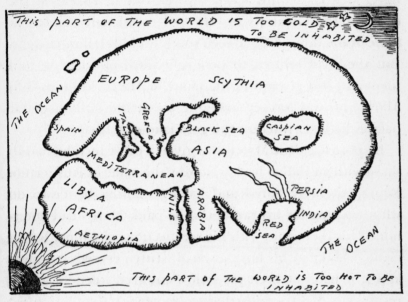

THE WORLD OF ARISTOTLE

licity and whole armies of ghost writers, we are very apt to forget that before the introduction of the printing press, the world was quite vocal but was not in the least addicted to expressing itself in a literary way. Even those who had had all sorts of interesting adventures, did not as a rule know how to communicate their ideas to others.

Marco Polo might have remained nothing but a name if he had not been such a good patriot. His love for his native city of Venice had made him enlist in an expedition against the rival republic of Genoa. The Venetian fleet was defeated in the naval battle off Curzola Island and Marco was among the prisoners taken to Genoa. Until then, he had never written a word about the years he had spent at the court of the Great Khan. He had occasionally hinted at some of the things he had seen to a few of his fellow-citizens. But they had refused to believe a word of what he told them and had given him the name of Marco Millions—old Mark who was forever bragging about the million dollar palaces he had visited in the gold-land of Cathay.

By pure accident Marco was given a cell which he had to share with an Italian hack writer by the name of Rusticiano. Being miserably bored and having nothing better to do while waiting for his ransom to be paid, Marco had entertained his roommate with his recollections of China. Rusticiano, who knew his business, had written everything down and if it had not been for Polo's enforced idleness, as the result of a disastrous battle between two Italian cities, we might never have heard a word about that most fascinating voyage to the court of Kubla Khan.

It was the same with Columbus. Imagine Columbus coming home today after having done what he did and try to imagine the scene—boatloads of reporters meeting his ships way down the harbor—offers of profitable syndicate contracts—of movie contracts—of radio contracts and book rights with first and second and third serial privileges! Overnight the whole world would have become familiar with the name of the Genoese admiral. But what did the world of Ferdinand and Isabella ever learn about the man who had discovered an entirely new world? Next to nothing! One sixteen page pamphlet had appeared in print shortly after his return. It was said to be an accurate translation of a letter written originally in Spanish by Columbus himself on February 14, 1493, when he was still on board his flagship.

This letter had been meant for the head of the Royal Exchequer, so that dignitary might be duly impressed by the importance of the discoveries which Don Cristoforo had made in India "above the river Ganges." As for the original, no one has ever been able to find it. We only know it from a Latin version and of the editions that have survived, only one bears the name of the town in which it was printed and the date of publication—Rome, MCCCCXCIII.

Besides this meagre literary effort on the part of the man who discovered us, we have a few letters which are usually appeals for some sort of official recognition or for the money the court owed him. Finally, there is a signature to a will and to a codicil to that will, but the world at large remained so completely unaware of the significance of this man's work that not a single voice seems to have been raised in protest when fifteen years after his first voyage, the world he had discovered began to appear on the maps under the name of someone else.

But we should remember that Columbus had been primarily a dreamer whereas Amerigo Vespucci, the Spanish

representative of the Medici interests on the Iberian peninsula, had been a practical man of business. Having been
instructed by his employers in Florence to find out what
chances of profitable investment there might be in this
newly opened-up territory, Vespucci thereupon had hastily
published two pamphlets, which gave full and very flattering details about the economic possibilities of the *mundus
novus*.

Here at last was something concrete, which the average
citizen could understand, and this time the public took
due notice. What those contemporaries could not know was
this: that, according to the most reliable information now
at hand, Vespucci had never taken part in that expedition
of the year 1497, which he so eloquently described in his
prospectus. We have gradually come to regard him as a
clever fraud with a fine flair for words. But in spite of all
this, we live on a continent which bears his name and not
that of the man who found it. And outside of a few patriotic
Italian societies, nobody cares.

I am giving these few rather flagrant examples of how
geographical information (correct or otherwise) will sometimes get around to show you how much still remains to
be done within this field. To make matters worse, once the
Spaniards had appeared upon the scene, everything had to
be referred back to the authorities in Seville and these were
notoriously lax in their business methods. It was perfectly
possible that a report upon some very important subject,
such as the discovery of the Torres Strait, could be filed

away in a pigeonhole to remain forgotten for almost three
entire centuries. But such negligence was part of the Span-

POMPENIUS MELA 40 A.D.
THE FIRST SUSPICION OF LAND AT THE OTHER SIDE OF THE
OCEAN

ish tradition. Had not the Azores and Madeira and the
Cape Verde Islands been known for more than five centuries and hadn't they thereupon been so completely forgotten that they might never have existed at all? Indeed

they had, except that during the period which intervened between their discovery and their rediscovery, there must have been hundreds of sailors who vaguely remembered how their own grandfathers or a friend of a friend of their own grandfathers had known a man who had once known a man who had actually set foot on one of these bits of land, way out towards the west. Some of their neighbors would merely shrug their shoulders and call them liars behind their backs, but others would undoubtedly think that after all, there must be something to these stories which were too full of concrete details to have been entirely invented. And professional cartographers, trying to give their customers something new, would eagerly incorporate the more plausible aspects of these mysterious accounts into their new maps, giving names and dates as if they had actually been there. Sometimes they guessed wrong but sometimes they guessed right and this led to some very curious charts on which we find certain parts of the world definitely located and outlined hundreds of years before they were actually discovered.

And now we might see how all this audacious guessing had affected the Pacific Ocean.

Most people seem to be under the impression that the most important discoveries in the Pacific were not made until during the second half of the eighteenth century. That is true to a certain extent but apparently a great deal of preparatory work had been done, about which we shall never have any details.

Today most geographers feel convinced that several centuries before the discovery of Hawaii by Captain Cook, certain Spanish galleons, bound from the Philippines to Panama, had been shipwrecked on the shores of those islands and that their crews, after the loss of their ship, had

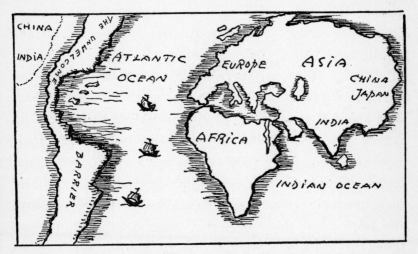

THE UNCOMFORTABLE DISCOVERIES OF THE FIFTEENTH CENTURY WHICH
UPSET ALL THE OLD MAPS

remained there until the end of their days. On the other hand, a few of them may have reached one of the other islands, like the Fijis or the Ladrones. And it is even possible that eventually they had found their way back to Europe, like a few of the men of Magellan's *Trinidad,* who had returned to Spain years after the others and who in the meantime had been taken all over Melanesia.

You will remember the Filipino I mentioned on board one of Magellan's ships, who had been the first man to circumnavigate our planet. For all we know, there must have been others like him, but being simple sailors, they remained mute, inglorious and unsung. Even so, a mute and inglorious boatswain who has been places can impart an awful lot of information, or at least he can suggest things which in the hands of an experienced geographer may prove to be of real scientific importance.

✦

You may well ask, "Why this meditation upon the philosophy of discovery when all you needed to have done was to give us the actual facts?" "Between the years 1616 and 1618, a Dutchman at last discovered the continent of Australia." I agree. I could have done just that, but please observe the words "at last." They are used in connection with a period of more than seventeen hundred years, during which there had always been more or less talk about the existence of a great continent that must lie somewhere far south of the Indies.

In order not to complicate matters any further, let us start with the year 1600. By then the road to the Indies by way of the Cape of Good Hope had already become an old story. On the continent of America, cities had been built, civil and ecclesiastic authorities had been duly installed, churches had been erected, universities had been founded and printing presses were at work on books that bore the imprint of the New World.

The impossibility of a short cut to the Indies by way of the polar regions had been definitely demonstrated by the disastrous expedition of the Dutch to Nova Zembla. Both the Indies and the Spice Islands had already enriched four generations of white investigators. Ships of a dozen nations were busily exploring every cove and bay of Asia, Africa and the Americas and maps of the Atlantic and Pacific Oceans showed that the geographers had made excellent use of the information brought home by their skippers and pilots.

The people of Europe had reason to be proud of themselves. Within the memory of man, all the old barriers had been broken down and the planet had increased a hundredfold. It was a time of terrific commercial activity and almost every vessel that came back brought fresh tales of new discoveries, of convenient short cuts to still other treasure chests, and every month saw the formation of more trading companies, companies going after the whales of Greenland, companies specializing in the pepper and nutmeg of the Moluccas, companies to find and explore the last gold mines of the Andes.

It was a period of unbounded opportunities, of marvelous achievements and dreadful disasters, of shoestring speculations and thousand percent dividends, of heroes and blackguards, but above all things, it was an era of glorious adventure.

Yet whenever old sailors came together to drink their ale and to swap stories of strange lands and miraculous escapes, there was one subject which would always, sooner or later, creep into the conversation and make them shake their heads and mumble, "Yes, but how about that great continent of the south? It is true, we don't know anything more about it now than we did a thousand years ago. Some even claim it does not exist—that it is just another fable like that of the island of St. Brandon, but even the old Greeks knew about it and those old folks were usually right, when they hinted at something like that. And since then, too many others have come back who said that they had been there or had been near it to let it go as just so much foolish talk. And some day, some lucky fellow will find it too!"

In the end, they proved right. After Abel Tasman had returned from his famous voyage of the year 1642, the existence of the Southern Continent was no longer a matter of speculation. It did exist. It had been seen and it had been visited and it had been claimed as part of another country's territory. But it had taken all of seventeen centuries to solve the puzzle of *Terra Australis Incognita*.

✦

The ancient world had been the world of one inland sea, the Mediterranean, and quite naturally it thought in terms of inland seas. There was an ocean in the Greek scheme of things, but that name was reserved for the *okeanos,* that wide river which was supposed to run way around all the dry land of the world. All the other seas were either lakes or inland seas, just like the Mediterranean, the Black Sea, the Caspian Sea, the Sea of Marmora, the Red Sea or the Persian Sea. During the fourth century B.C. another inland sea was added to this collection when Alexander the Great marched his men eastward until at the mouth of the Indus

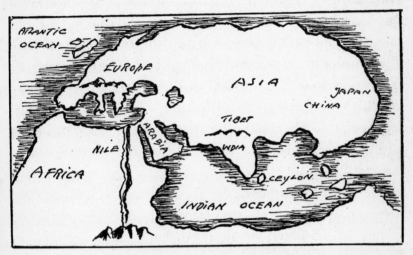

ARABIC MAP OF THE MIDDLE AGES

River they were stopped by the waters of what we now call the Indian Ocean.

The Greeks had already known about the existence of India, but they had considered it a part of Ethiopia. That was the name then given to the whole of northern Africa and still to be found as such on the maps of Europe until three centuries ago, when it was beginning to be used exclusively for the realm of the Negus of Abyssinia.

Since the world came to an end in southern Ethiopia, the waters seen by the troops of Alexander must be part of the all-encircling *okeanos*. That hypothesis made sense and was quite readily accepted by the geographers of the west. But according to the stories brought back by those who had been in the fleet of Nearchus, the Macedonian general who sailed from the mouth of the Indus to the Persian Gulf and discovered the mouths of the Tigris and the Euphrates, there was no noticeable change in the tides of these seas. That contradicted reports about the real *okeanos* where the differences in tides were said to be very great. And so the Greek philosophers (their word for what we call "professor") came to the conclusion that they had been mistaken and that Alexander had merely discovered another inland sea.

For centuries afterwards, the learned world accepted these findings, and on the maps appeared an additional inland sea, bordered on the north by India and China, on the west by Africa (or Ethiopia, as it was then called) and on the south and east by a *terra australis nondum cognita,* or an "as yet undiscovered land of the South."

That was the beginning of a problem which was to keep the civilized world mildly worried during the whole of the Middle Ages—the problem of the Great South Land.

It would be very pleasant if we could persuade ourselves that all this excitement about an unknown country had been due to a deep scientific interest on the part of our ancestors, but they were very much like ourselves. A few of them could take a detached view of the matter, but the majority were much more prosaic in dealing with such problems. They knew that a few people had become immensely rich because they had been the first to be on the spot when new countries were discovered. They hoped that

THE POPULAR BELIEF IN THIS MYSTERIOUS SOUTHERN CONTINENT MADE THE PROMOTERS OF SOUTH SEA ENTERPRISES RICH

some time in the future they would be just as lucky. If only they could know when to invest their money and when to say no, when some high-pressure salesman came around to let them in on the ground floor of that tremendous boom that was going to happen when the Exchange heard of those rich gold mines that were just said to have been found in Estremadura del Oro, five weeks north of the silver mines of Miraflores del Inspiracion! And they were also like ourselves in that they could never learn from experience.

Our history books devote inspiring chapters to the East India Companies of England and Holland, to the West India Company and the Greenland Company of the Netherlands, to the few groups of Gentlemen Adventurers who helped to enrich Boston and Bristol. But they never mention the hundreds of other little organizations which were founded in every town and village that had access to the sea, which swallowed up the entire savings of the community and thereafter and most effectively ruined everyone who had either directly or indirectly been in any way connected with the unfortunate enterprise.

I wish that some student in economics would sometime delve into the archives and would give us an account of the amount of money lost by the unsuccessful trading companies of the era of the great colonial expansion. It must have been enormous, much larger than the profits that accrued from the few successful enterprises. But this no more deterred the relatives of the victims from speculating in the same sort of stock than knowledge about the uneven chances in some Irish sweepstake will prevent the scrub-ladies of New York from wasting their hard-earned dollars in this lottery, and no sooner had one small and independent company gone to the wall than there were a half dozen others ready to take its place. For when an entire nation

NOT THE LEAST FASCINATING PART OF THOSE PACIFIC ISLANDS
WAS THE FACT THAT THEY WERE SITUATED AT THE OTHER SIDE
OF THE WORLD

or continent is attacked by one of those mass delusions which makes them believe that "this time they will be lucky," there is nothing that can stop the spread of the disease until it has worked itself out. In which case, it will be immediately followed by some other form of lunacy, like the absurd tulip speculation of the Low Countries during the early half of the seventeenth century or the wild scramble for Mississippi stock a hundred years later.

The widespread interest therefore in the unknown southern continent, which began to show itself shortly after Magellan had sailed across the Pacific, was not primarily a scientific one, but it was the old story repeating itself. People once more (and perhaps for the last time) saw a chance of getting something for nothing.

In the popular imagination of that time, every newly discovered piece of desert must necessarily lead up to another Ophir, the Land of Gold. No matter how often these great hopes had been dashed to pieces, no matter how many of the expeditions from these different Dorados had never returned at all, it made not the slightest difference to those who wanted to risk their dollars and pennies. For after every fresh disappointment, they would merely remark, "Of course, all that may be true, but how about that expedition of 1530, when a fellow who had been a swineherd over here found a country where the king wore gold dust in his hair and sat on a throne of solid gold and lived in a golden palace? Well, Sir-ee, he came back with thirty large ships, all of them full of gold and pearls and dia-

monds! How about him?" And that one exception kept all
the others in a state of perpetual suspense and excitement,
for the man who has never had quite enough to eat will of
course forever be dreaming of rich meals and tankards full
of ale. Those dreams of course won't fill his tummy, but
they will make him feel much happier, so perhaps it is just
as well, for what is life if you can't ever fool yourself?

By the middle of the seventeenth century, the possibilities of profitable speculations had greatly dwindled. The
richer parts of the Indies had been divided among the nations strong enough and solvent enough to hold their own
against their rivals. The new continent discovered by
Columbus had, by and large, proved a very decided disappointment. The few gold mines belonged to the government and no outsider was allowed to come near them. He
could risk his money and his life among the forests and
plains of the north, but unless he had some very decided
purpose in leaving home (a quarrel with his local landlord
or bishop), he had better stay right where he was, for the
reports that came from the other side of the ocean were
one endless tale of woe—of entire colonies that had been
swallowed up by the wilderness—of women and children
abducted by the savages—of towns that were never again
found when relief expeditions were sent out to bring them
arms and provisions.

Africa was out of the question on account of the heat
and sickness and the wild animals and evil spirits. And so
there remained only one final hope for the disinherited—

that unknown land that must lie somewhere beyond the southern islands of the great inland sea of India—the *terra australis*—as yet *incognita*.

The voyage of Magellan had given the European world some hazy ideas about its gigantic dimensions. It had also shown that the Southern Continent was not, as Ptolemy had supposed, a continuation of Siam and Ceylon. Ptolemy, as a matter of fact, the great Alexandrian cartographer of the second century, whose maps had dominated all geographical speculations during the whole of the Middle Ages, was now beginning to lose a great deal of his former prestige. The voyages of Vasco da Gama had conclusively proved that Africa was not connected with Asia except by a narrow strip of land in the north and as for Asia, that continent too had now been revealed as a gigantic island with water on all sides except in the west.

But ideas, no matter how erroneous, once they have finally incorporated themselves firmly into man's mentality, are not very easily dislocated. Columbus, for example, remained a convinced disciple of Ptolemy until the end of his days and although hundreds of Portuguese, following the trail of Vasco da Gama, had now sailed around the Cape of Good Hope and had explored the ocean for hundreds of miles south of that cape without ever finding any trace of land, the belief in the Southern Continent refused to die.

The maps grew more and more vague about it, moved it hither and yon, but no one dared to suggest that it was merely a myth. For that, even during the sixteenth century, might have got them into conflict with the Church. It had now become the last refuge of paradise. Did not Genesis II:10 speak emphatically about a river that "went out of Eden to water the garden"? Suppose (as many people believed) that river was the Nile? Suppose the sources of the Nile, which were not discovered until a generation ago, were really located in Eden? And although, after all the explorations of the last two hundred years, it seemed impossible that there should be any actual contact between Africa and the Great Southern Continent, it was better to stay on the safe side and not hint too openly that the Holy Book once more had proved to be wrong.

To us, accustomed to accept the findings of science without a qualm of doubt, this mentality, which refused to face facts even after they had been proved over and over again, seems incredible. But let us remember that we ourselves may still be the victims of delusions which will seem just as incredible to the people of a thousand years hence as these notions of otherwise reasonable men of three hundred years ago. But it seems to depend more upon what one wants to believe than what one should believe and so we should be lenient in our judgment of the men and women of the seventeenth century who in spite of Magellan's proof to the contrary continued to insist that the Pacific must be a vast inland sea, bounded on the south by an enormous continent, and who therefore greatly welcomed any new incidents which seemed to show that, after all, they might be right.

Let a hurricane blow a ship out of its course and let the frightened crew catch a hasty glimpse of a coast which did not as yet appear on any of the maps and at once all the stories about the mysterious Southland would be revived with great jubilation.

As early as the year 1526 a certain Jorge de Menezes had been driven southward by adverse winds and had finally reached a large island inhabited not by Malays (such as were to be found in every other part of Indonesia) but by a people who were unmistakably related to the Negroes of Africa and everybody was certain that now at last the problem had been solved.

In 1546 a Spaniard, Ortiz de Retez, returning from the Philippines to the Isthmus of Panama, had also been greatly driven out of his course and had reached the same island which Menezes had first found twenty years before. He stayed there long enough to give it a name and he called it New Guinea. Since the original Guinea was situated on the west coast of Africa between the Senegal and Niger Rivers, it showed how the fable which connected Africa with the unknown Southland continued to spook around in people's heads.

In the year 1567 the problem of the unknown Southland was once more tackled, but this time from a scientific angle. The Viceroy of Peru, Alvaro Mendaña de Neyra, noticing that the available supply of gold was beginning to grow very low, decided to make another attempt to find the unknown continent that he might convert the natives to Christianity and incidentally tap a few new sources of riches. His expedition crossed the Pacific just south of the Equator and reached a new group of islands. The skipper, in an outburst of entirely unwarranted enthusiasm, was so delighted with what he had found that he called them the Solomon Islands in honor of the biblical discoverer of the land of Ophir.

Unfortunately, these bits of land did not in the least live up to his expectations. They were found to be inhabited by a very low class of Negro-like aborigines who had not the slightest idea what these white visitors meant when they showed them a small piece of gold. But the name has stuck and this entire group, several hundred miles east of New Guinea, is still known as the Solomon Islands and is still inhabited by a low class of aborigines, who in spite of their Australian officials would greatly love to try their hand once more at their favorite old pastime of cannibalism and head-hunting.

In the meantime, news reached Peru of still another discovery. It had come to Lima by way of Mexico and it had taken a long time to reach civilization. It appeared that an expedition sent from Mexico to find the shortest route to the Moluccas had been shipwrecked on the coast of an island that as yet failed to appear on any of the maps. That island, as far as we can guess, was no other than our own beloved isle of Hawaii.

The discoverer was a certain Alvaro de Saavedra. He had been followed a few years later by another Spaniard, a certain Juan Gaetano, who was said to have visited this part of the Pacific in or around the year 1555. However, I hasten to mention that many historians positively deny these claims on the part of the Spaniards and insist that Captain Cook was the first white man to have set foot on Hawaiian soil in the year 1778. I shall take no sides, for we shall probably never find out.

At the same time, in view of the inexcusably careless methods which prevailed in the Spanish colonial office, it is well within the realm of possibilities that Spanish ships actually reached the Hawaiian Islands, sent reports home about their discovery and that thereupon some colonial official wrote "no gold" on the margin and went out for his afternoon nap and then forgot all about it.

But the persistent rumors about all these new islands seem to have inspired Mendaña de Neyra to try his luck once more and so in 1595 a second expedition left Peru for the great unknown. This time the expedition did not even get as far as the Solomons. It was forced to stop at the Marquesas where de Neyra died. His widow thereupon guided the ships to the Philippines and made no further personal attempts to solve the Southland problem. She delegated this task to one Pedro Fernandez de Quieroz, a Portuguese who after he had taken service with the Spaniards had changed his name to Quirós. Why Senhor Quieroz had decided to become Señor Quirós we do not know, but from his later record, we feel inclined to say that Portugal had not lost very much when he went over to the enemy, for he proved himself to be a most unreliable citizen.

Maybe he was not really a "liar" as many of his contemporaries called him. Perhaps he was only endowed with too much imagination, a failing of a great many other members of his craft. But whatever his accomplishments as a navigator, he did stumble upon several new pieces of land and as a result he has his own little page in all handbooks of geography.

Quirós began his independent career by writing several highfalutin' letters to the Pope and to the King of Spain. In these he proposed to go forth on a new expedition that would make everything Columbus, Vasco da Gama and Magellan had done look like the work of so many amateurs. The Pope was not interested, but the Spanish crown, as always desperately in need of funds, decided to give him a chance.

On December 21 of the year 1605 Quirós left Callao as pilot of an expedition of three ships under actual command of Luis de Torres. In the year 1606, Pilot de Quirós guided his squadron to what are now called the New Hebrides. If you will look on the map, you will see that one of these islands is still known as Espiritu Santo. It owes this noble appellation to the fertile brain of its discoverer. He lived just three centuries too soon. Today Quirós would have made a fortune as an advertising man, for he called this godforsaken isle La Austrialia del Espiritu Santo. Observe the Austrialia instead of Australis. That was de Quirós' delicate little way of flattering the King of Spain who as a member of the House of Habsburg belonged to the family which also ruled over Austria. For some reasons unknown, the foolish name stuck and when in the year 1802 Matthew Flinders, the great English navigator who was the first to give us a correct survey of the coast of the new continent, looked for a name to replace New Holland (as it had been known until now) he suggested Australia.

As for the original perpetrator of this joke, he did not mean to let his commander run away with the credit for his discovery. He resorted to the old trick of getting himself lost from the rest of the squadron and hastened back to the civilized world to reap the rewards which were his due. But whether he was just a little too smart for his own good or did not lie skillfully enough, this much we know—that his account was not received with any noticeable outbursts of enthusiasm and after that, we lose track of the noble Señor de Quirós.

Meanwhile de Torres, ignorant of any plot against him, had wasted considerable time waiting for his lost pilot and had thereupon decided to sail for the Philippines, which he knew to lie somewhere towards the north. It was on this occasion that he sailed through the strait which still bears his name and which separates New Guinea from Australia proper. De Torres did not set foot on either of these two coasts, having his hands full trying to navigate safely between those treacherous coral reefs, which even today force all steamers which ply between Sydney and Batavia to provide themselves with a special Torres Strait pilot. But he duly reported what he had seen to the home government.

Alas, either the Spaniards just then had had enough trouble with the untrustworthy de Quirós or it was once again a case of that slothful negligence which was so characteristic of all Spanish colonial methods, but nothing was done about this Torres report. For nearly three hundred years it lay forgotten in a monastery in Manila. Then by sheer accident it was unearthed by an inquisitive historian and today de Torres receives all the honor he deserves for his memorable discovery.

# 8. ABEL TASMAN PUTS NEW HOLLAND ON THE MAP

During the middle of the sixteenth century a young Dutchman by the name of Jan Huyghen van Linschoten had, for reasons unknown to us, left the shores of the Zuyder Zee for the banks of the Tagus, had learned the language and had taken service as a sort of secretary and butler with the newly appointed Bishop of Goa. Together with him he had sailed for the Indies by way of the Cape of Good Hope and in this way he had been able to visit a part of the world which no foreigners were supposed to see.

What had made this boy of sixteen go forth and leave his home town is as much of a mystery as the attack of homesickness, which in the year 1589 had suddenly made him give up his comfortable position and return to the Low Countries. There he was welcomed as a true gift from Heaven, for here at last was someone who might be supposed to know all about the road to the Indies and such information was then worth its weight in gold.

Linschoten was not exactly handy with a pen but several of the local geographers offered to assist him and together they produced his famous *Itinerary*. In this he not only told

A NEW WORLD—NO MAPS—NOTHING TO GO BY

what he himself had seen but he also mentioned everything he had heard others tell about the best way to navigate between the islands of the Indian archipelago. Among the odds and ends of the observations he thus bestowed upon his delighted compatriots were several references to a continent which was supposed to be part of what then was called Java Major, or Greater Java. Linschoten even hinted that by sailing due east after one had left the Cape of Good Hope, it would be possible to reach this unknown continent without first stopping at Java.

Almost half a century was to go by before the Dutch were able to take this matter up seriously. During that period they had been much too busy taking the Spice Islands away from the Portuguese to do anything else. But during the middle of the seventeenth century, when they had conquered the greater part of the Indian Archipelago, they bethought themselves of what Linschoten had written in his *Itinerary* about the unknown Southland and decided to equip a fleet, that this problem about the unknown Southern Continent might at last be solved and solved once and for all. For the mysterious Southland had again forced itself upon the attention of the European geographers and people were getting impatient to know what the real truth might be.

In the year 1503 a Frenchman, who was supposed to be bound for the Indies, had been blown out of his way and had reported that he had set foot on *Terra Australis Incognita*. It seems very unlikely that he had ever done anything of the sort. From his descriptions, we rather suspect that he had only visited Madagascar. The existence of this island, by name at least, had been known to Europe ever since the days of Marco Polo, who in his travels had mentioned a country called "Madeigascar" which was supposed to be a part of Africa. Also in the year 1500 a Portuguese, Diogo Diaz, also bound for the Indies and also blown out of his course, had seen the coasts of a new island which undoubtedly had been Polo's Madagascar.

Thirty years later, still another Frenchman, Guillaume le Testu, also put in his claim that he had reached the unknown Southland. Modern historical research, however, is not willing to support him, although it is difficult to decide where exactly he had been. But the ever alert geographers had not allowed these disjointed scraps of information to go by unnoticed and when in the year 1597 the Dutchman Wytfliet published his geography, he definitely stated that the *Terra Australis Incognita* was situated due south of New Guinea and separated from the latter by a wide strait (correct!), that it was situated two or three degrees from the Equator (fairly correct!) and that it was so large that it must be considered a continent in its own right (also correct!).

Wytfliet's book was published nine years before de Torres had actually passed through the strait that separated Australia from New Guinea and the name of this discovery (as I just told you) did not get published until years later. Therefore Wytfliet was either an awfully good guesser or

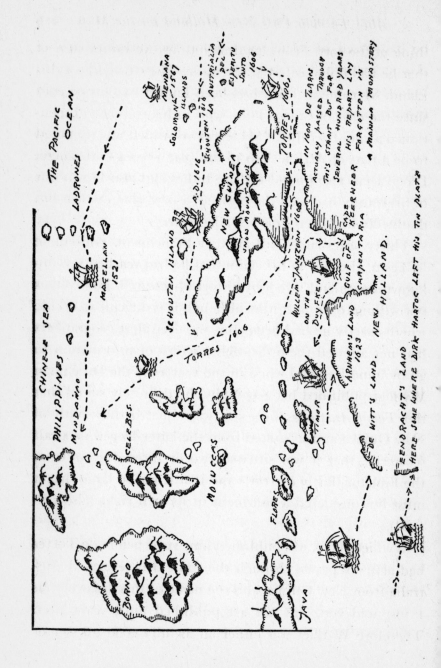

he had based his conclusions upon the verbal reports of skippers who had actually been in this part of the world but who had never felt the urge to give any written account of their adventures.

We should also remember that in those days it was not at all to the advantage of a successful navigator or of his employers to give too much publicity to their discoveries. New sea routes were the trade secrets of these early companies of merchant adventurers and they would no more have thought of telling a rival how to get from Amsterdam to Amboina than a modern manufacturer would think of informing his competitors how to make that synthetic rubber to which he owed his fortune.

The mystery with which the Dutch surrounded their first scientific expeditions to the new continent shows this very clearly. It was in the year 1606 that Captain Willem Janszoon was sent out from Bantam on the yacht *Duyfken* to explore the whole of New Guinea. Having followed the coast of the island as far as the Fly River, he had changed his course in a southern direction and one fine morning he had found himself in what is now known as the Gulf of Carpentaria.

Keeping close to the coast of the York peninsula, he had finally reached a cape which he had called Cape Keerweer, or Turn-Again. It was a most inhospitable piece of land and as soon as possible he had hastened back to his beloved Java.

But neither he nor de Torres, who was to pass through

this same region a short time afterwards, had the slightest idea of what they had done. We now know that they had conclusively proved that *Terra Australis* was not connected with New Guinea, but as they remained completely ignorant of the fact that they had actually been in sight of the new continent, their voyages gained them neither fame nor riches. They had seen a fine new continent. What of it? Almost any skipper during the first half of the seventeenth century had done as much. Why get excited about such an unimportant piece of news?

Ten years later another Dutchman was to have a similar experience. His name was Dirk Hartog and on the good ship *De Eendracht* he was proceeding from the Cape of Good Hope to Java. But he had taken his course a little too far towards the south and instead of landing in Java he had reached a coast which appeared to be completely uninhabited and of which, as a matter of routine, he had taken possession by means of a tin plate fastened to a pole. On this plate the following legend had been engraved by one of the sailors: "On October 25, A.D. 1616, the ship *De Eendracht* has arrived here." In the year 1696 this plate was found by another Dutchman, Willem de Vlamingh, master of the *Geelvinck*. He took it back with him to Holland and if you are interested you can still see it in the Rijksmuseum in Amsterdam. De Vlamingh in turn left a tin plate of his own on that inhospitable coast, which since then has been known as Eendrachtsland with a Dirk Hartog Island and a Geelvinck Channel as additional evidence of

A.D. 1616

DIRK HARTOG LEAVES A TIN PLATE ON THE COAST OF NEW HOLLAND

the fact that in those early days the Australian mainland
had actually been visited by the Dutch.

The report of skipper Hartog seems to have made some
slight impression upon the merchants of Amsterdam. Not
that anybody grew very excited about the prospect of add-
ing still further territories to a colonial empire that was
already much too large to be successfully administered. But
the Dutch still felt themselves to be intruders in the Indies,
where the Portuguese had already been established for
nearly a century when the first vessels from Holland had at
last made their appearance, and they were still worrying
about the safety of the route they had to follow to reach
Java.

Nobody had as yet thought of the possibility of fortifying
the Cape of Good Hope. That was not done until the year
1652 when the Dutch, having lost St. Helena to the British after they had taken it from the Portuguese, founded
Cape Town as a convenient spot where their ships could
take on fresh water and fresh vegetables. But the Portuguese, although they had lost most of their former power
in the Indies, were very apt to lie in wait for their Dutch
enemies in the neighborhood of the island of Mauritius
and the Dutch therefore were gravely considering the possibility of instructing their vessels to give the Cape a wide
berth, to steer about a hundred miles further towards the
south and then to proceed eastward to Java by way of
Amsterdam Island, which had been discovered in 1633 by
Anthonie van Diemen.

Times may occasionally change but men and their motives remain very much the same and no sooner had the Dutch stumbled upon the west coast of Australia in their desire to avoid conflicts with the Portuguese than certain London merchants were busy petitioning James I for permission to equip an expedition to explore the unknown Southland and to take possession of it in the name of the British crown. The English minister in the Hague had kept his home government well informed about the latest discoveries of the Dutch in that part of the world and the London merchants wanted their share of the profits, if any profits were going to be made. James, however, had already troubles enough of his own and he therefore advised Sir William Courten to desist, as the Dutch East India Company was even more jealous of its monopoly than the Portuguese had been and as such intrusions on the part of the English might lead to war with this inconvenient neighbor.

And so the Dutch were left in full possession of their southern route and as time went on more and more ships began to arrive in Java with stories about reefs and sandy coasts and a country without a single inhabitant.

The names on the modern map of Australia bear witness to these visits. There is Edelland, so called after Johan Edel, who in 1619 had reached this part of western Australia, together with Captain Frederick de Houtman, who in turn had given his name to the dangerous Houtman Rocks, just outside of the harbor of the modern city of Geraldton. Incidentally, these Houtman Rocks were responsible for the first white settlement of Australia. In the year 1629 another Dutch ship, commanded by François Pelsaert, bound for Java, had been shipwrecked on these rocks. The crew had remained behind while Pelsaert in an open boat had set forth in search of help. When he returned he found that the crew had mutinied and had behaved so outrageously —murdering each other—that he took two of the leaders and left them behind on the coast of the nearby mainland. No one knows what became of these scoundrels, but undoubtedly they had the honor of being the first white settlers of the Australian continent.

Another Dutch name on the map of Australia, Cape Leeuwin, proves that the Dutch had also begun to explore the southern coast of Australia, and Nuyt's Archipelago just off Eyre peninsula (so called after a director of the Dutch East India Company) shows that they would have been able to give us a very nice outline of at least half of the coast of the unknown continent if they had only realized that they had long since found what they were supposed to be looking for.

Partly their lack of understanding of what they were doing may have been due to the pressure under which they lived, for these skippers, sent out by the authorities in Batavia, were always admonished to observe the greatest possible haste. There was good reason why the Dutch East India governors should want to have the problem of the southern seas settled. They remembered what almost a century before had happened to the Portuguese. The Portu-

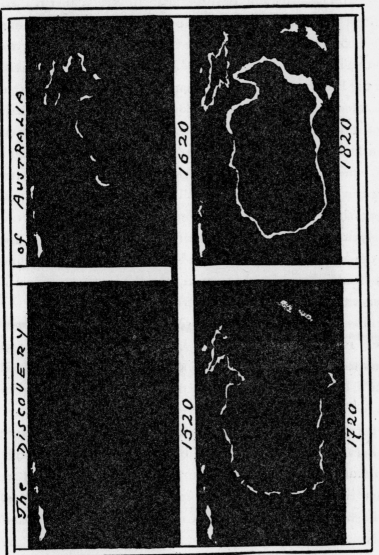

AUSTRALIA APPEARS UPON THE MAP

guese too had happily lived under the impression that their control of the African sea route to the Moluccas was sufficient to protect them against any surprise attack from the east. The sudden arrival of Magellan's squadron in that part of the world had shown them their mistake. The Portuguese monopoly of the Spice Islands had now been replaced by a monopoly on the part of the Dutch. But they too lived in a constant state of fear. What had happened before might happen again and they were forever scanning the eastern horizon lest an "unprivileged" intruder appear to challenge their highly questionable rights upon Java and the Moluccas. Therefore the sooner they knew the actual lay of the land in the southern and eastern part of the Pacific the better, for then they could take the necessary precautions against a surprise attack from the east.

This belief in the necessity of a rigid monopoly was entirely medieval, for today the Dutch East Indies are wide open to foreign capital as long as it does not organize little bands of Nazi boys who use their freedom of action to preach Hitlerism to the natives and establish a Greater Germany beneath the Equator. But all during the sixteenth and seventeenth centuries, the opinion prevailed that both individuals and nations could grow rich only if they had an exclusive hold upon certain commodities. It now makes us smile when we read that the leaders of that famous voyage to Nova Zembla of the year 1596 had at once suggested to their employers in Amsterdam that a few fortifications, built on both sides of the Vaygach Strait, which led from the Arctic Ocean into the Kara Sea, would assure the Dutch the absolute control over the route which some day (as they fully expected) would allow ships from Europe to reach the Indies by following the coast of northern Asia. And

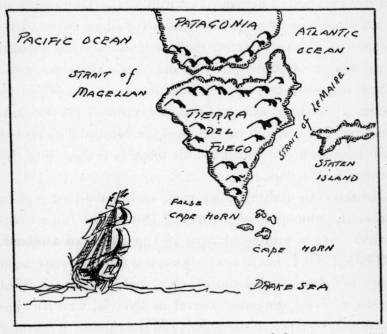

THE ROUTE OF SCHOUTEN IN 1616

Magellan too seems to have thought of the possibilities of fortifying the famous strait between South America and Tierra del Fuego, so that in the future the Spaniards would be able to exclude all other nations from the eastern half of the Pacific.

We should also remember that there was a good deal of the gangster spirit among those hardy gentlemen-adven-

turers who since they were able to lay the foundations for
the future wealth and glory of England and Holland have
since been promoted to the rank of noble and useful patriots. The Dutch realized very clearly that their position
in the East Indies depended entirely upon their ability to
hold by means of arms that which they had obtained by
means of violence. Hence the whole colony was thrown
into a state of panic when in the year 1616 two "scab"
ships, equipped by complete outsiders and commanded by
Schouten and Lemaire, had actually repeated the performance of Magellan and had reached the Moluccas by way of
still another route which led far towards the south of the
Strait of Magellan.

In the end, nothing much came of this bold attempt to
break the monopoly of the official Dutch East India Company. After a prolonged fight in the courts of Holland,
Schouten and Lemaire's expedition was found to have been
"out of bounds" and the courts upheld the highhanded
decision of the governor-general in Batavia, who had immediately confiscated the vessels and the cargoes of his most
unwelcome competitor. Eventually the ships were returned
to their rightful owners. Too late to do them any good but
for a short while at least, this incident had caused a terrific
anxiety among the Gentlemen Seventeen, the board of directors responsible for the conduct of the company's affairs,
and quite rightly so.

As for this expedition of the year 1616, which still survives in the names of Cape Horn, the southernmost point

of the American continent, and in that of many islands and bays along the coast of Tierra del Fuego, it was one of the most memorable voyages of all times. Having left their home port on the Zuyder Zee, Schouten and Lemaire had for the first seven thousand miles followed the route of Magellan. But when they reached the Strait of Magellan, they decided to try their luck further towards the south.

In the year 1616 all the maps still showed South America as being directly connected with either the South Pole or the unknown Southland and the Strait of Magellan was merely supposed to be a gap in the barrier. Now Schouten and Lemaire were primarily intent upon settling a point of law. The monopoly which the Estates of Holland had bestowed upon the Dutch East India Company spoke of the exclusive use the vessels of that concern might make of the route to the Indies by following the eastern route via the Cape of Good Hope. By following the western route via South America, Schouten and Lemaire expected to acquire the right of trading with the Moluccas without in any way interfering with the monopoly of their big rivals. They therefore proceeded most carefully, avoiding everything that might fail to give them a clear title to their own short cut. They even refrained from passing through the Strait of Magellan, as this might be claimed by the Spaniards. They pushed further towards the south, gave the coast of Tierra del Fuego a wide berth and thereupon discovered that this was really an island and in no way connected with the mythical continent of the south.

**CAPE HORN**

The last promontory they saw they called Cape Hoorn, after their native town of Hoorn on the Zuyder Zee. The name therefore has nothing to do with a horn (on account of its pointed shape) nor with the Portuguese word *horno,* which means an "oven" (again on account of its shape). It is just another one of those Dutch names which lie sprinkled all over the map and which have given us a Staten Island, N. Y., and a Staten Island which lies just north of Cape Horn and which is separated from Tierra del Fuego by the Strait of Lemaire.

At first it looked as if the Dutch East India Company had come out holding the long end of the stick. There was indeed nothing in their original charter which forbade other Dutch trading companies from doing business in the Indies as long as they did not follow the African route. They expected that eventually the courts of Holland would find some loophole which would allow them to decide in favor of the almighty company which had the backing of all the richest men in the Republic.

In the meantime, such infringements upon their monopoly were extremely annoying and measures must be taken against any possible repetitions. Hence the decision of the authorities in Batavia to reach an immediate solution of the entire problem of the western Pacific and to find out, once and for all, what they might have to fear from the side of that great continent which for all they knew might exist somewhere in that ocean which was beginning to look larger and larger as time went on and might still hide God knew what secrets.

And so, after very careful and long-winded deliberations, it was decided in the year of grace 1642 that a certain Abel Janszoon Tasman, in command of two ships, the *Zeehaen* and the *Heemskerk,* should leave Java and should proceed first of all in a western direction until he should have reached the island of Mauritius; that from there, he should return upon his tracks and should sail due east until he came upon the different bits of land which had already been sighted by Willem Janszoon, Hartog and de Hout-man.

Having located this territory, he should continue in a southern direction and following the coastline as far as it reached, he should try to establish whether New Guinea was an island or part of the great Southland. This would carry him to Cape Keerweer and from there he could decide for himself what course to follow.

As several historians have pointed out (and quite rightly, it seems to me), this insistence of the Council of India that Tasman must begin his search for *Terra Australis* right from the coast of Africa (the island of Mauritius lies not far east from Madagascar) shows how even then the old maps of Ptolemy continued to exercise a profound influence upon the mentality of even the most modern of geographers. We sometimes wonder why the doctors of the seventeenth century went on diagnosing their cases according to the rules of practice laid down by Hippocrates, who had

lived in the fifth century B.C. We dismiss their case because
they lived in a little world of their own. But then we watch
hardheaded merchants sending a man out to explore an almost completely unknown part of the world and asking him
to let himself be guided by a map that was more than fifteen
hundred years old! Well, in New York today we still kill
our chickens by a method that goes back to the days of
Moses. So what is the difference?

As for Abel Tasman, he was a native of Groningen. He
was born in the year 1603 and in his early thirties we find
him as a minor official of the Dutch East India Company,
doing business in the recently founded city of Batavia and
in the Moluccas. We know very little about him, but he
seems to have been a man of considerable ability, for he
was chosen by the Governor-General, Anthonie van Diemen, to head an expedition that was to locate certain islands
said to be very rich in gold and silver and supposed to lie
somewhere east of Japan. What these were supposed to have
been, we do not know. Perhaps they referred to Hawaii,
which had been visited by a couple of Spanish ships. But
after their adventure with Schouten and Lemaire, the
Dutch East India Company decided to leave nothing to
chance and if such islands actually existed, they meant to get
hold of them before they fell into the hands of the Spanish
crown.

That expedition had failed to find any islands "full of
gold and silver," but it did a fairly thorough job in exploring the Philippines and thereupon went northward to

Japan. With this then still flowery kingdom, the Dutch had· always maintained a rather curious relationship.

From the moment the White Man had appeared upon the scene, the Japanese had suffered from missionary trouble. In the year 1549, an advance guard of members of the Society of Jesus had reached the Nipponese shores. They had been rather more than usually slow in coming, because the Portuguese had already known about the existence of Japan for some seven years, but they had kept their discovery to themselves. In the beginning, these humble Christians had been received with great cordiality. But the moment they got a sufficient number of converts, they used their influence to attack the established form of religion, and since the established religion was an integral part of the established political order of things, the Japanese authorities had done what every government since the beginning of time has done when it felt itself threatened in its existence—it had insisted that the Jesuits stick to the business of saving souls and leave politics alone.

To make a delicate question still more complicated, the Jesuits in the year 1593 had been followed by large numbers of Spanish Franciscans. At once the question was raised whether they had any right to be there, for according to the treaty of Tordesillas, the Portuguese were to be the undisputed masters of all the territories that were to be discovered in that half of the world. And now, in spite of that papal bull, here were Spanish Franciscans, competing openly with the Portuguese Jesuits!

One can hardly blame the poor heathen if they did not quite know what to make of such a state of affairs. But when these two competing groups of soul-savers began to quarrel among each other and fought for converts, like modern promoters who are struggling for oil fields or coal mines, the Japanese government decided to make an end to all further difficulties by expelling every single Christian from their domain. An empire within an empire was about the last thing they wanted.

In all fairness to the Japanese authorities we should stress the fact that until then they had been quite tolerant in matters of the spirit. They seem to have felt no particular animosity towards the new creed, but they did not in the least like its political implications. When a Spanish pilot, in a sudden outburst of honesty, told one of his friends that that was the way the pioneers of Europe always proceeded— "First we let our missionaries convert the natives; then we train these converted natives to fight their own masters and then our soldiers come in and do the rest,"—they decided the time had come for drastic action.

First of all, the Jesuits were requested to leave and when they refused to do so, a large number of them were executed, their chapels were destroyed and their native followers were told to return to their old faith. That was the beginning of a period of friction and wrangling which lasted for almost twenty years. The Jesuits had no sooner been thrown out of the front door than they returned through the back door. The recently founded Society of Jesus was still full of zeal. Its founder had been dead a little over half a century but his almost superhuman energy and his intense devotion to his task had so completely imparted itself to all of his followers that a great many of them were actively in search of martyrdom. The Japanese showed themselves most obliging.

Then in the year 1616 a new Shogun came to power. It may have been true that the Japanese understood very little about their European guests, but these in turn were completely bewildered by the form of government which seemed to prevail in that distant island. Had they known their history a little better, it would have reminded them of the curious arrangement which had existed in France during the last of the Merovingian kings, when their Masters of the Palace (or prime ministers, as we would call them today) had exercised all the power, while the kings themselves were living in seclusion behind the wooden palisades of their royal residence and were excluded from all active participation in affairs of state.

But in France, this condition had lasted a comparatively short time, for in the year 751 Pepin the Short, the son of Charles Martel (the man who at Poitiers had saved Europe from the Mohammedans), had quite reasonably come to the conclusion that since he was the ruler of all Gaul in all but name, he might just as well legalize his position by assuming the title which went with the job. He had discreetly discussed the problem with the Pope and His Holiness had agreed that it seemed a most sensible arrangement.

The last of the Merovingians had thereupon been relegated to a quiet monastery in Rome and the former Masters of the Palace had become kings of France and founders of the famous dynasty of the Carolingians.

But in Japan when the Europeans arrived, this curious dual form of government had been going on for almost five hundred years. There still was an emperor, a Mikado. He still was honored as the head of the nation and as commander-in-chief of the army, but he lived somewhere in the heart of a palace which no ordinary mortal was ever allowed to visit and the real power was in the hands of a Shogun.

Originally that word seems to have been merely the title given to a military chieftain, but gradually it had come to mean a great deal more and when the Europeans arrived in Japan, the Shogun was the official with whom they dealt, although it was always made clear to these visitors that somewhere there also existed a real emperor in whose name the Shogun was merely supposed to exercise his power.

The Shogunate having in this way become the most profitable office in Japan, it had always been a subject of dispute between the more influential families of the Japanese islands. In the eleventh century the office had been held by the Fujiwara clan. Next the Minamotos had risen to glory. In the fourteenth century they in turn had been succeeded by the house of Ashikaga. When the missionary issue finally came to a crisis, the clan of the Tokugawa was holding sway and it was a member of the Tokugawa family who was re-sponsible for the final expulsion of all Christians.

I realize that this sounds rather complicated even to us, who since then have learned a great deal about Japanese history. Needless to say, to the Europeans of the early half of the seventeenth century it offered a puzzle which they were never quite able to understand. The Portuguese and the Spaniards had tried to make sense of it and they had only succeeded in getting further and further away from the actual truth. But the Dutch, who always considered themselves to be merely traders and who therefore never asked questions and never undertook to convert anybody to anything except when they were trying to persuade a customer to let them have a better bargain—they grasped the situation much better than their predecessors from Portugal and Spain.

In consequence whereof, when in the year 1616 a new Shogun came to power and put an end to all further missionary efforts by burning and beheading every Jesuit, Franciscan or Dominican he could lay his hands upon, the Hollanders felt that at last their chance had come and that they might now be able to succeed to the business which until then had been a monopoly of the Portuguese. They generously placed their vessels at the disposal of the Japanese authorities and cheerfully assisted them when they set out to destroy the last of the Christian strongholds. And when a law was passed which ordered all Japanese once a year to express their horror of Christianity by stepping upon

pictures of Christ and the Virgin, they expressed no senti-
ments of disapproval, for like all good Calvinists they too
abhorred the idea of image worship, and their own fathers,
only a few years before, had smashed every holy statue and
had destroyed every holy picture to be found in the
churches of their native land.

They did not openly encourage this practice of the Japanese (which continued officially until the year 1856), but
they held themselves aloof, considering it no affair of theirs
what the Japanese wished to do in their own country and
carefully minding their own business, which was trade and
not religion. At first they were still obliged to watch their
step, for the Spaniards did not lose the last of their trading
posts in Japan until 1624. Meanwhile the few remaining
Portuguese had been forced to withdraw to a small artificial
island that had been constructed in front of the old Portuguese settlement on the mainland. The name of this little
island was Deshima, or Decima, and in order to discourage
the Japanese from trading with the enemy, an edict had
been issued forbidding all Japanese, under pain of death,
from setting foot on it. When it was found impossible to
enforce this rule, since many Japanese were curious to see
the world and smuggled themselves on board foreign vessels, the matter was settled by the threat that anyone in
Japan who dared to construct a ship large enough to cross
the ocean would be beheaded.

Next, all half-breeds with Spanish or Portuguese blood
in their veins were expelled from the empire. Again two

years later when it was discovered that in spite of these drastic regulations Portuguese Jesuits continued to smuggle themselves into Japan, an order was given that every Portuguese ship found within the jurisdiction of the Mikado should be burned after the crew had been put to death.

All this seemed so completely opposed to the leniency formerly exhibited by the Japanese officials that the Portuguese in nearby Macao on the Chinese mainland felt that it could not last. They hated to lose their excellent Japanese connections which had been most profitable and so they decided to send a delegation to plead with the Japanese and to convince them that from now on there would be no further trouble with any Jesuits. The Japanese did not object. They permitted this peace expedition to land. Then they decapitated the four envoys and fifty-seven of their suite and sent the remaining thirteen back to Macao with the message: "Please forget about us and just behave as if we did not exist."

When news of this terrible disaster spread abroad, the Dutch felt that now perhaps the moment had come for them to take a more direct interest in the affairs of their good neighbors, the Japanese. For meanwhile they had established themselves on the nearby island of Formosa and their fleet, protected by the guns of the fortress of Zeelandia, was within easy sailing distance from Nagasaki. The Japanese however were by now in such a fury against all foreigners (an old Nipponese custom) that at first the Dutch envoys got nowhere at all. They were not actually beheaded, strangled, dismembered or burned as the Portuguese had been, but there was always some convenient excuse when the Shogun could not receive them, or he made them wait

WHEN SCURVY HIT THE SHIP

endlessly and forced them to undergo all those humiliations which the Japanese warriors of today know how to bestow in such generous measure upon the English residents of the Chinese treaty ports.

It was about this time that Governor van Diemen sent Tasman to find out about those islands which were said to lie just east of Japan. It may have been accident that Tas-

man appeared upon the scene at the exact moment the
Portuguese had been driven out for good and all. We don't
know, but it proved to be a very wise move, for the Dutch
were given permission to establish a trading post on Deshima.

The little island offered few attractions as a place of residence, being a square of three hundred paces in all direc-
tions and connected with the mainland by means of a bridge
which was always guarded by Japanese soldiers. As for the
representatives of the East India Company, who now went
to live there, they were never allowed to leave their St.
Helena. Neither were they allowed to bring their Dutch
wives with them or any other European women, a measure
which may account for the fact that so many of them
learned to speak perfect Japanese. Furthermore they were
strictly forbidden to own any Bibles or other Christian
books. Indeed, on one occasion when they had built themselves a new warehouse and had put the date on it prefaced
by an innocent A.D., or Anno Domini, the entire structure
had to be pulled down, for the Japanese had made up their
minds that nothing that could even remotely remind them
of the Christian religion could henceforth be tolerated on
Nipponese soil.

Once a year a delegation of Dutchmen was allowed to set
foot on the mainland and to proceed to Yedo to offer pres-
ents to the Shogun. Even then they were invariably sub-
jected to all sorts of indignities. They were made to sing
funny songs in their funny barbaric jargon and to dance

and to give imitations of drunken European sailors, rolling over the floor or staggering around the room and the more realistic these performances were, the better pleased the Japanese showed themselves.

It was not exactly a flattering arrangement for these dignified representatives of the mighty East India Company but it meant money in their pockets and so they submitted to the inevitable, meanwhile bleeding their Japanese customers and taking so much gold out of their country that at the end of two centuries, Japan seems to have been so completely deprived of that valuable metal that the government was forced to choose between bankruptcy and opening its frontiers once more to foreign commerce.

This economic crisis, which is said to have been brought about by the gradual disappearance of all gold from the Japanese islands, is a subject about which I would like to know something more. For it would help explain Japan's decision of the year 1853 to make an end to its policy of self-enforced isolation and its willingness to conclude a commercial treaty with the United States of America.

✦

Here we had better stop a moment and come up for a little air. This chapter, I know it, is somewhat lacking in sequence. But how could I have done it differently? Try and imagine the width, breadth, depth and altitude of the problem before us!

Here we have the Pacific Ocean, the largest body of water

on our planet. It is thousands of miles removed from the European centre of civilization. As there were few intermediary stations along the road, it was quite customary for half the crews of the ships which undertook the voyage to be either dead or sick before they got as far as the Cape of Good Hope. After that, they had to spend from six weeks to two months to cross the Indian Ocean and then at last they reached the Malayan archipelago, those islands which now form part of the Netherlands East Indies and which cover a territory the length of which is about equal to the distance between San Francisco and Boston.

Having safely navigated these islands, they would at last reach the outskirts of the Pacific and then they entered upon a part of the world which even today has not yet been fully explored, for it is quite possible that there may still be a few small islands which either have never been sighted at all or which have been so completely forgotten that they are not mentioned on our maps.

This will give you a fairly clear idea of the difficulties that awaited the contestants for Pacific honors. In addition to the dangers they would run for lack of dependable charts, there also was the chance that a storm would make them suffer shipwreck on one of those Melanesian or Micronesian islands where the people were still practicing cannibalism.

Now it is one thing to be told on board a modern liner, "See that island! Isn't it interesting? There are still cannibals in them thar hills." But it was quite a different story when you were one of a crew of twenty or thirty men on board a converted yacht of perhaps fifty or sixty tons and obliged to find your way through this maze of islands and atolls, through racing channels, between foaming reefs— none of them properly buoyed, none of them indicated on the existing charts and not a single one of them provided with a lighthouse.

There is a dreadful chapter in *The Australian Encyclopaedia*. You will find it in Volume II under the letter W. It is called "Wrecks and Shipping Disasters." It consists of fifty-three pages, small print and double column. Therein you will find an account of all the ships that have been wrecked in that part of the world since the year 1622. Just to read through that record is an experience in itself and a very harassing one. The few details which follow the names of the unfortunate vessels are sober and concise, but what stories of hardships and torture and hairbreadth escapes they conceal if you know how to read between the lines! Here are a few examples:

"*America,* cutter from Queensland to Bampton Reef, Coral Sea. On her return, in making Torres Strait, she was wrecked, . . . about April 1839. Her crew of 5 men were lost, but one woman was saved by the natives and lived with them until rescued by H.M.S. *Basilisk* in 1849." Imagine a white woman living for ten years with that sort of natives!

"*Otter,* Boston sealer, called at Port Jackson in 1796, took away with her one of the Scottish Martyrs, Muir, and was wrecked on the coast of British Columbia. Only Muir and 2 seamen survived, the rest of the crew being killed by Indians."

"*Jenny* . . . left Port Jackson for Fiji for sandalwood. On 29 July 1808, she left Fiji, leaving ashore . . . the well-known William Lockerby and 6 seamen. Lockerby re-

THE DANGEROUS COAST OF AUSTRALIA

mained there nearly 2 years before being rescued. . . ."

And again: "*Lady Shore*, convict ship. In 1798, when bound for Sydney, was seized by mutineers, who turned the loyal people adrift in boats. . . . The mutineers took the ship to Monte Video and gave her up to the Spaniards, who hanged the ringleader and surrendered the others to the British naval authorities. The loss of her stores occasioned much distress in Sydney."

Small wonder that among all these thousands of distressing cases, the most famous of all the Pacific tragedies is reduced to a mere four lines: *"Bounty,* H.M.S., under Captain Bligh. After leaving Tahiti, the crew mutinied, April 1789. Eventually the mutineers took her to Pitcairn Island, where she was beached and burnt."

And so it goes on, column after column, page after page, until well within our own time when the worst of all disasters occurred in full sight of the entrance to Sydney harbor.

Read that list if ever you happen to come across a copy of *The Australian Encyclopaedia,* which the publishers, Angus and Robertson of Sydney, so generously presented to me and into which I dip whenever novels bore me and I want to read something really interesting. Then you will begin to understand the truly gigantic proportions of the problem with which we are dealing and you will realize that a chapter like this must by the very nature of its dimensions be somewhat disjointed and disconnected and sadly lacking in sequence. For during the seventeenth and eighteenth centuries all sorts of people from every corner of the earth were simultaneously trying to solve a problem that was much too vast for them and that could not possibly be solved in a hurry. Yet they were in a hurry, for time meant money to those who had risked their pennies upon these foolhardy expeditions in search of spice islands, gold islands and all sorts of hidden paradises. And so they continued searching, exploring, inquiring, examining and getting themselves drowned, but ever again tackling the

THE HIDDEN REEF

problem from a new angle, sailing now from east to west, next from west to east or from south to north, and starting all over again as soon as they had been able to borrow a few thousand guilders or pounds.

The discovery of the Pacific Ocean is the most dramatic and fascinating chapter in the whole dramatic and fascinating story of navigation and exploration. For all these voyages were enacted against a background of utter loneliness, the loneliness of the Pacific. It is a loneliness such as is not to be found in any other part of the world. It is a loneliness that seems to cut man completely off from the rest of his fellow-men. And once you have experienced that loneliness, you wonder how anyone ever had the courage to hoist sail and boldly enter upon this watery desert when he had not the slightest idea of the fate that awaited him and when he realized that the chances of his ever returning were about one against nine.

After this short interlude, we must return to Abel Janszoon Tasman. He has meanwhile been able to prepare himself for his second voyage—the voyage that was to make him sail clear around Australia and which was to give us a fair outline of at least three sides of the last of our continents, the *Terra Australis* of the ancient maps.

According to his instructions (which I have already mentioned), Tasman was to take his five ships, the *Zeehaen* and the *Heemskerk* first of all, to Mauritius and was thereupon to proceed in an eastern direction. For seven long weeks he sailed across the placid Indian Ocean. Then he caught his

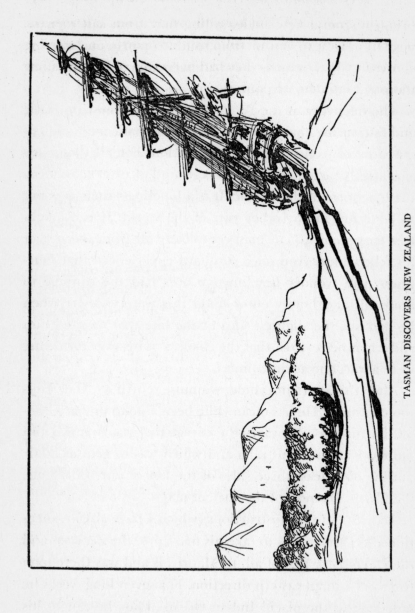

TASMAN DISCOVERS NEW ZEALAND

first glimpse of land. Not knowing what it was but ever the obedient servant of the almighty Company, he called it Anthonie van Diemen's land after his employer. But luck was not with him. He had set his course a little too far towards the south and as a result he missed the continent of Australia itself and the first land he sighted was the island of Tasmania, about one hundred and twenty miles south of Australia.

We still have Tasman's report upon his voyage with this entry: "On November 24, 1642, at the fall of evening, we saw two high mountains towards the northeast." In the year 1798, Captain Flinders called these two mountains Mt. Zeehaen and Mt. Heemskerk in honor of their discoverer.

On December 1, 1642, Tasman set foot on shore and explored the coast. He thought that he had heard the sound of drums but he found no other direct evidence that the island was inhabited. Neither did he catch sight of any animals. But trees that showed "steps hacked into them by human hands" and a plentiful supply of manure proved that the islands were not devoid of either human nor animal life. It seems to us that he might have continued his researches a little further, but we should remember that his instructions bade him to hurry.

He therefore hoisted the flag of the Estates General of the Seven United Provinces (the same flag you may still see flying over New York City) and proceeded further southward until he came to the end of the coast, whereupon he followed a northeastern course until on December 13, 1642, he beheld a chain of high mountains suddenly arising from the sea. They were about fifteen miles towards the east. The *Heemskerk* and the *Zeehaen* dropped anchor in a bay

**WHY THE WHITE MAN PREFERRED NOT TO LAND IN
NEW ZEALAND**

which was apparently surrounded by native villages, as the Dutch sailors could see smoke arise from the woods.

The next morning the officers of the *Zeehaen* rowed over to the *Heemskerk* to make plans for a landing party. While they were meeting in Tasman's cabin they noticed a lot of war canoes leaving shore. The captain of the *Zeehaen* therefore sent his boat back to his own ship to warn the crew that they must not allow any of the aborigines to come on board. But on the way back, this sloop was rammed by the Maoris and four of the seven sailors were killed with clubs while they were struggling in the water. The other three managed to escape. Tasman gave orders to fire at the native canoes. This was done but the Maoris merely laughed and made off with the bodies of their victims.

Such an incident would not have caused great surprise if it had happened on one of the islands where the population had already come in contact with the White Man, for as a rule the visitors began by killing off a couple of the natives, "so as to teach the others a lesson." But in this case Tasman was quite certain that he was the first European to appear upon the scene and therefore this unexpected outbreak of violence on the part of the islanders caused him considerable surprise. And not having enough sailors on board to risk a repetition of such a disastrous encounter, he called the harbor in which he had found shelter Murderers' Bay and continued his voyage without making any further efforts to come in contact with these dangerous barbarians.

Almost three centuries were to go by before a solution of this curious incident was fished out of the mud of the harbor of Wellington. This exhibit A consisted of a Spanish helmet dating back to the end of the sixteenth century. Since Spanish helmets do not travel by themselves, it followed that a Spanish ship must have been in that part of the world long before the arrival of Abel Tasman. We have not the vaguest idea what the name of this vessel may have been nor do we know what became of it. But most likely

the Spaniards who were in the habit of treating all natives
like vermin had behaved in their customary fashion. Most
likely they had indulged in their favorite sport of hanging
a few of them from the yardarms of their ships and had
thereupon departed in search of more profitable shores. To

them it had been but an incident but most primitive people
are possessed of far-reaching memories and when fifty or
sixty years later another ship arrived bearing a vague resemblance to the Spanish galleon, the poor benighted
Maoris had decided that now was the time to get even and
had slaughtered and eaten four Dutchmen to avenge their
ancestors who had been killed by those selfsame Spaniards
who were the sworn enemies of the later arrivals.

This may seem a rather farfetched yarn built upon as
slender a premise as a single steel helmet fished casually out
of the harbor of the city of Wellington. But anyone at all

familiar with the history of discovery will know the strange
subterranean courses which are sometimes followed by
these vague native memories which have become part of the
tribal folklore. There must have been some very definite
reason why the Maoris should have acted with such fury
against these unexpected visitors. I am convinced that for
several years they had had a grievance and now the chance
seemed to have come to get even. They took their chance
and Tasman, minus four of his sailors, made haste to get
away from this disastrous spot. At that moment he was
just 1,200 miles away from the continent he had set out to
find. Surely, the Pacific was no easy sea to explore.

From New Zealand Tasman went northward until he
reached the Tonga Islands. They are also known as the
Friendly Islands and Tasman found that the natives of this
region were indeed a much pleasanter sort of people to
deal with than those he had encountered while exploring
the coast of New Zealand. But he also observed that they
were completely devoid of any sense of private property.
They were complete communists in the way they shared
each other's and especially other people's property. But they
were perfectly good-natured about it. As soon as you noticed
that they had stolen your property (all sorts of odds and
ends left lying around in your boat) you went to their huts
and reclaimed what was yours and everybody took it as part
of a fine joke and nobody showed any hard feelings at losing that precious steel axe or knife of which he had been
the proud possessor for only a few hours, though such axes

and knives must have been a veritable godsend to a people who had never seen a piece of metal.

Here as in New Zealand Tasman tried to appeal to the souls of the natives by means of sweet music. This time he organized a regular symphony orchestra among his sailors and his fiddles and flutes and trumpets were such a success that even some of the native ladies joined the audience and showed themselves delighted by the performance.

From the Tongas, Tasman sailed westward until he reached the Fijis and from there, following an almost complete circle which kept him several hundred miles north of the Solomon Islands and New Guinea, he had reached Celebes; from there he had proceeded to Batavia.

In a sense, he had done what he had been told to do. He had sailed all the way around the Great Southland. He had discovered a lot of new territory, but he had never caught sight of the mainland. However, his trip had been of real value to our geographical knowledge. It had definitely shown that the mysterious continent must lie somewhere within a circle which, roughly speaking, touched Java, Tasmania, New Zealand, the Tonga Islands and Celebes and the map makers now agreed that from now on, it would be comparatively easy to find the elusive continent. All one had to do was to narrow down on one's circles until at last one reached the centre. If then one failed to find a core of dry land, it followed that the story about an unknown Southland had been nothing but a myth.

For this purpose, Anthonie van Diemen, who seems to

have been a man of considerable imagination, equipped a new expedition and in the year 1644 Tasman once more set sail, this time at the head of a squadron of three ships, the *Zeemeeuw,* the *Limmen* and the *Brak.* Being a true Hollander of the seventeenth century, van Diemen also expected to derive some slight concrete profit from his extensive geographical explorations and suggested that Tasman, after he should have found his Southland, proceed further eastward until he reached the coast of Chile, where he could thereupon establish "cordial relations" with the Spaniards. But on his return voyage he might incidentally conquer those islands which were said to lie just west of the South American mainland, in order that the Dutch East India Company should henceforth have a trading post of its own in that part of the world and be more or less in command of the whole of the southern half of the Pacific Ocean.

It was an ambitious scheme but unfortunately the directors of the East India Company at home said no. Those gentlemen never left their native haunts. They had never seen a tropical island and hoped that they would never be obliged to do so. And they informed Anthonie van Diemen by return mail (a matter of about ten months) that enough was enough and that he had better forget about his old continent.

The directors (to give them their due) had probably come to the conclusion that by now they had learned enough about Australia to realize that it was of no particular value. Throwing good money after bad money had never

WHAT THE FICTION WRITERS OF THE EIGHTEENTH CENTURY HAD
CAUSED THE VISITORS OF THE GREAT SOUTHLAND TO EXPECT

WHAT THEY ACTUALLY FOUND
ONCE THEY GOT THERE

been one of the weaknesses of the Dutch and perhaps they were right. Had they supported van Diemen just a few years longer, undoubtedly Tasman would have added hundreds of thousands of square miles to the possessions of the Dutch East India Company and the flag of the Estates General would have flown over an entire new continent. But the problem of turning Australia into a paying proposition has never yet been solved, not even in our own day. It therefore would have meant a constant drain on the exchequer of the Company and where would the Dutch Republic, with only 1,200,000 inhabitants, have found the men necessary to administer all this territory when they did not have enough people to take care of their holdings in America? And so New Holland went the way of the New Netherlands and Brazil and numerous other settlements in every nook and corner of the Seven Seas.

The Dutch Republic, during the first half century of its independent existence, had over-expanded its holdings at a reckless rate of speed. The time had come to do a little consolidating and word was sent to Batavia to stop wasting money on further explorations.

We of the present generation are apt to blame the directors of the Dutch East India Company for their short-sightedness, but in this, I fear, we are not quite fair. Those solemn-faced gentlemen who frown down upon us from the canvases of the great masters of the seventeenth century did what they considered best for the interests of their stockholders, which like all good businessmen they identified with the public interest.

They were realists who rarely indulged in vague daydreams. They very clearly realized just how far they could go and at that point they stopped. As a result, they have bestowed upon their descendants a closely knit, well-organized colonial empire which can be handled with comparative ease and which therefore may outlast a great many other ventures of a similar nature, but which were conceived upon a much more ambitious scale.

And surely we should give full credit to Anthonie van Diemen and his faithful subordinate Tasman at the head of this mission. It seems rather a pity that neither van Diemen nor Tasman ever received any particular rewards for their labors, but that is an old complaint within the realm of pioneering, and it will probably remain that way until the end of time.

✦

As for Tasman's final journey, I will now give it to you in a brief outline. This time he found Australia and followed the northern coast until he reached Torres Strait. That strait had been the weak point in all the earlier explorations of this part of the world. Tasman had been given explicit orders to try and find Cape Keerweer, which skipper Willem Janszoon of the *Duyfken* had discovered thirty-eight years before, and then solve the problem whether New Guinea and the Southern Continent were one and the same or were separate units. The report of de Torres had never been published. Most likely it had never yet been read. Tasman therefore had no definite data by which he could let himself be guided. And in addition he was handicapped by a considerable amount of incorrect information which had gradually been accumulated in Batavia.

Most of this had been gathered by two Dutch sailors, Jan Carstenszoon and Joosten van Coolsteerdt. They had visited the coast of northern Australia in the year 1623 with two ships called the *Pera* and the *Arnhem*. They had given the name of Arnhemsland to all that part of the Australian continent which lay west of the Gulf of Carpentaria but thereupon they had returned to Batavia with the startling news that the strait which was supposed to separate New Guinea from the Great Southland had run "too dry to allow them to proceed any further." What they had probably meant was that they had been unable to find a way through the maze of reefs and small islands which make this narrow passage so dangerous and so difficult to navigate.

Tasman may have come to the same conclusion, for when he reached the point now known as Cape York he decided to go southward and enter the Gulf of Carpentaria. He made a fairly accurate map of this vast inland sea and once more following the north coast of the Great Southland in a western direction, he finally reached the Timor Sea. He then stuck closely to the western coast of the mainland until at last he reached the island where Dirk Hartog in the year 1616 had hammered his tin plate to his wooden stake, claiming all the territory for the Republic of the Netherlands.

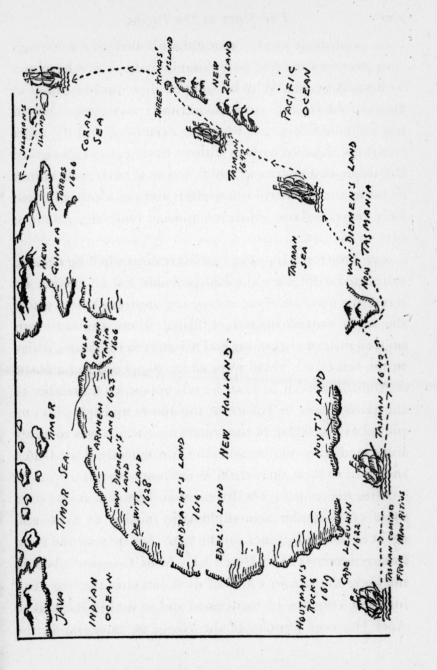

Tasman made careful soundings all along his route and thus gave us the first fairly reliable maps of northern and western Australia. Why he stopped there and returned to Batavia, we do not know. Governor van Diemen showed considerable annoyance when the *Zeemeeuw* and the other two ships returned to Java without having circumnavigated the whole of a continent which was now fairly well known so far as the northern, the western and the southern coasts were concerned but which remained as much of a puzzle as ever in the east.

But Tasman, I suppose, had his reasons when he decided to return to Java, and he had probably lost all further interest in a country where everything was topsy-turvy, where the birds walked instead of flying, where the mammals hopped instead of running and where even the swans, which in the rest of the world were white, happened to be black.

After his return to Java, he was appointed a member of the High Court of Justice of the Indies and was also employed as a delegate of the commission which was to establish a *modus vivendi* between the Portuguese and the Dutch in regard to their operations in the Spice Islands.

After his return from this mission, he was sent out once more on a similar semi-diplomatic mission to Siam and again to the Philippines. In the year 1653 he resigned from further service in the Dutch East India Company. We do not know the year in which he died, but after the year 1659 his name ceases to be mentioned and so we bid farewell to Abel Janszoon Tasman of the village of Lutjegast in the

Province of Groningen, whose name will remain forever associated with the discovery of that continent, the existence of which had plagued all geographers for almost twenty centuries and which now was shown to be a rather useless desert and by no means the paradise people had expected to find.

The last of the casual Dutch explorers of Australia's west coast was so delighted when he was able to get away from that dreadful land where he had actually run across Dirk Hartog's tin plate on its pole but had found nothing else of any importance, that he fired all his guns as a final token of farewell and malediction when he hoisted sail to return to Java. And that, I regret to say, was the way everybody seems to have felt about this glamorous land of Ophir until we reach the year 1688, when another candidate for Australian honors appeared upon the scene. But this fellow had good reason to keep away from civilization and an absolutely deserted part of the world was what he was looking for at that moment as he was "wanted" on charges of piracy.

He was an Englishman and his name was William Dampier. I can give you only a very brief outline of his career for if I let myself go and followed this hero through all the details of his incredible life, he would fill the greater part of this book.

William Dampier was born in 1652 and he had been "intended for trade." That meant life in a shop and little William felt no inclination for the humdrum existence of a respectable merchant. And so, after he had lost both his father and his mother, while still in his teens, he persuaded his guardians to let him follow his "own inclinations" and start out to make his fortune for himself.

These guardians apparently were only too happy to rid themselves of their responsibilities towards this headstrong child and at the age of fifteen, William signed up as a cabin boy and sailed for Newfoundland. At the age of twenty-one he was an able-bodied seaman on board a man-of-war and made a trip to Java, but he got sick and was sent home to recover. As soon as he had recovered from his affliction, he went to Jamaica. From there he found his way to Yucatan in Mexico to engage in the logwood business. Yucatan was under Spanish jurisdiction and therefore no foreigners were allowed and those who came in ran the risk of losing their heads. William did not lose his head, but as he might as well be hanged for buccaneering as for buying and selling logwood, he decided to turn pirate.

He joined a gang of derelict Englishmen who worked out plans to attack and plunder the rich city of Panama and together with his lusty mates he marched across the Isthmus of Panama, bound for that ancient stronghold. Unfortunately, the Spaniards had been warned and the project came to nothing. Whereafter the Englishmen turned pirates and having stolen four ships began to raid the coast of Colombia. Once more the Spaniards proved too much for them and having lost their ships, they were forced to march back across the isthmus. Most of them died on the way but the survivors somehow or other managed to reach Virginia.

There William remained for thirteen months and then, once more falling a victim to his indomitable wanderlust, he took service on board a buccaneer and left for the west coast of South America by way of Cape Horn.

While sailing southward and living on booty, they fell in with another English pirate vessel called the *Cygnet* and commanded by a Captain Swan. Together, the two vessels thought they were strong enough to try their luck in the Caribbean. On the way northward they plundered Spanish cities and captured Spanish coastal vessels until their supplies began to dwindle, whereupon Dampier joined Swan on the *Cygnet* and with him once more made for the Pacific.

Early in March, 1686, the two outlaws had reached the west coast of Mexico and from there they crossed the Pacific until they reached Guam at the southern end of the Ladrones. Here the crew, having almost died of hunger and thirst, was quickly revived, but the sailors had grown so exasperated at the brutality of their commander (Swan) that they put him in a boat, rowed him ashore and left him there to shift for himself.

The next year they spent sailing leisurely through the Malay Archipelago. They paid visits to Cochin-China and to Tonkin, and lived pleasantly and comfortably upon whatever plunder fell into their hands. What suddenly made them decide to go southward in search of the country that now appeared upon the maps under the name of New Holland, we do not know. Most likely they felt that the time had come for them to drop out of sight for a short

RAROTONGA

while. Early in January of 1688 they saw land. They had reached the Lacepede Islands, just off what is now called Dampier Land in northwestern Australia.

After having been at sea for so many years, it had become absolutely necessary to overhaul the *Cygnet* and the ship was therefore beached in Cygnet Bay and Dampier made use of his enforced idleness to study the surrounding countryside. And so, almost eighty years after this part of the coast of Australia had been first sighted, the White Man at last caught a glimpse of the inhabitants of this mysterious continent.

The meeting was very disappointing. Dampier, whose claim to fame rests more upon his powers of observation than his talents as a navigator, dismissed the aborigines with a few highly descriptive sentences.

"They were the most miserable people in the world I have ever seen," he wrote in the book he published a few years later. So miserable that even the aborigines of the lowest islands he had visited, nasty as they looked, were yet "for wealth gentlemen" when compared to these terrible creatures.

In March, the *Cygnet* thought it safe to return to civilization. By way of Sumatra the vessel sailed for India, but it stopped long enough at the Nicobar Islands to rid itself once more of several of its less popular passengers by the simple process of marooning them. Dampier was among those who were ejected but it seems to have been a fairly good-natured arrangement, for the victims had enough money with which to buy themselves a native canoe.

In spite of many hurricanes they were able to sail their frail craft across the Malabar current and to reach Sumatra. They followed the coast of that island until they came to Bencoolen and there Dampier was lucky enough to find a vessel willing to take him back to England by way of the Cape. It must have been a matter of considerable satisfaction to him to hear that two years before the *Cygnet* had been shipwrecked on the coast of Madagascar with everyone lost!

When Dampier set foot on English soil, he was not alone. Being an inventive sort of fellow, he had invested his last pennies in a beautifully tattooed native from the Philippines whom he had discovered in the market place of Bencoolen and had forthwith bought from his previous owner. He felt sure that there would be a fortune in exhibiting his "painted prince" to the London public, but lacking the necessary capital with which to hire a hall, he was obliged to sell his walking picture gallery to another panhandler and then (for after all, he had to eat) he bethought himself of the profits that were being made just then out of travel books, and he turned author and published a volume entitled *A New Voyage round the World*. This volume he dedicated to the Earl of Halifax and it came at exactly the right moment, for the English government was seriously considering the possibilities of establishing a colony on the Isthmus of Panama. This plan fell through, but

Dampier, making use of the knowledge he had acquired of that part of America during his buccaneering days, set himself up as an expert and managed to be called upon as a witness by the Isthmian Commission.

He was a man with a fluent tongue and he did so well and made such a good impression that soon afterwards he was approached by two officials of the Admiralty who were thinking of sending him back to the Pacific to arrange for an English colony on the coast of New Holland.

Fifty years before, van Diemen, the governor-general of the Dutch East Indies, had wanted to take possession of the Great Southland as part of the Company's defenses against England. Only this time it was the English who wanted to occupy New Holland to protect themselves against the Dutch. A British fortress just south of Java would be a constant menace to the safety of the Hollanders in the north. Was Master Dampier willing to go back to New Holland and find out what could be done along that line?

Master Dampier, who was impatiently chafing under his enforced idleness, was more than willing to do anything that would take him back to sea. On January 14 of the year 1699, more than half a century after Tasman had set forth upon his famous voyage, William Dampier sailed from England. He surely had come up in the world, for he now was Captain Dampier, R.N., in command of H.M.S. *Roebuck,* a vessel of some two hundred tons, armed with twelve cannon and provisioned for two years with a crew of fifty sailors.

All this sounded very fair on paper but once out of sight
of land, Dampier had to confess that his new employers
had treated him rather shabbily. For the crew was without
any training, lazy, obstinate and mutinous, and the *Roebuck* was in such a state of neglect that Dampier was soon
obliged to give up all hope of following the western route
and had to proceed by way of the Cape of Good Hope,
where he could count on better weather than in the vicinity
of Cape Horn.

Luck was with him and after eight months he reached
the Houtman Abrolhos (discovered in 1619 by Frederick
de Houtman) and a few days later he entered a bay which
he called Sharks Bay on account of the multitude of those
unpleasant creatures which welcomed him there. He tried
to find fresh water in that neighborhood but failed and so
he hoisted sail and followed the coast until he reached Roebuck Bay, where again there was no water but a lot of natives, "the same sort of miserable creatures" as those he had
seen thirteen years before. By now his crew was being rapidly decimated by scurvy and Dampier had to beat a pre-
cipitous retreat to the island of Timor. It took him three
months to get his men back on their feet.

As soon as they had sufficiently recovered to hoist a sail
and pull an oar, Dampier was off once more, but this time
he meant to tackle his problem from the east. Still under
the impression that New Guinea was part of the Southern
Mainland, he went as far north as Schouten Island and
from there he sailed eastward until he reached New Ireland

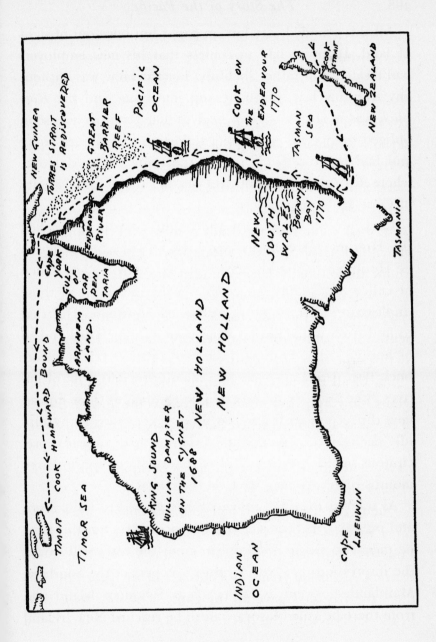

and New Britain, both of which he mistook for parts of New Guinea.

At that point he was surprised by the sight of a magnificent volcano fully 2,500 feet high and busily belching flames and smoke. The volcano still exists, but it is now no longer a landmark. During the period of time that separates us from Dampier, it has blown itself almost completely to pieces and has now dwindled down to a mere 250 feet.

All these explorations had taken considerable time and April had come and the trade winds were beginning to blow the English ship the wrong way. Otherwise Dampier would undoubtedly have rounded the easternmost point of New Guinea and in that case he would eventually have been driven to the east coast of the great Southern Continent, anticipating the discoveries of Captain James Cook by three-quarters of a century.

But of all this he knew nothing and so he let the trade winds blow him back whence he had come and on July 3 of the year 1700 he reached Batavia, where he insisted that his ship, as a regular vessel of His Majesty's navy, be received with all due honors, the firing of salutes, the striking of flags and all the rest of it.

Due to the hard wear it had seen, his noble craft needed three months before it was seaworthy again. From Java, Dampier returned to England by way of the Cape. He reached Ascension Island in February of the year 1701 but there the *Roebuck* gave up the ghost. The ship foundered in the harbor with the loss of practically all of Dampier's papers and sketches. The crew managed to reach shore and there the sailors camped out until they were saved two months later by a British man-of-war.

Dampier was now fifty years old, but being hale and hearty he did not think of resigning himself to a life of ease as a country squire. His career as a pioneer of the Pacific had come to an end. After he had reported upon his discoveries, the British Admiralty felt convinced that there was nothing in this idea of fortifying New Holland and using it as a sort of Gibraltar, a pistol pointed at the ample chest of the Dutch governor-general in Batavia. The scheme was therefore dropped for good and all, but in 1703 Dampier was given command of two vessels to do a little discreet pirating along the west coast of South America. That voyage was to play a role in the lives of all of us, for it was during this trip that the mate of the second privateer, an unruly and cantankerous fellow by the name of Alexander Selkirk, was put on shore and left behind on the island of Juan Fernandez, four hundred miles west of the Chilean coast. Five years later another expedition of which Dampier was the pilot (he never gave much satisfaction when in command but he was a good subordinate) visited Juan Fernandez and to their great surprise they found Selkirk to be still alive. And so they forgave him, thinking that he had probably learned his lesson and they brought him back to England.

As for this voyage, it was the most profitable one of Dampier's whole career. It had netted the investors one

ROBINSON CRUSOE'S ISLAND AS PEOPLE IMAGINED IT WAS

AND AS IT REALLY LOOKED

million dollars in cash. But the division of the spoils took a lot of time and when finally the crew received its share (in the year 1719), poor Dampier had been dead and buried for more than four years.

His former victim, Alexander Selkirk, was more fortunate, for he lived until 1723 and when he went to his final reward he was not only a lieutenant in His Majesty's navy but also the hero of one of the most popular best sellers of all times. It bore the title of *The Life and Strange Surprizing Adventures of Robinson Crusoe.* The first part made its appearance on April 25 of the year 1719 and the second half within a few months. Its author was a certain Daniel Defoe.

At the time his masterpiece appeared, Defoe was no longer a young man (he was born in 1661) and his career had been a turbulent one. Born into a family of traditional dissenters, he had forever been at loggerheads with the established authorities. He had greatly approved of William III, who also professed the wrong religion, being a member of the Dutch Reformed Church. His ironical pamphlet, *The Shortest Way with the Dissenters,* had been so little appreciated that it had got him a very stiff sentence, a heavy fine, an indefinite term of imprisonment and as an extra expression of the court's disapproval he was also condemned to be shown three times in the public pillory. As an act of grace, he did not lose his ears (until the beginning of the eighteenth century people who were pilloried used to have their ears cut off) and his misfortune proved to be a blessing in disguise. For it made him a hero in the eyes of the public, which after Dutch William's years of tolerance hated to see the high church bishops come back into power and the Defoe scandal assumed such proportions that he was soon released and henceforth was left alone.

The moment he left prison he started to publish his famous *Review,* a paper written entirely by himself and published three times a week, an enterprise which (as every modern writer will agree) gave evidence of extraordinary industry, for even with a typewriter and a dictaphone that number of words is an all-day and all-night job. This *Review* was not a great success and only one copy of the entire publication survives. But it was this little sheet of Defoe which apparently inspired Dick Steele and Joseph Addison to start their *Tatler* and their *Spectator* and in this way Defoe became the founder of that little school of moralizing literature which eventually was to degenerate into our gossip columns of today.

Only in the days of Defoe that sort of work did not pay very well and Defoe was forever on the lookout for something that would allow him to settle his debts. Then came this windfall of *Robinson Crusoe.*

According to the best available information, Defoe had met Selkirk at the house of a certain Mrs. Damaris Daniel at Bristol and according to that lady, Selkirk had given his prospective biographer all his private papers. What the "private papers" of a common British sailor in the year

1710 may have been is something beyond our comprehension, for even the captains in the days of Nelson were hardly able to write a letter. However, it sounded well as a piece of publicity, "this book is based upon the private papers of Robinson Crusoe himself," and it fooled no one but the public, which is after all the main purpose of all good publicity.

Meanwhile Defoe, being a first-rate craftsman, knew that he would need a lot of detailed background to give his hero an air of authenticity and for his "local color" he went to William Dampier's *New Voyage round the World*, published in the year 1697 and never very much of a success as it was not very entertainingly written.

Since Juan Fernandez had been (and still is) a pretty barren sort of place, Defoe had taken the liberty of moving his hero several thousand miles towards the northeast and had shipwrecked him on an island at the mouth of the Orinoco in Venezuela. That, of course, had been his good right as a novelist. William Shakespeare had never bothered about facts in his plays and nobody loses any sleep over his grotesque historical and geographical misstatements. But Defoe did something which was not quite pardonable from an ethical point of view. He failed to acknowledge his indebtedness to a fellow-writer who, believe it or not, had chosen Australia—of all places!—as the locale for a similar plot and in which New Holland had been depicted as paradise itself.

The name of this pioneer of the *Robinson Crusoe* school of literature was Hans Jakob Christoffel von Grimmelshausen. He was a native of north Germany. At the age of ten he had been kidnapped by a roving band of soldiers, who had dragged him through the thirteen last (and worst) years of the Thirty Years' War. In 1667 Grimmelshausen had been appointed a magistrate in a small village in Baden and there he had written his epoch-making life of *The Adventuresome Simplicissimus,* being in reality a true account of the wondrous wanderings of the famous vagabond, Melchior Sternfels von Fuchsheim.

In this volume, which appeared in 1669, Grimmelshausen had gathered together everything he himself had seen and experienced during those hideous years when the whole of central Germany had been turned into a slaughterhouse by the nations of Europe making war upon each other for the sake of their religious beliefs. In the end, despairing as completely of the future of civilization as we do today, Grimmelshausen had added a rather farfetched yarn about a mysterious traveler who had taken passage on a Portuguese ship to proceed to the Indies by way of the Cape. Adverse winds had driven his vessel southward where it had been shipwrecked on the coast of the unknown Southland. But whereas all other Robinson Crusoes of subsequent vintages have immediately set to work to prepare themselves for a trip back to their old haunts, the hero of Grimmelshausen had so completely fallen in love with his new surroundings that he had vowed that never, under any circumstances, would he return to a world that was in every way inferior to the paradise in which he then found himself and where he expected to spend the rest of his days.

OUT OF THE HORROR AND MISERY OF THE THIRTY YEARS' WAR CAME THE DESIRE OF THE PEOPLE OF EUROPE TO ESCAPE INTO SOME IMAGINARY PARADISE SITUATED IN THE MYSTERIOUS GREAT SOUTH SEA

A careful study of Grimmelshausen's description of this mysterious paradise shows us that the stories about New Holland which the Dutch navigators of the first half of the seventeenth century had brought back with them had already become common knowledge among the people of northern Europe, for all the queer creatures they had seen, the giant geese and the black swans and the hopping and skipping birds and mammals and marsupials of the Australian desert were duly enumerated by the industrious Grimmelshausen.

Defoe greatly improved upon the work of his German predecessor and when Robinson Crusoe was added to Simplicius Simplicissimus, the world found itself possessed of two volumes which, each in its own way, were to contribute in a most disastrous measure to the old misconception that man, in his primitive state and untrammeled by civilization, had been a creature of unlimited goodness, kindness, generosity, spending his days in blissful happiness and content practicing Virtue (with a capital "V") and contemplating the beauties of Nature in some distant Garden of Eden.

This nonsense which the literary genius of Grimmelshausen and Defoe had been able to extract out of the prosaic journals of a dozen hard-boiled and prosaic Dutch and English skippers—like bees getting honey out of thistles—was to play a very important and disastrous role in the history of the next two centuries. For they indirectly inspired Jean Jacques Rousseau to indulge in some of his most absurd psalms of praise about primitive man. By the time this muddleheaded Swiss had started the conflagration known as the Great French Revolution, the sad truth about Australia was beginning to reveal itself. But then it was too late. For James Cook was only twenty-one years old when Jean Jacques Rousseau won international renown by publishing his prize essay on the superiority of man living in a

savage state. And when Captain Cook's *Voyages* were published (the books which for the first time told the complete
and unadorned story about this unhappy part of the world),
the sentimental poison of Rousseau's absurd imaginings had
already entered into the souls of most civilized Europeans.

Those who went to the scaffold during the days of the
Terror of the year 1793 were not the sort of people who
had wasted much of their time upon historical speculations and most of them were probably very vague in what
they knew about the mysterious Continent of the South.
Otherwise they would have realized that that ideal society,
for. the establishment of which they were now being
slaughtered, had been the direct product of a dream—of a
delightful literary dream based upon the actual but far
from delightful adventures of a number of old Dutch and
English sea captains whose bones for many centuries had
lain bleaching on a dozen desolate shores. These poor fellows had died cursing the fate that had carried them to
this hell on earth. With a last fever-stricken effort they had
penned their dying messages, warning all others to keep
away from this Gehenna, and behold! by that strange
alchemy of the imagination which is one of the profound
mysteries of human civilization, these tales of woe had
within a couple of centuries been converted into hymns of
joy and praise, and hazy visions of the Elysian Fields situated at the other end of the earth made drunken harpies
gloat over the blood that flowed from the guillotine and

that was being shed to bring about the triumphant rebirth
of man, regenerated in the image of his primitive self.

Meanwhile that image, a naked Australian bushman, was
sitting shivering among the offal of his oyster middens. For
he had not yet learned how to cook a meal or build himself
a house. More miserable than the beasts of the field, he was
starving to death while all along the banks of the Seine the
booksellers were growing rich, turning out their voyages to
the glamorous Utopia of the great Southern Continent.

## 9. JACOB ROGGEVEEN

*The last of the Dutch explorers, followed by
many French competitors*

AFTER the disappearance of William Dampier, the Pacific
enjoyed a period of undisturbed rest for almost
seventy years. Only occasionally—very occasionally—the
White Man now ventured into this perilous region where
he ran a thousand risks of perishing from thirst, from shipwreck or from the violence of the natives.

The most important among the voyages of this period
was that undertaken in the year 1721 by still another
Dutchman (the last one) by the name of Jacob Roggeveen.
He was the son of a native of Zeeland and an inhabitant
of the city of Middelburg. An ardent devotee of the science
of geography, the father was all his life long fascinated by
the problem of the unknown Southland and not at all satisfied with the work his fellow-countrymen had done along
the coast of New Holland, almost three-quarters of a century before.

He was not a navigator. Indeed, it is doubtful whether
he ever set foot on board a ship, but he was a map fanatic,
just as today we have a great many radio fanatics who have
never broadcasted and airplane fanatics who have never

been up in the air. And so he spent all his life dreaming of that mysterious Southland, "where undoubtedly," as he wrote, "the sun always shines brightly but which meanwhile remains hidden from our view as if covered with a hazy curtain or a dark cloud on account of the great distance."

The old fellow got as far as publishing an atlas of the west coast of America but he was never able to make his neighbors share his enthusiasm sufficiently to let him have the money necessary for a regular expedition and so he spent his days dreaming strange dreams about his beloved continent and it was left to his son to put his father's name on the map of the Pacific.

This son, Jacob Roggeveen, was a lawyer. Whether it was filial piety that sent him forth upon his famous voyage or hope of gain, that I do not know. Most likely it was a little of both. For during the first half of the eighteenth century, the Pacific problem was once again beginning to attract the attention of the investors. The fortunes lost by the earlier pioneers had been forgotten. Once more the Pacific had become a subject of discussion in Edward Lloyd's well-known coffeehouse on Tower Street and in the taverns along the Dam of Amsterdam and once again the House of Habsburg was at the bottom of all the excitement.

It is curious to reflect that only two members of this dynasty, which ruled for so many years over that entire part of the world, ever set foot on American soil. One of them was the unfortunate Maximilian, who came here to meet his death. The other was the Archduke Ferdinand, who came as a private traveler, crossed the United States in a special train, insulted everybody he met and then hastened back to the Old World, where he in turn was to be killed a few years afterwards. But in the year 1700, Charles II, the last descendant of King Philip of Spain, had died. It was found that he had left the whole of the Spanish monarchy, including the southern part of the Netherlands (which had remained in Catholic hands in 1648) to the grandson of King Louis XIV of France. That meant a direct menace to the safety of both England and Holland, and it led to the outbreak of the so-called "War of the Spanish Succession."

By the Peace of Utrecht of the year 1713, the southern Netherlands had been ceded to Charles VI, the head of the Austrian branch of the Habsburg dynasty.

This was not at all welcomed by the merchants of the Republic of the United Seven Netherlands. Until then they had been able to keep the port of Antwerp closed, but now it looked as if once more they were to be exposed to the commercial rivalry of those neighbors along the banks of the Scheldt River. Having now become a race of inveterate investors, the Dutch were as loath to risk their prosperity in battle as the English of the present era. But this time they felt that they had to take some sort of action. The new emperor might not be a man of outstanding ability or energy, but he was said to be only half asleep, whereas the Spanish Habsburgs had been so completely lost in their

DAWN IN TAHITI

slumbers that no one had given them a serious thought for almost a century and a half.

Soon rumors began to reach Amsterdam about certain grandiose plans that were being hatched in Vienna and which meant nothing less than the establishment of a regular Austrian East India Company with headquarters to be located in Ostend and to be financed with Antwerp money.

Ostend, as soon as the new company functioned, was to be connected by a system of canals with both the Rhine and the Meuse and in this way, central Europe would at last be able to rid itself of the spice monopoly of the Dutch.

In 1717 this Ostend Company was actually founded and several ships, flying the Habsburg flag, were sent out to the east. Two of them were captured by the Dutch East India Company and then the trouble started in all seriousness. It lasted until the year 1727 when under pressure of England, France, Holland and Prussia (which greatly preferred to see its Habsburg neighbors in a state of perpetual bankruptcy), the emperor was at last persuaded to give up his Indian ventures. But before surrendering his rights and prerogatives, the Habsburg ruler insisted that in exchange for his generous act, the four great powers give him their solemn promise that they would offer no objection if after his death he was succeeded by his daughter, Maria Theresa.

This redoubtable lady should really have been a boy. She had been born a girl by mistake and therefore she could not really succeed her father to the throne. The so-called Pragmatic Sanction of the year 1724 regulated all this to everybody's apparent satisfaction and nothing more was heard of the Ostend Company.

All this does not sound very important to us except perhaps that we smile rather pityingly when we read that by withdrawing his ships from the Indies, the Austrian emperor was really convinced that by sacrificing his own interests for the sake of the peace of Europe he had laid the foundations for a lasting peace. We know all about such sacrifices and what they are apt to lead up to, but the people of the first part of the eighteenth century did not and they shared their emperor's belief that from that moment on, peace was assured.

One would have expected that in the face of such a menace, the Dutch East and West India Companies would have made common cause, but their mutual jealousy was too great. The D.E.I. Company had by now grown so rich that it was too indolent (or too proud, if you will) to fight for its own interests. The D.W.I. Company on the other hand, having lost both Brazil and the New Netherlands and depending for its continued existence entirely upon the profits it continued to make from the nefarious trade in slaves, experienced a sudden new lease of life. During the preparatory discussions about the financing of the Ostend Company, the possibilities of establishing colonies of white men on the great Southern Continent had been delicately touched upon and had been eagerly discussed by the shareholders of the D.W.I. Company, who were facing bankruptcy. Why not scrape together a few thousand

guilders, carry on the investigations of Tasman which the
D.E.I. Company had allowed to lapse almost eighty years
before and then hoist the flag of the old Zeeland over New
Zeeland and New Holland?

Young Roggeveen found the directors of the D.W.I.
Company more than willing to listen to this last argument.
That company had always been more closely identified with
the Province of Zeeland than any other part of the Republic and in the year 1721 Roggeveen, backed up by Zeeland
capital, sailed for Australia. He chose the western route by
way of Cape Horn, thereby following the precedent of
Schouten and Lemaire when, more than a century before,
they had ventured to intrude upon the territory of the
D.E.I. Company.

Roggeveen had been given enough money to equip three
ships. They were called the *Arend,* which Roggeveen himself commanded, the *Thienhoven* and the *African Galley,*
a smaller vessel. Near the mouth of the Rio de la Plata, the
*Thienhoven* had got separated from the *Arend,* but the two
vessels were to meet again near Juan Fernandez, and so this
was not a farewell forever. Roggeveen had experienced ex-
ceptionally good weather on his way to Cape Horn and he
had been able to gather interesting information about certain islands which a previous visitor, the Dutch captain,
Sebald de Wert, had called the Sebald Islands. Even then,
de Wert had not been their discoverer as they had first been
seen by John Davis in the year 1592.

This is the first time I have been able to mention John

Davis in connection with the Pacific. These early navigators were an incredible breed of men. Nothing could discourage them nor kill them. Having been defeated in his attempts to find the northwestern passage by way of the Davis Strait, which still bears his name, Davis had next tried his luck by way of the Strait of Magellan and it was on this occasion that he had discovered the Falklands. In between those activities he had found time to command a vessel in the fleet that had attacked the Spanish Armada, had made further investigations in the Greenland seas, had published two highly popular books on the art of navigation, *The Seaman's Secrets* and *The World's Hydrographical Description* and had invented the Davis quadrant which all skippers used for several hundred years afterwards. Quite appropriately he had finally lost his life in the year 1605 in a fight with Japanese pirates somewhere off the coast of Sumatra.

Once past Cape Horn, Roggeveen had steered a course due south. According to his father's calculations, the Great Southern Continent not only existed but its easternmost point was only a few hundred miles removed from the west coast of South America. And Jacob Roggeveen was convinced that all he had to do was to sail due south until he saw land. Thereupon, by following that coast in a western direction he must eventually come upon the territory seen by Tasman and Dampier and so many others and mentioned on the maps as New Holland. But in spite of all his efforts he found nothing but water—water everywhere and not a drop to drink—and thirst finally forced him to return northward, bound for Juan Fernandez where the *Thienhoven* had been waiting for him for a considerable length of time.

So far the voyage had contributed nothing new, but after the combined fleet had bidden farewell to Selkirk's island, things began to happen.

On April 6 of the year 1722, Roggeveen sighted a new island not mentioned on any of the existing charts. In honor of the day, Easter, he called it Paasch Eiland. His crew was delighted. Here at last was something that must be an outpost of the Great Southland.

A native came paddling out to the White Man's ship. He was stark naked, which so greatly shocked the Dutch sailors that they hastened to hoist him on board and to provide him with a loincloth, hastily improvised out of a piece of an old sail. After that, other natives hastened to be similarly garbed. They climbed over the sides, they stole the hats off the sailors' heads and they dived into the sea before one could say "Booh!" Once in the water, they were gone, for they were stout swimmers and it seemed a bit risky to shoot at them and kill them merely for the sake of a few old hats.

Roggeveen remembered Tasman's disastrous experiences in New Zealand and to prevent any unfortunate incidents with those light-fingered communists, he fired off all his guns before he decided to set foot on land. This proved to be a waste of valuable gunpowder. The natives were most hospitable and Roggeveen was amply rewarded for all his troubles by the sight that awaited him when he explored the hills just back of the native village.

The fantastic tales about the Southern Seas which had appeared in the popular literature of that day had so thoroughly filled the minds of most Europeans with visions of a weird terrestrial paradise that they were ready for almost anything. But these dark-browed stone monsters arising in awesome silence from the soil of an island way at the other end of the earth were almost too much for them. And I must confess that I share their feelings. I have never been near Easter Island but I still remember the first time I stood before one of these Easter Island idols in the courtyard of the British Museum. It was a hazy and misty morning and the light was bad. There in a little gallery and far removed from his original surroundings stood one of these stone men from Easter Island.

Even so, without any trappings and against a commonplace background of London brick, this God of the Empty Spaces made me feel exceedingly uncomfortable. He seemed to belong to another world—a world completely foreign to me. Afterwards, when I had caught a little of the spirit of the Pacific, I came to understand this stone monster better, but I would have hated to spend a night alone under the open sky with a dozen of these South Sea Rübezahls as my only companions.

We know from Roggeveen's description that the statues made a deep impression on him, but he was a lawyer and not a trained anthropologist and without years of training, the amateur anthropologist can commit more blunders than even an amateur doctor. He observed that the statues were made of clay and that they crumbled to the touch of the fingers, whereas they were cut out of the lava of one of the local craters. He expressed no particular wonder how those fifty-ton contraptions had ever been hoisted into their erect positions but he is careful to inform us that the natives paid great reverence to these idols and prayed before them at night amidst the smoke and flames of big fires. But when half a century later, Cook and La Pérouse visited Easter Island, they found the people completely indifferent about their stone images and no one was able to tell them what they meant, when they had been made or why they were there anyway.

But these mysterious idols fitted so beautifully into the mentality of an eighteenth-century European, who had absorbed all the nonsense about the Great Southland, that he must immediately connect them with a biblical prophecy. "Wherefore glorify ye the Lord in the fires, even the name of the Lord God of Israel in the isles of the sea" (Isaiah XXIV:15).

Modern scholarship feels inclined to agree with the version of Cook and of La Pérouse and has come to the conclusion that these statues were made by a race of Polynesians who had lived on the island long before the arrival of the people who were in possession of the premises when Roggeveen visited them.

From Easter Island, Roggeveen sailed due west. He missed Tahiti and the Marquesas, but had the good luck

VIEW FROM STEVENSON'S HOUSE
IN SAMOA

to discover Samoa, which he called Baaumann Island after his second in command.

From Samoa, following the northern coast of New Guinea and without so much as catching a single glimpse of the Great Southland, Roggeveen proceeded to Java.

There his ship and its cargo were at once confiscated by the authorities of the Dutch East India Company and that was all Roggeveen, like Schouten and Lemaire, ever got for all his troubles. In his case too, the highhanded procedure of the D.E.I. Company caused considerable resentment in the mother country and this time it looked as if something could be done about it, for "monopoly" was no longer a sacred term but was rapidly becoming Public Enemy No. 1.

Encouraged by the rising tides of public indignation, the D.W.I. Company took the matter to court and after many years of litigation, the D.E.I. Company was ordered to pay an indemnity of 120,000 guilders and to reimburse Roggeveen for the wages he owed his sailors. And so the expedition did not end as disastrously as that of Schouten and Lemaire but Roggeveen's name was the last Dutch name to appear upon any of the maps.

The old fires were dwindling. Rich people have no incentive to risk life and limb on little ships which sail forth into the unknown. The old swords have been hammered down into scissors with which to cut coupons. The Republic, which a hundred years before had dictated its will upon the rest of the world, was now obliged to follow a policy of hesitation and appeasement, of palavering and cajoling and apologizing, which was as disgraceful as it was futile, for the more Their High and Mightinesses appeased and palavered, the less mercy they were shown by their enemies, until in the end a brutal realist by the name of Napoléon Buonaparte threw their whole paper house of stocks and bonds and debentures upon the scrap heap, stole their accumulated hoardings and turned their country into a political dependency of his own empire.

✦

From a practical point of view, Roggeveen had accomplished nothing but indirectly his expedition had been of some value. Once again it had been shown that in spite of the old geographers, there existed no connection of any sort between South America and the unknown Southland. That legend had persisted in spite of everything Tasman and Dampier had already done. It had been somewhat weakened by the adventures of a French naval officer, Pierre Bouvet, who in the year 1739 had been sent out to take possession of the Southern Continent for the crown of France and who, with the exception of Bouvet Island, had found nothing but thousands of miles of open sea and a barrier of ice which had forced him to return whence he had come. And now it was to be destroyed for good and all by a number of Frenchmen and Englishmen who at last succeeded in proving that this mighty continent was nothing but a vast island, situated between Java and New Zealand.

The first to follow in the tracks of Roggeveen was a Frenchman by the name of Louis Antoine de Bougainville. Like Roggeveen he had originally been intended for the law but having switched over to soldiering he had been aide-de-camp to the Marquis de Montcalm, who had com-

**MOREA**
**AS SEEN FROM TAHITI**

manded the king's forces in Canada. After the end of the
Seven Years' War, de Bougainville had tired of life in the
barracks and had obtained permission to colonize the Falk-
land Islands, provided he did so at his own expense.

The Spanish government, not wishing to have the French
so near to their own possessions, had most strenuously ob-
jected and finally had got rid of him by a promise that they
would indemnify him for his losses. Still having no desire
to return to the monotony of a soldier's life, de Bougainville had thereupon (in 1766) prevailed upon the government in Paris to send him to the Pacific to see what he
could do to solve the many problems which still mystified
the geographers.

He passed safely through the Strait of Magellan, explored the Tuamotu group, paid a pleasant visit to Tahiti,
passed through the Samoan Islands, whose name he changed
for reasons unknown to Navigators Islands and from there
he made for the New Hebrides and the Solomon Islands,
parts of which are still called after him.

After an uneventful voyage of over two years, he returned safely to France and gave us not only a new flower,
the lovely bougainvillea, but also the first travel book of
the Pacific that was written with so much good humor
that it could be read for entertainment as well as instruc-
tion.

De Bougainville, when he turned author, was still in his
early forties and he had no intention of spending the rest
of his days entertaining the court of Versailles with elegant

little tales about his adventures with the Tahitian belles. Two whole years he stuck to his writing table and then in sheer despair he asked to be sent on a visit to the North

PAPEETE
WHERE THE FRENCH INFLUENCE MAKES ITSELF VERY
DECIDEDLY FELT

Pole. But the government of France, already fighting to stave off bankruptcy, was in no position to finance such an expedition and Monsieur de Bougainville was forced to remain at home. He somehow survived the Revolution and the Terror and managed to bring himself to the attention of the Emperor Napoleon, who made him a senator and a count of the empire. In the year 1811, this old Frenchman, who had fought with Montcalm on the Plains of Abraham and who had been the first to give us some idea of life among the Tahitians, died peacefully and in his own bed. He had reached the venerable age of eighty-two.

The next time you see a house buried in bougainvilleas, give the old gentleman a thought. He will like it and will bestow upon you his most polite bow, done with all the grace of the old regime.

✦

The example of a man like de Bougainville was bound to find imitators in the France of Louis XVI and during the early seventies of the eighteenth century we find another French explorer busily engaged in trying to prove that Bouvet had been wrong when he reported that south of the 55th latitude there was nothing but water and ice.

This new candidate for Pacific honors was Yves Joseph de Kerguelen-Trémarec, a Breton nobleman, as you may already have guessed from his name. It was de Kerguelen who in the year 1772 discovered an island some two thousand miles southeast of Madagascar, and so big and high and forbidding-looking that it reminded him of Norway. The centre consisted of a number of mountains, some of which rose as high as six thousand feet and were partly covered with glaciers and snow fields. But glaciers and snow fields were not what de Kerguelen had come to look for and so, in deep disappointment, he called it the Isle of Desolation, a name which later explorers, out of respect for its discoverer, have since then changed to Kerguelen Island.

To us, the island is mainly important because it has still further contributed to the confusion already existing in respect to the Pacific Ocean. For if there never has been any connection between South America and the Antarctic mainland, then why should Kerguelen, situated at the other end of the Pacific, have a vegetation which is much closer to that of the American continent than to that of Africa?

Sailors however have a more direct reason to appreciate its existence, for here, right in the heart of the most lonely part of the world, lies an island which raises a kind of cabbage, the famous Kerguelen cabbage, or *Pringlea antiscorbutica,* which is one of the best remedies against scurvy. Perhaps I ought to say that it "used to raise," rather than "raises," for one day some bright fellow had the cheerful idea of introducing rabbits on this bit of land. He thought that they would provide food for the shipwrecked sailors who landed on Kerguelen. His intentions therefore were of the best but unfortunately, the rabbits ate most of the cabbages and there are not enough shipwrecked sailors to consume the rabbits. But as Kerguelen lies thousands of miles out of the way of all modern shipping lanes, it does not really matter very much. The rabbits, however, make an excellent stew for the Norwegian whalers who occasionally venture that far south, and so all is well again with this most extraordinary of worlds, but I would very much like to know how, in the name of the great Jehovah, the penguin ever got here, all the way from the South Pole? And how did all the insects get here, since most of them belong to the non-flying variety?

But these are questions for the zoologists to worry about and this is merely a history of discoveries in the Pacific Ocean.

# 10. CAPTAIN JAMES COOK, R.N.

## *The man who solved the problem*

JAMES COOK was the son of a farm laborer and he started his career as a stableboy, until he was promoted to be a clerk in a grocery store. Yet had he survived his last voyage to the Pacific, he would undoubtedly have been made a baronet and he might have ended the Lord only knows where!

That shows conclusively that this young Yorkshireman was a person of exceptional ability. For if England in the days of Disraeli, almost a century later, was still a country of the few—the very few—what must it have been in the era of the Georges when a poor devil could still be hanged for killing His Lordship's fox, even if he could prove that His Lordship's fox had just eaten the last of his pet chickens, and when a nobleman's son must under no circumstances be plucked in any of his university examinations, even if he were too dumb to spell his own name correctly!

If, in spite of his social handicaps, James Cook rose to such high honors, this merely proves that talent will invariably find a way out, even in the England of the first four Georges. And Cook was not only one of the greatest

navigators of all time, but he was also one of the most
humane men that ever set foot on the quarter-deck. Some
day the world may forget his discoveries, but among all
sailors the story will continue to be told of an eighteenth-
century captain who never lost a single member of his crew
through scurvy while he was on his dangerous expeditions
in a completely unknown part of the world and who
actually flogged those members of his crew who deliberately
refused to eat the food which was to protect them against
this hideous disease and insisted upon a diet of salt pork
while they should have been eating fresh vegetables.

At the age of sixteen, young James Cook had had more
than enough of a commercial career (some authorities claim
that he worked for a grocer and others say that he worked
for a haberdasher) and he quietly got himself apprenticed
to a firm of Whitby shipowners known as the Walker
Brothers. His immediate employer, John Walker, happened to be engaged in the Baltic trade with occasional
excursions to the coast of Norway and it was under his
superintendence that young James learned his trade. After
three years of the messy work of an apprentice, James Cook
began his slow rise to fame. He became a mate. He had
been fortunate indeed in choosing his master, for John
Walker was a humane old patriarch who in every way encouraged his intelligent pupil to improve his mind and who
spent the long winter evenings reading him chapters from
those old travel books which he had collected for his private
entertainment. In the eighteenth century there were very

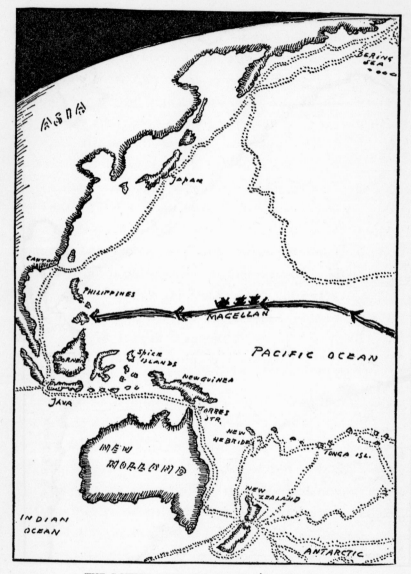

THE DOTTED LINE SHOWS COOK'S VOYAGES

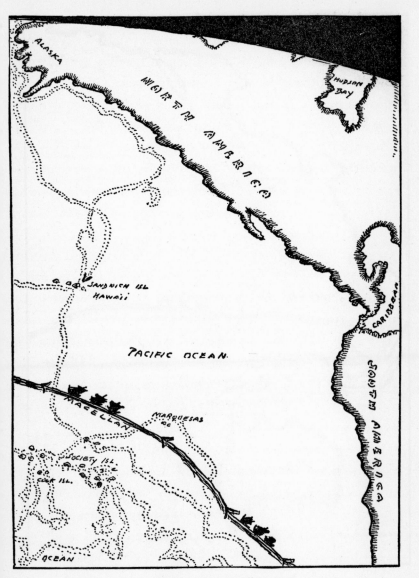

ACROSS THE PACIFIC

few schools and a prospective doctor or painter or musician or carpenter learned his trade from spending from nine to ten years in the home of a competent teacher until he had absorbed all the older man could give him. This made education a highly personal affair and it may explain why the people of that age were often so extremely well educated.

Master James' great chance came in the year 1756 with the outbreak of the Seven Years' War. England, fearing that France might attack the Hanoverian possessions of its own sovereign on the mainland, took the side of Prussia. James Cook at once volunteered for service and he started his career in the royal navy as an A.B., or able-bodied seaman. Five weeks later he was already promoted to the rank of a master's mate and in that capacity he crossed the ocean for the first time and on the *Pembroke*. He arrived in time to assist at the attack on Quebec in 1759 and there on the St. Lawrence River he gave the first evidence of that ability which soon afterwards was to take him out of the common run of sailors and eventually was to associate his name forever with that of the Pacific Ocean.

For when the hostilities had come to an end, he was recommended by Admiral Lord Colville to survey the newly acquired territories, as he was "a man of genius and capacity, well qualified for undertakings of that kind." And so began James Cook's American career which made him spend four years of his life in our part of the world, surveying the coast of Newfoundland and the other islands in that neighborhood and doing his job so well that, according to those who are familiar with those waters, many of his maps are as good now as on the day they were made, more than a century and a half ago.

This is beginning to sound like a Horatio Alger story. But young James Cook had one quality which made him an ideal candidate for a good old-fashioned success story. He always did a little more than was expected of him and therefore he sometimes received a little more than he had expected. This is undoubtedly a platitude, long since discovered by the moralists of the new economic dispensation. But in the year 1766 it worked and when in August of that year James Cook had performed certain observations on a local eclipse of the sun, he did his job so well that his report somehow or other found its way to the Royal Society and this august body, when it needed someone to lead an expedition to the Pacific Ocean to observe the transit of the planet Venus across the face of the sun, selected James Cook to act as commander-in-chief.

The Admiralty obligingly bestowed upon him the rank of a lieutenant and on August 26 of the year 1768 he left on board the good ship *Endeavour*. The *Endeavour* was a bark of 370 tons. It had an uncoppered bottom of peculiar shape which would make it an excellent craft to navigate shallow water and this was the main reason Lieutenant Cook selected the vessel. Otherwise it was not exactly the most comfortable type of vessel for service in the tropics. In view of what it accomplished, however, the *Endeavour* gained such great renown that it became a sort of maritime

CAPTAIN COOK IN THE "ENDEAVOUR" LEAVING TAHITI

curiosity and a favorite topic with the writers of sea yarns. But in spite of the great amount of literature that exists upon the subject, no one has ever been able to discover what became of her. One claim to fame of the city of Newport in Rhode Island was a legend about Cook's *Endeavour,* which was said to have spent the last of its days on a local beach. But there never was any proof of this and the ultimate fate of the *Endeavour* is as uncertain as that of the *Mayflower.*

This could hardly have been avoided as the name of "Endeavour" was a very common one in England during the eighteenth century. The city of Whitby alone (where Cook's *Endeavour* was built) turned out not less than eleven Endeavours in half a century. And for all we know, the real *Endeavour* may now be a coal barge in almost any colonial port and may be patiently awaiting the arrival of an enterprising promoter who will thereupon make a fortune showing her alongside of the vessel in which the British used to send their earliest pioneers to that continent which James Cook had added to the Empire.

After an uneventful trip, Lieutenant Cook and his scientists safely reached Tahiti. While the astronomers observed their little planet, Cook explored the entire group of islands situated in this part of the Pacific. He called them the Society Islands. The name had nothing to do with the sociable qualities of the local terrestrial Venuses. It was chosen to give expression of his gratitude for the honor which the Royal Society had done him when it elected him ahead of all other candidates and made him the leader of their famous expedition. This little incident, by the way, is very typical of the man. James Cook comes as near to being the Perfect Gentleman as any other representative of his race and there again he gave even more than was expected of him.

As soon as the telescopes had once more been packed, the *Endeavour* continued upon its course and this time Cook steered directly for the spot where in the year 1642 Abel Tasman was said to have found a land covered with very high mountains and where he had had that disastrous encounter with the natives which had cost him the lives of several of his men. Cook, having been warned by the name of Murderers' Bay, took all possible precautions but in spite of these, when he finally landed in Poverty Bay it was necessary to kill four Maoris before the others were willing to let him land and refill his water barrels.

The *Endeavour* had left the Society Islands on August 9 and she reached New Zealand on October 7. She therefore had needed almost two months to cover the distance. This gives us a very high opinion of the seamanship of the earliest Polynesian explorers who must have followed exactly the same route as that of Cook but who had done so seven hundred years before, at a time therefore when even as powerful a chieftain as William the Conqueror had experienced great difficulties in finding enough boats to take him and his army from France to England.

This is no mere guesswork on my part. As early as the

year 1150 we find mention in reliable Polynesian chronicles (preserved orally by the Wise Men of the different tribes) of a certain Tahitian chief who had come to New Zealand in search of one of his sons who had disappeared and who was said to have settled there and to have become the ancestor of a great many Maori heroes. It was, of course, possible that the first arrival in New Zealand had been blown there by adverse winds. But the presence in New Zealand of the sweet potato and the yam and of dogs, none of which were native to that land but which must have been imported from elsewhere, show us that subsequent expeditions from Tahiti must have been as carefully planned as those which were organized in the seventeenth century between the different European countries and their colonies in the New World.

Therefore, while the people of central Europe were still considering a trip of four or five days as the limit of their sailing capacity, their contemporaries of the Pacific Ocean were able to cover distances which kept them at sea for several months at a time and they did this in open boats with cargoes of women and children, livestock and plants.

When Cook explored the Pacific, the Polynesians, already an old race, had started on the downward grade. Life had become too easy and they were beginning to show unmistakable signs of degeneration. But they must have come from a race of surpassing courage and magnificent strength. That strength is still there, as you may observe when you give some native boy in the harbor of Honolulu a quarter

**COOK SAILS AROUND NEW ZEALAND**

to amuse you by diving down from the deck of your steamer. But whereas his grandpa was a mighty mariner, who covered thousands of miles in an open boat at a time when our own grandsires sailed by following the church steeples on land—the tables have now been turned. And the handsome brown fellow is glad to make a living by clowning for the benefit of the foreign tourist.

Fortunately, these islands are located within the volcanic belt. Some day the Good Lord will realize what he has done and leave it to Mauna Loa to set things straight.

From Poverty Bay (I have seen it and it lived up to its name!) Cook sailed southward as far as Cape Turn-Again. There he changed his course and now, following the coast in a northern direction, he finally, at Christmas time of 1768, reached the Three Kings Islands, just north of New Zealand. He then proceeded southward past Cape Maria van Diemen and in February he sailed through the strait that still bears his name and which separates the North Island of New Zealand from the South Island. From there he once more followed a northern course until he reached Cape Turn-Again for a second time and knew for a certainty that he was dealing with an island and not with anything resembling a continent.

From Cape Turn-Again, traveling with unusual speed for those days, he sailed southward until he reached Stewart Island. He thereupon stuck close to the western shore until he found himself off Cape Farewell just west of Tasman Bay. It had taken him a little less than seven months to cover 2,400 miles of a sea which until then had been completely unknown to the White Man. In this case, his genius as a cartographer once more manifested itself. In spite of a

COOK IN NEW ZEALAND

great deal of bad weather and a lot of fog and rain, Cook returned to England with a set of maps that were far superior to any similar work ever done during a first trip in a new part of the world.

Having now clearly demonstrated that New Zealand con-

sisted of two separate islands and that those were not connected with any other piece of land, Cook bade farewell
to this inhospitable territory (the Maoris remained hostile
until the end) and sailed due west to see whether in this
way it would prove possible to reach the east coast of Tasman's New Holland.

It was the year 1770, only six years before our own Declaration of Independence, but Australia continued to guard
most of its secrets. The Dutch had by now visited most of
the western coast. The Dutch also had a pretty thorough
idea about the northern part of the continent situated between the Gulf of Carpentaria and van Diemen's Land,
now the Kimberley Division of western Australia. They had
seen parts of the southern coast and Tasman had stumbled
upon the island of Tasmania. But from there he had sailed
directly to New Zealand and therefore no one as yet knew
what that part of the world might have kept hidden from
the White Man's eyes.

Cook himself felt convinced that New Holland was not
part of New Guinea. But neither he nor anyone else knew.
And therefore, when Cook finally decided to leave New
Zealand and sail westward, he entered upon a part of the
world which was still as completely unknown as America
had been before the arrival of Columbus.

✦

First of all, Cook made for Tasmania, but not far from
the northernmost point of that island he turned sharply

northward. It was at the exact spot where Tasman had changed his course a little too far towards the east, a mistake which had prevented him from becoming the real discoverer of Australia. Cook, going about his purpose in a much more scientific fashion, did not commit the same error. From that point on, he sailed due north and early in the morning of April 20 of the year 1770 his senior lieutenant, Zachary Hicks, saw land, eight miles towards the north. It was a low hill about a thousand feet high. It is still there and it is known as Point Hicks Hill and you can find it on any map if you will look for it in the neighborhood of Sydenham Inlet on the southeastern coast of the Province of Victoria.

From there on Cook followed the coast in a northern direction, looking all the time for a suitable place to land but everywhere encountering such a heavy surf that it was impossible to lower the boats. Finally, on Sunday, April 29, 1770, he reached a wide bay which the *Endeavour* could enter and where the ship dropped anchor about half a mile from shore.

Botany Bay is still very much as it was on the day of its discovery. According to a legend with which every one of Macaulay's "typical schoolboys" is familiar, the name was chosen on account of the profusion of wildflowers which were to be found along its shores. Maybe the flowers have since then died, for when I set foot on this interesting historic spot, it looked about as exciting as the harbor of New London or Bridgeport, Conn. The bay itself has of

BOTANY BAY

course not changed. It still is essentially a bay, greatly resembling that artificial harbor which our War Department
has caused to be constructed on Block Island. There is a
narrow opening which leads to the sea and the rest is a
large pond, surrounded by low hills, meagre vegetation, a
road, cars, filling stations, a number of those nondescript
little houses which are to be found all over Australia and
New Zealand and which remind one of the architectural
horrors of the French-Canadian part of Montreal. The
commonplace character of this historic spot is further en-
hanced by a few smokestacks and the remnants of bill-
boards, giving the dates of last year's racing encounters in
nearby Sydney.

The Australian government however has done its duty
by this landmark and has now turned part of Botany Bay
into a reservation where no hot-dog stands and chewing-
gum automats are allowed. But it is all pretty dreary. That
is to say, it is dreary to those of us to whom the name of
Botany Bay will be forever associated with the cruelty and
brutality of the earliest days of Australia when the mother
country was in the habit of dumping its criminals and its
labor union leaders upon the shores of this bay and thereupon submitting them to a life of such rigors and horrors
that many of them preferred to join the aborigines rather
than stay in the prisons of their own people.

Of all this, Cook was most fortunately ignorant on that
lovely Sunday afternoon in April of the year 1770 when at
three o'clock of the afternoon he landed with three of his

officers and a native Tahitian (a bright boy who wanted to see the world) to take possession of the new continent on behalf of His British Majesty. The natives, never having heard of His British Majesty, showed the White Man's delegation very little respect and welcomed these emissaries with spears and stones. As always happens in such cases, the firing of a few muskets was enough to put the fear of God into the naked savages who immediately fled into the bushes and were never seen again while the *Endeavour* remained in port.

For those interested in such details, the first White Man to set foot on the east coast of Australia was a midshipman by the name of Isaac Smith. But this fact need not disturb Herr Hitler's sensitive feelings about the young man's possible racial antecedents. Young Isaac was a hundred per cent Aryan. He happened to be a cousin of Captain Cook's wife and he was considered a member of the family, for after Captain Cook's untimely death he devoted himself with touching fidelity to looking after the widow of his former commander and when he retired from the navy with the rank of a rear admiral, he took full charge of her affairs and saw to it that she never was in need, as a grateful government had forgotten to take any adequate measures that might have provided for her support and that of her six children. Three of these had died in infancy. Of the other three, James, the eldest, had been drowned off the Isle of Wight in the year 1794 while he was in command of a small sloop of war. The second one, Nathaniel, had been lost at the age of sixteen in H.M.S. *Thunderer,* which had gone to the bottom of the ocean with all on board, while the third one, destined for the Church, had died while a student at Cambridge. And so the old lady had been left alone with her husband's gold medals and his ornamental swords and her slender royal pension and somebody had had to look after her, which the excellent Isaac Smith (himself a most expert surveyor and map maker) had done most faithfully until the year 1831, when he had joined his beloved chief, leaving old Mrs. Cook, then in her dotage, to the care of her trusted servants. She reached the age of ninety-three and died, of all places, in the village of Clapham, just two years before Queen Victoria ascended the throne.

A strange hodgepodge of names! Tahiti, Cook Islands, New Zealand, Botany Bay, Hawaii, Kamchatka, Tongatabu, Rarotonga and then finally Clapham. But such things must happen when a small island of less than 90,000 square miles undertakes to rule almost 14,000,000 square miles of dry land in the rest of the world, and we shall continue to find Chelseas and Upper and Lower Peckhams and Nether and Higher Sheepwarks in all sorts of unexpected places. Until the cards are reshuffled and these villages are revaluated into Ober and Unter Pfurzheims and Sheepwarkojes, when I for one shall make straightway for the pleasant burial ground of what then (if the Lord is good to us) will still be Old Greenwich.

And since we are on this lugubrious subject, let me give

you another little detail in connection with the discovery of the Great Southern Continent. It had already become the home of the White Man when one of the Dutch captains, almost a century and a half before, had been obliged to leave a mutinous member of his crew on the eastern coast. Now the west coast too was to receive its first permanent occupant of the White Man's race. For on the very day the *Endeavour* had reached Botany Bay, a member of the crew by the name of Forbes Sutherland had died of consumption. On May 1 he was buried at Point Sutherland. A suitable inscription was left behind on a nearby tree and thereupon the *Endeavour* continued its northward voyage to Port Jackson and Broken Bay at the mouth of the Hawkesbury River, just north of the present city of Sydney.

From there on Cook continued surveying the coast line in his usual meticulous fashion until on June 11, after sounding twenty fathoms of water, his vessel suddenly struck a hidden coral reef. This was absolutely contrary to the true Cook tradition, for few explorers have ever been more careful than James Cook while exploring new territory and nothing was ever left to chance. But in this unpleasant emergency, Cook, as always, knew immediately what to do. Thirty casks of fresh water were dumped into the ocean. All the stores that somehow could be spared, all the iron and stone ballast and six guns, together with their carriages, followed them in quick order until the *Endeavour* had lost sufficient weight to get once more afloat. And then it was discovered that the sharp reef had cut such a big hole in her bottom that it was necessary to beach her.

The situation was becoming desperate. In spite of the fact that all the pumps were being worked day and night, there were almost fifty inches of water in the hold. And so a boat was launched to look for a nice sandy beach where the necessary repairs could be made and it was found at the mouth of the Endeavour River. It took two weeks to get the ship in order but after a few hours at sea, it was found that so much water still poured into the hold that the whole job had to be done all over again.

At last on July 20 everything seemed to be in order and so, after taking on a new load of fresh water and a large number of live turtles, Cook once more set sail.

During their enforced stay on Australian soil, Cook and his officers had spent their time surveying the surrounding country and had tried to learn something about the natives. But just as in Botany Bay, the ugly little black men were found to be extremely unfriendly. They refused to engage in barter, but they were forever trying to steal fresh turtle meat from the shipwrecked white sailors and they could only be driven away by the constant firing of muskets. Not liking this artificial thunder very much, they made an effort to drive their visitors away by setting fire to the surrounding grass and bushes. Therefore everybody felt considerably relieved when finally on July 20 the *Endeavour* was once more considered seaworthy and ready to depart.

In spite of the unfriendly attitude of the aborigines, Cook

had recognized the great fertility of the land he had discovered and when he came back to England he reported that, with proper care, all this territory was extremely well fitted

THE GREAT BARRIER REEF

for permanent settlement on the part of the White Man. In this prediction he was, as usual, entirely right, for today the eastern coast of Australia is densely populated and the home of a number of large cities, whereas the western half of the continent has remained an almost complete wilderness and most likely will continue to be so until the end of time.

Today every atlas will give you the exact location of the
so-called Great Barrier Reef, but in the days of Cook it was
not even suspected. This is the largest coral reef in the
world, being more than twelve hundred miles in length.
In the south it lies 150 miles away from shore, whereas
in the north it comes very close to the dry land and leaves
only a narrow opening through which vessels can pass without being smashed to pieces.

The Barrier region is a world for and in and by itself,
a world of magnificent aspects, for the foaming white streak
of water, appearing suddenly above the smooth surface of
the ocean, is a sight never to be forgotten. But not all of
the Reef lies hidden beneath the surface of the sea, for
there are thousands of little specks of dry land, ranging
all the way from mere rocks to regular islands covered with
pine and palm trees.

James Cook of course had not exactly set out to see the
sights. He was at the head of a scientific expedition which
had achieved significant results and it was now his business
to bring his vessel back to England and surrender his report to his employers, the governors of the Royal Society,
and now to his dismay, he found himself caught in a trap
of coral reefs. It was up to him to find a means of escape.
This he finally did, just north of Lizard Island, by coming
upon a passage which is still known as Cook's Passage, and
at last he found himself in the deep water that lay east of
the Coral Sea. But then he had to face another problem—
one that had puzzled the world for more than two hundred

years—for he was now somewhere in the neighborhood of the Cape York peninsula and he would have to find out once and for all whether New Holland was part of New Guinea or a continent by itself.

Cook, a most methodical person in everything he did, had been careful to collect all the books which until then had been published upon the problem of the problematic Strait of Torres. He had the latest available maps on board and these were only fourteen years old. They were printed in a history of all the expeditions that had ever been made to the southern Pacific, the work of a man who was to play quite a role in the politics of France just before the outbreak of the great revolution. This was the learned Charles de Brosses, who had started his literary career by giving the world the first popular account of "the subterranean city of Herculaneum," which was then at last being brought back to life, not as an immediate result of any deep archaeological curiosity on the part of the Neapolitan authorities but because a foreign visitor had become suspicious about the origin of their almost unlimited supply of crushed marble which they were selling to the people of the city for building purposes and which they obtained by smashing ancient statues to pieces at a disastrous rate of speed.

De Brosses, a man of universal interests, had been convinced from the previous investigations in this part of the Pacific made by the Spaniards and the Dutch, that New Guinea and New Holland were actually two large islands, separated from each other just north of the Gulf of Carpentaria, and Cook fully shared this view. And so, on the fifteenth of August of the year 1770 he began the most perilous part of his entire voyage, the navigation of the treacherous Torres Strait, a name which ever since the days

TAHITI

of Dampier (and at his particular suggestion) had been bestowed upon that narrow stretch of water just north of New Holland.

The first two days, all went well with the expedition but then the wind suddenly ceased to blow and the *Endeavour* was rapidly drifting towards one of the innumerable reefs. There was only one way in which the ship could be saved and Cook knew it. He manned his boats and had his sailors pull the *Endeavour* away from the breakers. After all, she was only 370 tons and no bigger than a ferryboat, but it shows the sort of navigation that had to be practiced in the days before the introduction of steam and gasoline.

Having by means of his man power saved his ship from destruction, Cook dropped anchor and early the next morning the big sloop once more preceded the mother ship to show the way.

On August 22, the channel broadened and Cook realized that he was about to bid farewell to his newly discovered territories. He therefore tried to make a landing on Cape York, but the natives gathered together and forced him to look elsewhere for the final ceremony by which he meant to take official occupancy of the whole of New Holland for the benefit of the English crown.

And so Cook performed this ceremony on a little island, instead of the mainland. It is known as Possession Island and is situated two miles off the western shores of Cape York. There, at six o'clock in the evening, the flag of England was hoisted while Captain Cook, in the name of His British Majesty, took possession of the whole of New Wales, as Cook had called the entire eastern half of New Holland. Cook had chosen this name because the coast near Port Jackson had borne a very close resemblance to that of the real Wales. There was no local patriotism in the transaction, as Cook was a Yorkshireman, but in the character of this extraordinary man there seems to have been no room for personal vanity. And Dumont d'Urville was right when in the book he wrote on his own two voyages through the Pacific, undertaken during the twenties and thirties of the last century, he said that Captain James Cook would ever be regarded as the most illustrious navigator of both the past and future ages and that his name will forever remain at the head of the list of the sailors of all nations, as much on account of his personal traits as his ability as a navigator.

This was no small praise but already another Frenchman, whose name also stands writ large upon the maps of the Pacific, had given expression to a similar sentiment. When the famous Captain La Pérouse sailed from Botany Bay on his last and fateful voyage in the year 1788, he turned to the English officer who bade him farewell and remarked rather sadly, "But what can I hope to do? Your Mr. Cook has done so much that he has left me nothing but to admire his work."

Speaking of these two gallant Frenchmen, I feel tempted once more to stress the peculiarities of the breed of men who gave us the Pacific. Others who had pushed forth into unknown parts of the world had of course been people of remarkable courage and endowed with tremendous powers of endurance, for otherwise they would never have been able to do what they did. But those who chose the Pacific as their experimental territory were more than that. Almost invariably they were also people of some imagination and many of them were scholars and scientists of outstanding merit. This may of course have been due to the fact that the

Pacific was the last of all oceans to be explored, when the general level of culture was considerably higher than it had been in the days of Elizabeth or the early East India Company. But it is also possible that the Pacific attracted a different type of person.

After the last failure of Tasman, it was pretty generally agreed among those in the know that the Pacific, contrary to the beliefs of the ancients, hid no *Dorados* and no lands of Ophir. Therefore, direct economic gain was out of the question. Businessmen might still play with the idea of getting hold of some hitherto unsuspected Cathay, but they are the last to learn any sort of lesson, so we might leave them out of the discussion. Neither could the Spanish Conquistador hope to enrich himself here overnight, and as for the Church, why waste time upon a few handfuls of heathen when there were hundreds of millions of unsaved souls available in nearby Asia, Africa and America?

Therefore, with the exception of certain bestial acts committed by a few of the earlier Portuguese and several of my own ancestors during the days of the great spice boom, one does not come across any of those harrowing tales of premeditated assassination and unnecessary bloodshed which were so common in every other part of the world while they were being brought within the realm of progress. And also, perhaps because the Pacific began to loom upon the European horizon at such a late date and just when in so many countries people had begun to read books for the purpose of entertainment rather than subsequent salvation

—the more amusing passages of popular travel literature and picaresque novels—it was possible to endow this entire region with an atmosphere of that unspoiled simplicity and those qualities of a primitive gracefulness which appealed so immensely to the men and women of the age of the rococo.

For the sake of absolute fairness I should of course mention the name of William Bligh, who was responsible for not one but an endless series of Pacific tragedies. But Bligh was a psychopath. He was an incurable sadist, a most competent man with a sextant and absolutely brave in battle, as he showed upon several occasions, notably in the battle of Camperdown, but totally unfit to deal with normal, ordinary sailors. He served for two years under Cook on board the *Resolution* but even the example of that humane and ever considerate and courteous leader had left no lasting impression upon his violent and uncontrollable temper. He should never have been entrusted with any sort of independent command and the British Admiralty was to blame for the fact that he had not long before been dismissed from the service and in spite of the support he received from his superiors, who only thought of maintaining discipline and to whom all sailors were merely so much scum and riffraff, he came to a bad end, for having been appointed governor of New South Wales, he was taken prisoner by his own subjects and kept on board a man-of-war in Tasmania for almost a year before he was allowed to return to England. Bligh therefore was not only far from typical but he was almost the exception to prove the rule that by and large, the Pacific had attracted a type of men of superior qualities when finally it allowed itself to be really discovered.

Compare the way the early navigators had shot and hacked their way through the territories of the Black Man to the grand manner in which James Cook dealt with the natives. When on one occasion—and in absolute self-defense —it had been necessary to kill four Maoris (during the attempt to land in Poverty Bay on New Zealand), you will find this astonishing reference to the incident made by Joseph Banks, the scientist of the expedition: "This was the most disagreeable day my life has yet seen." A hundred years before, during the struggle for Java, the Dutch commander-in-chief would have slaughtered whole armies of Jacatrans and would have rejoiced in God's mercy as it had manifested itself in the destruction of his enemies. Not to mention our own beloved Puritans, who had accepted the wholesale demise of the New England natives as the result of an illness they themselves had imported as a sign of the Divine approval of their cause.

Or take another example. During the sixteenth and seventeenth centuries, every other European you met on the high seas was your natural enemy and if you had been able to send his ship to the bottom, then you quietly lit a pipe while you watched the sailors struggling for their lives amidst the wreckage of their sunken craft, or took pot shots at them while they tried to keep afloat on empty barrels. But when our own Benjamin Franklin, the representative of the rebellious colonists to the court of France, heard that Captain James Cook had started forth upon a scientific expedition to the southern Pacific, he immediately asked that instructions should be given to the commanders of all American warships that they should treat him as a friend if they were to encounter him or his squadron anywhere on the high seas.

Yes, in many ways it was a gracious age. It was an era of gentlemen who considered the art of living as the highest of all forms of art and that is what bestows a certain lustre upon this final act of the discovery of the Pacific.

✦

I believe that I started this little soliloquy à propos of a Frenchman, a certain Dumont d'Urville, the man who solved the problem of what had become of La Pérouse by finding the remains of that unfortunate captain's vessel on one of the Santa Cruz Islands, fifty years after La Pérouse had disappeared. D'Urville did a great many other things, during a most active career as a French naval officer. But he was still a product of the eighteenth century in the many-sidedness of his talents. The next time (God only knows when that will be!) you stand before the statue called the Venus of Milo in the Museum of the Louvre, remember that you owe a debt of gratitude to this famous Pacific and Antarctic explorer, for it was he who had recognized its precious value the moment it had been unearthed.

He was then, in the year 1820, making a hydrographic

survey of the Mediterranean and if he had not promptly warned the French ambassador at Constantinople, the people of Melos might have used the lovely goddess as a doorstep or to fill a gap in their city walls.

A further curious detail, but to show you how short a time all these famous exploits in the Pacific lie behind us, this same Dumont d'Urville, who followed immediately in the ship tracks of Cook, was not killed by the spear of some Samoan native. It is true, he too died a violent death (together with his whole family) but it happened in a railroad accident near Meudon in France. But if you want to fix the date of Cook's most famous exploit firmly in your mind, there is an easy way of doing so. James Cook left Tahiti for Australia in the same year in which James Watt obtained his first patent for his steam engine—the year 1769—and the year, I feel convinced, from which the historians of the future will date the beginning of our modern era.

✦

To return to the hero of this chapter, after taking official possession of New Holland by landing on Possession Island, Cook sailed westward through the Strait of Torres and he would have explored the coast on both sides, except for the condition of his ship, which had not yet recovered from the leak it had sprung on the Great Barrier. And so he made for the Timor Sea, for he also had begun to notice signs of sickness among his men and their welfare, as always, came ahead of all personal considerations.

In October he reached Batavia on Java and on July 13 of the next year, 1771, he was back in England.

I regret to say that the visit to Batavia had been fatal to the health records of his expedition. While on shore leave, the sailors had indulged in all sorts of sailor delicacies which had been kept away from them as long as they were under their captain's immediate supervision. And in consequence of their excesses, a great many of them now fell ill and many of the men who had spent years on the high seas without a single day's discomfort now died from afflictions which were due to their intemperate mode of living on dry land.

In spite of this and in spite of his humble origin, the former haberdasher's assistant had every reason to be satisfied with the reception he received. The Admiralty advanced him in rank. King George III most kindly accorded him a private audience and showed himself "very mutch bleased mit so wunderful a foyage," and he graciously deigned to accept a copy of the *Endeavour's* journal and some of the original charts of the coasts of his newly acquired "derridories." And all of England for a while forgot the rising tide of discontent among the bothersome tradespeople and peasants of the colonies on the other side of the Atlantic Ocean to focus its thoughts upon the future possibilities of establishing a territorial substitute for America on the newly discovered continent in the Pacific.

Indeed, it was worry about the future of their American possessions which once again placed the problem of the

Southern Continent in the centre of discussion. There was still a large part of the Pacific which until then had never been explored. Australia was now fairly well known. But who could tell that somewhere in that watery desert there was not still another continent—a seventh one which awaited its European discoverers?

The British Admiralty therefore decided to try just once more but this time, so all Their Lordships felt, the job must be done in such a manner that there would never be any further reason for doubt. Every square mile of the whole of the southern Pacific must be searched and then checked off on the map until it had been shown beyond the shadow of a doubt that it was nothing but water.

The stay-at-home geographers immediately joined in the chorus that something more ought to be done. It was true that Captain Cook had rendered most valuable services to the advance of the science of geography, but just the same, there was that gigantic region east of New Zealand and south of Tahiti. Nobody had really ever paid any attention to these thousands and thousands of square miles. It was about time that they should be thoroughly explored, for then alone would it be possible to say that Captain Cook had really done what he pretended to have done and that his South Wales and Tasman's New Holland were really all there was to the old puzzle about the unknown Southern Continent.

It was mainly in order to put an end to all such talk that the Admiralty now decided to send out two vessels which should systematically search the entire region between the Antarctic, South America and New Zealand. Under the right sort of a commander, two ships would be just as useful as a whole fleet and now, if Captain Cook were willing to be the leader of this new venture, then everybody felt sure that the expedition would be a success.

The gallant captain was more than willing, for by then he had fallen into the hands of what in his day was called "fashion" and what today is known as "society." Perhaps some day someone with greater courage than I will give us a "History of Society" and its influence upon human progress. He would come to some very distressing conclusions. If Society (with a capital "S") were based only upon money (as so many people seem to believe), then we would not have to bother about its disastrous effect upon society (with a small "s"), for money is in a constant state of flux and the poor of today are the rich of tomorrow and *vice versa*. But there is more to Society as designated to mean a "higher social circle" than an unlimited bank account and ditto credit. What, ever since the beginning of recorded history, has kept this small number of fashionable people together and given them their power is something much more subtle than mere money. It is their ability to take themselves, their pleasures, pastimes and prejudices with complete and unquestioning seriousness. For they instinctively realize that they have nothing tangible to set themselves apart from the rest of the community. They are no better born, better mannered, better dressed or more intelligent than the average run of humanity. Often their women are most unattractive in appearance and have the manners usually associated with the ladies of the fish market. Yet they will be able to dictate to the public taste, to make and break artistic and literary reputations, to spoil scientific and political careers and to cause revolutions that shake empires as well as republics. But unless they become so arrogant and brazen in their pretensions and affectations that they cause an open outburst of discontent, as they did in France during the eighteenth century and in the Russia of the Romanovs, few serious historians have ever paid much attention to this highly destructive social organism and none of them has bothered to inquire very seriously into the real reason for its existence.

As far as I have been able to come to any definite conclusion (having for many years given the subject a great deal of thought), the strength of this sort of society lies solely in the gift of its members for making themselves and all they do "exclusive" and therefore "desirable" and worthy of the popular envy. They can accomplish this purpose quite easily by doing whatever they do just a little differently from the rest of their neighbors and in such a way that these neighbors shall feel slightly abashed and humiliated.

You would misunderstand me very sadly if from those remarks you were to conclude that I consider James Cook the sort of man who could possibly have fallen for all these hollow pretensions. Not at all. But neither does one fall for a toothache. One gets a toothache and even the wisest and most prudent of people will be influenced by the pain until the cause has been definitely removed.

In the case of Captain Cook, this was out of the question, as all the people who were to be his ultimate employers needed the good will of the court to obtain the money necessary for their second expedition. Therefore there was only one thing he could do—bid farewell to London and betake himself as soon as possible to the more congenial and less distressing surroundings of the bay of Papeete.

But there was a second reason why he was so anxious to be off. Cook was a sailor, not a writer. It was of course expected that as soon as possible he would publish a beautifully illustrated volume containing a description of his voyage. The scientific data he had brought back had been surrendered to the Royal Society, where the scientists could now ponder over them and digest them at leisure. Fashion was not interested in latitudes and longitudes and in currents and wind velocities. Society and its faithful slave, the reading public, wanted glamour. The reading public especially wanted something over which it could gush.

This was in the days before our cheap theatres, movies and magazines. A great many of the people who could read and write still lived in almost perfect seclusion on their country estates and during the long evenings of winter, they derived great pleasure from reading the latest travel books about strange and distant countries. Travel books, solid and substantial travel books, expensively printed and illustrated and even more expensively bound, were then at a premium. All the best publishers were engaged in that

HONOLULU

particular business, for it was considered the most lucrative branch of their ancient and honorable trade.

It was therefore a matter of the utmost importance that Captain Cook's voyage should be put upon the market before the fashionable interest in the Southern Continent had begun to wane. But as the gallant captain could not be expected to wield a goose quill as graciously as a sword, someone had to be found who could act as his ghost writer.

A great many candidates were tried and found wanting and when a final choice was made, it could not have been worse. For the ghost of *Cook's Voyages* was an empty-headed and foolish scribbler who owed his selection to "influence" rather than to ability.

His name was Hawkesworth, John Hawkesworth. He was an old hand at the game for in 1744 he had succeeded Samuel Johnson as the compiler of the parliamentary debates for the *Gentleman's Magazine* and afterwards, together with the Doctor and others, he had founded a periodical called *The Adventurer,* for which he had written most of the stories.

Being a fellow without any originality, he had studied the unpleasant mannerisms of Sam Johnson so faithfully that in the end, even that self-satisfied pedant had begun to object and had asked his assistant to leave his style alone. As the learned Doctor (who never allowed a chance to go by to make himself objectionable and obnoxious) had undoubtedly couched his request in the most objectionable terms, there had been an end to all further collaboration and Hawkesworth had struck out for himself.

At first he and his wife had run a school, and he also had set up as a free-lance penny-a-liner. In that capacity he had edited the first twelve volumes of Dean Swift's assembled works (twenty-seven were to come later) and now he pulled every possible wire to have a chance at getting Captain Cook's manuscripts ready for the press.

He made a terrible hash of the job. Cook, as honorable

a gentleman as the England of the eighteenth century produced, had merely written down what he had actually seen and observed. Such modesty was not at all to the taste of John Hawkesworth. He disregarded the data that had been

DIAMOND HEAD. OAHU

placed at his disposal and gave full rein to his considerable powers of imagination when it came to the more glamorous aspects of life among the South Sea Islanders.

No blame for the subsequent result attaches to Captain Cook. He was long since gone when his book appeared, for the Admiralty, having made up its mind to put him in command of its new expedition to the Pacific, had proceeded with such unusual speed and with such a complete absence of red tape that the ships had been got ready in less than half the usual time for such elaborate preparations.

Late in November of the year 1771 the *Resolution* and the *Adventure* had been handed over to James Cook and already in July of the next year, 1772, he was ready to leave for the Cape of Good Hope.

At the last moment there had been some slight difficulties about the scientific part of the expedition. At first it had been decided that Joseph Banks, who had accompanied Cook on his first expedition, would once more be in charge of the scientific arrangements. He had got along very well with his chief during their many months in the tropics, for James Cook was a man of even temper, not at all like that religious fanatic who afterwards was to cause so much discomfort to Charles Darwin on his voyage on board the *Beagle*. But primarily, Cook was a sailor. He was interested in the lands he discovered as outlines on a map. He wanted to explore their coast line so as to make the future navigation of the Pacific safer than it had been before. What sort of people and trees and animals lived in the countries he found were of secondary importance to him, as compared to the reefs and rocks that were a constant menace to safety. And so, although he had always been meticulously polite to Dr. Banks (Oxford, his former university, had made him a D.C.L. after his successful observations of Venus, transiting across the sun's face), the scientist had occasionally felt that he was only playing second fiddle.

And then, there were Cook's officers. They realized that Dr. Banks enjoyed the high protection of Lord Sandwich,

then First Lord of the Admiralty but now chiefly remembered as the inventor of the "ham on rye" and as the British
official during whose term of office, corruption and inca-
pacity reached a height never before equaled or surpassed
in a department which for centuries had been infamous

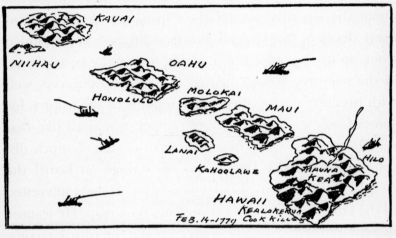

T. H.

for its unlimited possibilities as a grafter's paradise. These
officers, quite rightly, foresaw that all of them would have
to sacrifice their own quarters if Dr. Banks were able to persuade Lord Sandwich that he would need most of the ship's
highly limited space for laboratory purposes for himself and
his elaborate staff of assistants. Therefore they discouraged
the idea of Banks being a member of the party just as much
as they dared and when the doctor withdrew from the expedition (which he did shortly before Captain Cook sailed)
there was loud jubilation.

I should add however that Joseph Banks, in spite of his affiliations with the fourth Earl of Sandwich and a somewhat exaggerated view of his own importance, was an extremely able and highly accomplished gentleman. He always remained on the best of terms with Captain Cook and after the latter's murder, he became a most active champion of the new continent and established himself as a sort of minister without portfolio for Australian affairs, forever annoying the British Government with his plans to turn the country into a well-regulated and self-sustaining colony. Indeed, it was Dr. Banks who, after the loss of America, came forward with an elaborate project to remove all American loyalists forthwith to New Holland and there give them a new and better start in life. Nothing came of this scheme because the loyalists were about as anxious to move to that distant land as most of Mr. Hitler's victims are to settle down among the wide open spaces of the great West.

Banks, not to be discouraged, thereupon suggested that Chinese be imported to take care of all this empty territory. Only when the Chinese too had refused to go so far away from home was the decision made to turn the region around Botany Bay into a penal colony for the inmates of Britain's jails. Even then the new continent continued to enjoy his undivided care and loyalty and he used his wide botanical knowledge to send the successive governors all sorts of useful trees and shrubs and to encourage them in their efforts to introduce wool grazing as one of the main industries of the country.

As he grew older he also grew more set in his opinions and it is curious to reflect that it was one of the co-discover-

THE ISLAND OF HAWAII

ers of the new continent who afterwards tried to prevent Captain Flinders from calling this part of the world Australia and dropping the name New Holland, by which it was still known on most maps.

Matthew Flinders, by the way, was the man who between the years 1795-1799 and 1801-1803 navigated around both New Zealand and Australia and cleared up all the details which Cook, for lack of time, had been obliged to leave to his successors. Having performed his task in a most able fashion, he then, for convenience' sake, made the suggestion that all the old and conflicting appellations be dropped and that the whole of the continent be called Australia. But old Banks, paralyzed from the waist down and rapidly turning into a crabby old fellow, would have none of this nonsense and when Flinders' famous book appeared—the first reliable account of the sixth continent—it still bore the now almost prehistoric title of *A Voyage to Terra Australis.* That was in the year 1814, the year of the battle of New Orleans.

✦

An expedition of the sort which was now about to proceed to the unknown seas of the southern hemisphere could of course not sail without a duly qualified scientist. And it was then that Cook, who as a rule was an excellent judge of men, made the wrong choice. For the Forsters, father and son, who now asked to join him as his naturalists were a couple of bull-headed, obstreperous and tactless Germans and their presence on board led to continual friction, and although Cook was too tactful ever to let it come to an open breach, they were a constant source of irritation to everyone on board.

Even so, after the return from his second voyage, Cook prevailed upon the Admiralty not to permit the elder Forster to write the official story of the trip, as had been the original intention, but to let him do it himself.

To show you the sort of people the Forsters were, the

father thereupon told his son to write the volume and he brought it out just a few months before the book of his commander was put upon the market, so as to spoil the sale of the latter's labors.

Forster was of English origin but the family had lived long enough in German territory to have become completely Teutonized. He had started his career as a Lutheran minister in the Polish part of Prussia, but he had switched over to botany and after a visit to Russia, he had settled down in England as an assistant schoolmaster. He had drawn some attention to himself as an expert on matters pertaining to the Pacific by his translation of de Bougainville's *Voyage round the World* and when Banks had withdrawn from the expedition, he had got himself and his son appointed in his place as the official scientists of the second James Cook expedition.

The son was apparently just as unattractive a creature as his papa, and all during the trip, the two Heinies were either plotting against their commander or whining about the way they were treated. Cook would have been entirely within his rights if he had left them behind at some intermediary port. He was unfortunately too considerate to take such a drastic step. But when Forster circumvented the Admiralty's positive orders against his publishing a book of his own and let it appear with his son's name on the title page, the English public, aroused by such callous incivility, settled the matter by making it impossible for the Forsters to remain any longer on British soil. The Professor returned to the country of his adoption, where he spent the rest of his days teaching botany to the students of the University of Halle and translating the voyages of Cook and Bligh and the other popular Pacific explorers into the native vernacular.

Cook's second voyage was the least important of all three from a positive point of view. But it was most useful in that it provided the world with that negative information for which it had been looking for so many centuries. It proved once and for all, and definitely this time, that the old story about a vast southern continent, situated between Africa and South America, somewhere in the eastern half of the Pacific, was a myth. Or, as Cook observed after he had returned to England in 1775, if such a continent should after all exist, it must be situated so close to the South Pole that it must be forever covered by such a heavy layer of snow and ice as to be uninhabitable by man.

The *Resolution* and the *Adventure* (the latter commanded by Tobias Furneaux), after having taken on fresh supplies at the Cape, made at once for the Antarctic Circle and then, following the southern ice fields, the two ships sailed in an eastern direction until they had reached the neighborhood of Tasmania, where they separated. This being January and the height therefore of the summer of the southern hemisphere, they had encountered no great difficulties and they had met again in May in New Zealand.

Then it became clear from Furneaux's reports that he was still uncertain about the actual outlines of Tasmania.

He still suspected that there might be a land connection between that so-called island and Australia. For this he deserves no blame, for it was not until almost a generation later that Bass (the ex-apothecary assistant who had turned naval surgeon and was the lifelong friend of Flinders) definitely established the existence of such a strait by sailing through it.

After having studied Furneaux's report, Cook at first felt tempted to turn back on his trail to settle this matter before he proceeded further eastward. But time was getting short; it was now May and the southern winter would soon set in. And so Cook left Queen Charlotte Sound on the South Island of New Zealand and he entered a part of the Pacific into which no White Man until then had dared to penetrate. He made one short trip to Tahiti to hire a few of the natives who were known to be first-rate sailors and might be more familiar with these waters than he himself, and then he crossed and recrossed every part of the whole of the southeastern Pacific, but without finding trace of land.

When Cook returned to England in July, 1775, after an absence of three years, he had added only one new island to the map, Norfolk Island between New Zealand and New Caledonia. But now at last the world knew that contrary to the belief of the ancient mariners and geographers, there was absolutely nothing in all that part of the southern Pacific except water. There might be some more land in the neighborhood of the South Pole, but that was another question again and without any possible interest to anyone but a penguin or a sea gull.

When Cook reached England he found that Furneaux had been waiting for him a whole year. That was in the days when explorers did not bother about split seconds, but took time in their stride and when a wait of two or even half a dozen years meant nothing as long as one eventually got home. Furneaux too had had a fortunate voyage, although he had been engaged in a regular pitched battle with the Maoris of Queen Charlotte's Sound. He had made the return trip by way of Cape Horn and he too reported that he had discovered no evidences of any land in the southern Pacific.

This time, Cook wrote his own travel book. Hawkesworth was still alive but his services were not wanted. A clerical gentleman attended to the necessary grammatical details and Jimmie Boswell was delighted to report to Dr. Johnson that now at last some of Hawkesworth's nonsensical exaggerations had been brought back to their true proportions and that the famous circumnavigator of the world was a simple and pleasant-spoken gentleman, worthy of all the honors that were once more being bestowed upon him.

To us, accustomed to our Broadway and Grover Whalen receptions of every returning hero (rare, medium or just so-so), these honors do not seem very impressive. Cook was elected a fellow of the Royal Society and in this quality he was allowed to read a paper on the best methods of pre-

COOK'S SEARCH OF THE ANTARCTIC

venting scurvy. For Cook was the first of the great travelers who took an active scientific interest in the health of his subordinates. Until he published his report on his experiments with lemon juice or lime juice (which of the two he preferred, we do not yet know even today), it had been taken for granted that no long voyages could possibly be undertaken without a heavy loss of men through scurvy. The number of those who died ran usually from fifteen to thirty per cent. A voyage with less than ten per cent of the crew having succumbed to scurvy was accounted a great success.

Cook, during almost six years of constant traveling, had not lost a single man through that painful affliction while he was at sea. He had performed this miracle by feeding his sailors plenty of fresh and dried vegetables and by giving them lemon or lime juice instead of copious portions of rum. The other navies thought this was just too funny for words. The idea of a two-fisted tar drinking anything less hearty than rum became the standing joke of the age. In the end, of course, all other nations were obliged to follow Captain Cook's example, but the experiment survives in the name by which English seamen are still known to their seafaring colleagues. They are called "lime-juicers" or "limies" for short. This to differentiate them from the Scandinavian "square-heads," the Mediterranean "dagoes" and the "dumb Dutch" who hail from the ports of the North Sea and the Baltic.

✦

No sooner had Cook returned than rumors began to spread about still another, a third expedition, which the Admiralty wanted to send to the Pacific. There was no longer any interest in that mysterious Southern Continent, which now—even the most conservative among the theoretical geographers were forced to confess it—had been shown up as non-existent. But there were other aspects of the Pacific problem which had never yet been studied.

There was the old question of that Northeast Passage from the Pacific to the Atlantic for which the nations of Europe had been looking ever since the beginning of the sixteenth century, but then in the opposite direction, from west to east. Such a passage, if it existed, would be most valuable to those who could get hold of it and with England now in complete control of Canada, it would be very handy if London could also lay claim to this polar route between the two great oceans and in this way could control all territory adjacent to that part of the Arctic Ocean.

The Admiralty, in the belief that after almost six years at sea, James Cook would prefer to enjoy a short respite on dry land in some pleasant sinecure, had offered the command of this new expedition to Cook's former second-in-command, Charles Clerke. But the moment James Cook heard of these plans, he immediately offered his services, which quite naturally were most gratefully accepted.

And so, only a very short time after he had returned to the bosom of his family, James Cook, who does not exactly seem to have been what one might call a "family man," was busy getting the *Resolution* ready for the most ambitious trip he had so far ever undertaken. It was to be a voyage all the way to that New Albion (California to us) of which Sir Francis Drake had spoken with such eloquent words of praise after he had returned from that memorable voyage of his around the world of the year 1580, the occasion on which he had been able to present his royal mistress with booty to the tune of seven million dollars.

From New Albion, Cook was to return to Europe, following either the eastern or the western route as might seem most practicable, once he had arrived on the spot, but by preference he was to take the eastern route, the one therefore that followed the coast of North America.

The *Resolution* was no *Golden Hind* and King George was no Queen Elizabeth, but Cook set to work with the greatest possible energy, for this voyage, he felt sure, was to bring him his baronetcy and then as now, it was pleasanter to be called Sir James than plain Mr. Cook.

Charles Clerke, who had graciously withdrawn before his superior, was to accompany him on a second ship, the *Discovery*, and early in July of the year 1776, Cook left for the Cape of Good Hope, where shortly after his arrival he was joined by the *Discovery*.

From there the trip went southward, so as to make sure that there was no land in that part of the Pacific. First to Marion Island. Next to the Crozet Islands and Kerguelen. From Kerguelen to Tasmania and New Zealand and from

New Zealand to Tahiti by way of the Friendly and Cook
Islands.

In Tahiti, where by this time Cook must have known
most of the people by their first names, the ships stayed
almost five months and from there they went northward.

They now followed a very old Polynesian route which
led them directly to a group of islands which as yet had
been unknown to the White Man, or about which (in case
they had been visited) no news had reached the Old World.
Cook called them the Sandwich Islands in honor of the
First Lord of the Admiralty, who had sent him out upon
this last voyage.

The name maintained itself for more than a century, but
after the occupation of the islands by the United States, it
was quietly allowed to drop from the maps and the islands
became known as the Hawaiian Islands. Officially they are
termed T.H. or Territory of Hawaii, but as not one in a
thousand Americans seems to have the faintest idea what
that T.H. stands for, I shall stick to Hawaii or the Hawaiian
Islands.

Early in February, Cook left the islands for New Albion,
which then meant all the region that lay between California
and the state of Washington. In March he sailed northward
to find a passage to the Atlantic. All this happened in the
year 1778. The Declaration of Independence was therefore
nearly two years old. Burgoyne had surrendered his troops
to Gates the year before and France had just recognized
the independence of the United States. Along the western

shore of the Atlantic, therefore, civilization was making rapid strides. But in the west of America, all the territory between Mexico and Alaska was still practically unknown, and the fact that America and Asia were not one continent but were separated from each other by a strait fifty-six miles wide was not definitely established until the year 1741 when Bering explored this part of the northern Pacific and died on the island that still bears his name.

✦

Among the books I hope that someone will write some day is a history of the winning of the East, meaning the occupation of Siberia by the Russians. It would show us (what few Americans suspect) than when it came to the occupation of new territories, the Russians, of the old imperial days, performed feats of speed and endurance which make our own efforts at conquering the West look rather amateurish.

Siberia to most of us is merely a name and a vague one at that. Some day we may realize that it is quite a big piece of land, for it covers about five million square miles and is therefore almost twice as large as our own country. We settled along the western shore of the Atlantic during the early half of the seventeenth century and we did not reach the shores of the Pacific until almost two hundred years later. The Russians began a little earlier with their conquest of Siberia, for they crossed the Ural Mountains in 1580.

Some sixty years later they had penetrated as far as the Amur River, way at the other end of Asia. And in the year 1648 a Cossack by the name of Dejnev had reached the

BERING IN ALASKA

Bering Strait and the whole of Siberia had been visited by Russian travelers. In sixty-eight years, therefore, the Russians had occupied twice as much territory as we did between the year 1609, when Hudson first visited Manhattan Island, and 1805 when Lewis and Clark reached the mouth of the Columbia River.

In view of our ignorance of the general subject, it is only

natural that so few people should be familiar with the man who gave his name to the strait across which the earliest settlers of the American continent had marched on their way from Mongolia to Patagonia a great many thousand years before. At most they will tell you that he had probably been some sort of Roossian. Well, not exactly! It is true that he had taken service in the Russian navy which Peter the Great had imported from Holland to help him in his war against the Swedes. But by birth he was a Dane and he hailed from Jutland, where he had seen the light of day in 1680 and had been baptized as Vitus Jonassen Bering. He had joined the Danish navy and had visited the East Indies, but after his return to Denmark he had anticipated a more rapid promotion in Russia and he had served in the Swedish war as captain of a Russian frigate. In 1724, Peter the Great ordered him to cross Siberia, to build himself a vessel and then find out whether America and Asia were one continent or whether the Hollanders and English of the sixteenth century had been right when they had predicted the existence of a gap which would make it possible to cross from the Pacific to the Atlantic by way of Nova Zembla and Cape Chelyuskin.

Bering walked across Siberia, reached the coast of Kamchatka, built himself a small boat and sailed along the coast of Asia from the mouth of the Kamchatka River until he reached the Gulf of Anadyr. As he saw no evidence of any land in the east, he decided that the two continents must indeed be separated from each other and so he walked back to St. Petersburg and reported that without a fleet, Russia would never be able to conquer the northern part of America.

Meanwhile, not only Peter had died but his widow too, that lusty and shrewd old strumpet, Catherine Skovronska, had moved to an eternal reward, which must have been a most generous one if it is really true what the Good Book says about those who have loved much. She had been succeeded by Anna Ivanovna, the daughter of Peter's half-witted brother, also a lady who would hardly have been a success at the court of Queen Victoria, but who had the good sense to choose herself a sequence of very intelligent lovers, none of whom were Russians and who therefore worked all the more eagerly for the glory of their adopted country and the benefit of their own pocketbooks.

In the south, these gentlemen had at last broken the power of the Turks and then they seem to have toyed quite seriously with the idea of extending their power across at least part of the American continent. And so, in 1733, Bering had been sent once more to Kamchatka. But as most of his subordinates had been of Slavic stock, there had been endless quarrels, rows and drunken altercations. Therefore it had not been until seven years later that Bering at last had been able to set sail.

With two small boats, the *St. Peter* and the *St. Paul,* he had gone from Petropavlovsk to revisit the waters he had first visited in 1729. He soon lost track of the vessel that was supposed to accompany him and being left alone, he had preferred to follow an eastern course which had carried him past the Aleutian Islands without his ever becoming aware of their existence. But we know that he must have reached the American mainland because he left us a description of a volcano which he named Mount St. Elias and which is situated quite far to the south, near the present frontier between Alaska and British Columbia.

But Bering, with his procrastinating and unruly Russian crew, was way behind his schedule and the approach of winter forced him to return before he had a chance to penetrate inland. On the way back he was almost constantly in a heavy fog and, unable to reach Kamchatka itself, he was obliged to prepare some sort of winter quarters on one of the islands of the Komandor group. These islands were without trees and without population. When the rest of the crew was finally rescued, after six months of dreadful privations, the rock on which they had spent the winter had one permanent resident, Vitus Jonassen Bering, late of the Imperial Russian Navy and discoverer of Alaska, as well as of the strait which separates Asia from America.

✦

Cook, when he reached this northern region, experienced no better luck than Bering had had, thirty-seven years before. We do not know exactly how far north he got but he probably had been in the neighborhood of Wrangell Island, when the pack ice at last forced him to return.

From the general direction he had taken, it rather looks as if he had decided to give up all idea of using the northeastern passage and had tried to find the northwestern passage and connect with a number of British vessels that were supposed to be on the lookout for him near Nova Zembla. This passage was eventually made but not until almost a century after Cook had given it up as impossible. Between 1878 and 1879, the Swedish explorer Nordenskiöld on the good ship *Vega* actually sailed from the Atlantic to the Pacific by following the northeastern passage. As for the passage north of America, that had to wait even longer, for it was only in the years 1903-1906 that Amundsen on the *Gjöa* successfully crossed from the Atlantic to the Pacific by following that difficult route.

But no ship has as yet been able to sail from the Pacific to the Atlantic by way of the polar regions. And now that we can so much more comfortably do our exploring by airplane, it is highly doubtful whether anyone will ever be found willing to bury himself alive for two or three years on a small wooden tub, just for the honor of having been the first to etc., etc.

I once spent an hour in Oslo, sitting in the cabin of Nansen's *Fram*. My respect for the old polar explorers increased about ten thousand per cent. An hour of silent meditation was more than enough. A week of it would have driven me completely crazy.

In September, 1778, Cook returned to the south to spend the winter among the Hawaiian Islands. At first he chose the island of Maui, between Oahu (where Honolulu is now situated) and Hawaii itself, but in January of 1779 he crossed over to Hawaii and dropped anchor in Kealakekua Bay.

Cook had an uncanny gift of getting along with all sorts and varieties of people, both European and foreign. He recognized (what few Europeans before him had ever done) that a Polynesian, or for that matter, any other native, was not just another European with a slightly darker skin or a kinkier sort of hair. No, his entire psychological approach towards life was different from that of the White Man and therefore, in dealing with a native, one had to be very careful not to give offense when no offense whatsoever was meant, but when a great deal of it was taken in spite of all the White Man's precautions.

Perhaps his associations with the easy-going Russian settlers of the region he had just visited had made him a little careless. Or perhaps his honest Yorkshire background played him false when he had to deal with one of those difficult border cases in which the White Man will talk of a "theft" whereas his darker-skinned brother is under the impression that he has merely shared something.

Then again, the natives, having been obliged to feed the White Men for as long a time as they deemed necessary for the observation of their very strict rules of hospitality, felt slightly annoyed when the White God, after having hoisted

**COOK GOES ON SHORE FOR THE LAST TIME**

sail, returned a few days later with a request for still further supplies. Cook always took great pains to pay for everything he obtained. There was no question of "help yourselves" when James Cook's sailors went on shore. They paid in whatever the natives most wanted. The natives of all the Polynesian islands, still dwelling in the stone age and never having seen a scrap of metal until the White Man appeared upon the scene, were very eager to get hold of anything that was made of iron or steel.

We don't know the real reason but after his return to Kealakekua Bay (having been forced back by the gales of the open sea) Cook at once sensed a very noticeable change in the attitude of the Hawaiians, both towards him and towards his crew. A native, intent upon being insolent, has ways and means of giving vent to his feelings by a display of such offensive if subtle brazenness and such a manifestation of swaggering over-bearance that only a saint, in his more saintly moments, can withstand the temptation to knock him down. Cook had many saintly attributes but it was the saintliness of Yorkshire, which was mixed with certain highly practical considerations about the rights of property. When a few of the natives made away with the *Discovery's* cutter, Cook decided to put an end to all such further incidents by asking for a couple of hostages and by keeping them on board his flagship until the hour of his departure. By such an action he hoped to protect himself against further wholesale pilfering on the part of the light-fingered Hawaiians.

But in spite of his precautions there were all sorts of unpleasant little incidents between the visiting Englishmen and their unwilling Polynesian hosts. On February 14 of the year 1779, Cook landed with an armed guard to pay his respects to the local chieftain and to demand his hostages. The mood of the crowd that surrounded his boat was a very ugly one and it did not grow any better when someone spread the rumor that only a few minutes before, in another part of the bay, the English had shot one of the native chieftains.

Cook, realizing that for the moment at least he could accomplish nothing, seems to have given orders to his men to return to the boat. The mob had waited for that moment to rush him. Cook put up a stiff resistance, while giving the others a chance to escape. But just before he reached the boat he made the mistake! For a moment he turned his back upon his assailants. He was at once knocked down and killed.

During the struggle that followed, four mariners were also cut and hacked to pieces. The survivors, several of them badly wounded, made their escape to the *Resolution* and waited.

They were familiar with the habits of all Polynesian peoples. It was not pleasant, that night, to watch the glow from the fires on shore, for that meant that the body of their commander was now being prepared for a glorious repast.

At this moment, most historians discreetly draw the curtain upon this ghastly incident and hint at certain "ceremonial usages," which made it necessary for the native chief to eat the heart of his enemy as a token that he was a very great warrior and that he had now added his opponent's valor to his own by means of this old and widely honored ritual. One hates to be too realistic upon a subject which can only cause discomfort to one's friends who are descended from the men who had slaughtered the gallant captain.

But in the case of James Cook, I regret to say that the circumstantial evidence (offered to the English a few days after their commander's murder) points most ominously and most directly to a fate which it is not pleasant to contemplate, even after a distance of these many years. Already on the afternoon of the fifteenth of February, news had reached the sailors of the *Resolution* that their beloved Captain had gone the way of most Polynesian captives of war. They had thereupon fired several volleys at that village where this sacrilege was supposed to have taken place and had succeeded in setting the place on fire.

Whether fear of further reprisals or genuine remorse had thereupon inspired the natives to give some signs of repentance, we shall never know, but on the twenty-first of February, a party of natives, led by a chief, came to the shore and then returned unto the British what little there was left of their former commander. These relics consisted

of his hands, part of his skull, part of his scalp and some
of the bones of his legs. On the evening of the twenty-first,
Lieutenant Charles Clerke read the burial service over a
small casket containing these gruesome objects and thereupon he committed them to the care of that ocean with

THE LAST OF CAPTAIN COOK

which the name of James Cook will ever remain associated.

A short while later, Clerke also bade a final farewell to
his beloved Pacific, for he died on August 22, while trying
to finish the investigations of the Bering Strait region which
had been interrupted the previous year by the advent of
winter. Two young lieutenants, Gore and King, thereupon
brought the *Resolution* and the *Discovery* safely back to
England. They arrived there without any further incidents
on October 4, of the year 1780.

We have almost come to the end of these chapters on the White Man's discovery of the Great South Sea. Only one more voyage and then the explorers will retire from the stage, leaving the islands they had found and the sea routes they had charted and the continents they had outlined to the mercies of the trader and the whaler and the slave merchant and the pearl diver and the planter and the beachcomber. But we have one final candidate for honors, the Frenchman we have already mentioned, the glamorous Jean François de Galaup, Comte de la Pérouse.

He came from the country of the Albigensians and as a young boy he had joined the French navy, being one of the survivors on board the *Formidable* when in 1759 Admiral Hawke had attacked the French navy in Quiberon Bay, thereby preventing a French invasion of England. Later he had been in command of one of the vessels which had harried the eastern Canadian seaboard during the American Revolution. Not content with this comparatively harmless pastime, he had boldly sailed into the Hudson Bay and had there captured the two most important forts of the Hudson's Bay Company, Forts Prince of Wales and York. But his brilliant raiding expeditions had in no way influenced the course of the war. Canada had remained in British hands and the government of France had thereupon decided to try its luck in the Pacific.

The unexplored northwestern part of the American continent was still a no man's land and said to be richer in furs than any other part of the world, while the southern

Pacific might offer an excellent hunting ground for the French whalers from Brittany. In 1785 La Pérouse had sailed for the Great Southern Sea in command of two vessels, *L'Astrolabe* and *La Boussole*. His instructions had been rather vague but the French Admiralty had suggested that La Pérouse might try to do what Cook had just failed to accomplish and discover the Northwest Passage.

La Pérouse had faithfully followed the coast of America until he came to Mount St. Elias in Alaska. There bad weather had forced him to turn back and so, by way of Hawaii and Necker Island (the famous island where the ancient Hawaiians had gone to get the feathers for their royal robes and first seen by La Pérouse), he had gone to the Philippines.

From the Philippines he had crossed over to the mainland of Asia, where he had visited China, Korea and Japan. The name of the strait which separates Hokkaido, the most northern of the Japanese islands, and Sakhalin Island, which is still known as La Pérouse Strait, bears evidence of his presence in those unknown parts of the world.

From Japan, La Pérouse had proceeded to Kamchatka and from Bering's old city of Petropavlovsk he had sent one of his officers back to Paris, together with all his maps and journals and the miscellaneous information gathered during his two years in the Pacific.

After his departure from Petropavlovsk we hear of him only twice more. First when ten of his men were murdered in Samoa in December of 1787 and the next time when he

**THE SHIPWRECK OF LA PÉROUSE**

dropped anchor in Botany Bay in January of 1788. From Botany Bay he sent one more letter back to Paris and after that—silence.

In the year 1826, an English squadron called at the New Hebrides. The commander, Captain Peter Dillon, was greatly surprised when a member of his crew showed him the hilt of a European sword which the sailor had bought from one of the natives. He made a few investigations and soon came to the conclusion that this must be the neighborhood in which the ships of La Pérouse must have been shipwrecked.

As soon as this had become known in Europe, the French government sent Dumont d'Urville (whom you met a few pages ago) to the New Hebrides with instructions to make certain that Dillon had not been mistaken. It was due to the researches of d'Urville and his own *Astrolabe* (he had rebaptized his ship with that name in honor of La Pérouse) that we can now point to the reef of Vanikoro as the exact spot on which La Pérouse and all his men had perished during a severe storm some time in February or March of the year 1788.

✦

That was the way in which the White Man explored every nook and corner of the Great South Sea until he could safely say, "The job is done, for now we know all there is to be known." Occasionally we still hear stories of some whaling captain who reports that he has found an island "not mentioned on any of the available charts." Such a thing is of course still within the realm of possibilities, but it is far from likely and as a rule it develops that the whaler had either made the wrong observations or had mistaken a rock for an island or had sailed on a map of the days of Captain Beechey, the English naval officer who during the twenties of the last century had first of all made a scientific survey of the eastern Pacific.

✦

Yes, that was the way the White Man discovered the Pacific Ocean, following in the tracks of the Polynesian navigators who had preceded him by more than a thousand years. And what did it profit him that now he could at last remove the legend of *terra incognita* from so large a part of the map of the world?

It is too early to tell, for it is only since the official opening of the Panama Canal on July 12, 1920, that the Pacific Ocean has ceased to be a sort of backwater and been brought within easy reach of the Atlantic. But during the first four centuries of its existence as a field of exploration for European enterprise and greed, it produced remarkably few concrete results. It was too far away. It had neither gold nor silver. Its population, except in a few rare instances, could not be forced into slavery. And its agricultural products were negligible compared to those of America and the spice islands of the Indian archipelago. And so the Pacific remained a field of speculation for the writer of popular fiction and for the promoters of fantastic financial schemes. Its Utopian reputation greatly facilitated the labors of both these groups of men. But whereas the former at best derived some slender profits for themselves, the

THE WHOLE WORLD WENT MAD SPECULATING IN SOUTH SEA
VALUES WHICH DID NOT EXIST

latter used the mysterious appeal of these distant lands to ruin hundreds of thousands of their fellow-countrymen.

Talk of the great swindles of the past and "the South Sea Bubble" will be the first thing that comes to your mind. Even in our own day and age, when fraudulent speculations have assumed gigantic proportions, the Great South Sea Bubble commands a certain respect for the immense and complicated scale of its far-reaching ramifications.

It was in the year 1711. After prolonged and elaborate negotiations, a number of small trading companies, which had been doing business with the Spanish colonies of South America, were at last brought together into one large and powerful South Sea Company. Its charter gave the directors the right to deal not only with South America but also with the recently discovered islands in the Pacific.

The name appealed greatly to the people of Europe, for all of them had heard vague rumors about the tremendous riches that were said to lie hidden on the great continent, which almost any day now was sure to be found by some daring explorer, and everyone with a little surplus capital was eager to invest.

Seven years after its foundation, no one less than His Majesty the King deigned to accept its general directorship. After that, the sky was the limit and the profits were so enormous that the company approached the British government with a most ambitious scheme—something unheard of in these pre-Kreuger days. In return for still further concessions, the Company expressed its willingness to take over the entire national debt, amounting to more than $150,000,000! Most of the debt was then held by well-to-do citizens who in this way had hoped to provide themselves with a safe and sound annuity. The Company set to work to persuade those unsuspecting citizens to exchange their annuities for stock in the new company.

The idea seemed absolutely foolproof and it caused such a stir on the London money market that the Bank of England hastened to make a similar bid. In the end, the South Sea Company won by outbidding its competitors to the tune of several million dollars. And in return for an annual contribution of some forty million dollars, the South Sea Company was told to go ahead with its plans.

Nobody knew exactly where all this money was to come from, nor where these South Sea Islands were situated— these islands that were to produce these magic millions. But the name "South Sea" had caught hold of the popular imagination and the rest was easy. In less than a fortnight, more than half of the holders of government bonds had exchanged their annuities for stock in the South Sea Company. Early in 1720 the Company's stock still stood at 128. In June of the same year it had risen to 890. One month later it mounted to a thousand and $25,000,000 worth of fresh stock was immediately disposed of.

The whole of England participated in the gamble. The continent followed suit. The sad fate of John Law's Louisiana Company (the Mississippi Bubble) apparently taught nobody anything. One either speculated in South Sea stock or one became a traitor to the best interests of one's own family and children.

Already in August of the same year there were rumors

of difficulties. The Company managed to silence these and once more a heavy layer of paper millions began to cover every part of the British Kingdom. In September the explosion took place. Overnight the stock fell from over a

THE OLD GODS STILL LIVE

thousand to a mere 135. In December, it had dwindled down to nothing at all.

The exact number of people who were ruined will probably never be known, as thousands, unable to meet their obligations, left house and home and escaped to the continent. When an investigating committee, composed of members of the House of Commons, went through the Company's books, it discovered that the directors, in order to cover up their fraudulent dealings and statements, had bought up practically every member of the government. The Chancellor of the Exchequer, the Secretary of State, the Postmaster General, a Commissioner of the Treasury and a large number of less exalted personages had all of them shared in the booty. The private property of the directors and of two members of the government was confiscated by an act of Parliament. But what was a paltry ten million dollars compared to the hundreds of millions lost by the public at large? And what consolation could the poor dupes derive from the mild sentences that were eventually meted out to the real culprits?

It was a catastrophe of the first magnitude and it took England half a century to recover from this shock to its credit. In this way, the South Sea avenged itself upon those who had dared to disturb its age-old and undisturbed tranquillity for the sake of satisfying their own lust for money.

✦

And now it is the year 1833 and a small vessel, the *Beagle*, is leisurely cruising between Tahiti and New Zealand and Tasmania and Australia and all the other islands of the vast Pacific. The vessel is on a surveying expedition but there is a young naturalist on board by the name of Charles Darwin. On his mother's side, he is the grandson of Josiah Wedgwood, the founder of the English pottery industry, and on his father's side, of Erasmus Darwin, the noted botanist who so eloquently poured his scientific observations into a poetic form. Young Charles himself had been most carefully educated, first at Edinburgh, where he

DARWIN

soon discovered that he had no natural gift for the practice of medicine, and afterwards at Cambridge, where he despaired of ever becoming a good clergyman. And so he had volunteered to act as scientist on board H.M.S. *Beagle*, bound for a prolonged surveying voyage in the Pacific Ocean.

The captain of the *Beagle* was an austere Calvinist, but

Charles Darwin found congenial company among some of his shipmates, such as Conrad Martins, the artist, and a young midshipman by the name of Owen Stanley. During four endless years of endless seas and endless skies and apparently endless seasickness, young Darwin had a lot of time to study and to think and to draw a few conclusions of his own regarding the strange way this planet had come to be populated by the weird creatures which were brought to him for observation. And when he reached home, he continued his speculations upon the methods which Nature had chosen, her miracles to perform.

Twenty-three years after his return and among many misgivings, he at last published a book. The title of the volume is: *On the Origin of Species by Means of Natural Selection, or the Preservation of Favoured Races in the Struggle for Life.*

The deed had been done! Genesis had been boldly challenged. The definitely established creed of the Church was rocked to its very foundations. And in this way, the Great South Sea for the second time brought itself to the attention of the world at large.

✦

In the year 1891 the *paquebot* to Tahiti dropped a passenger at the capital city of Papeete and when this visitor registered with the police (for this was a French settlement and subject to a rigid form of bureaucracy) he gave his name as Paul Gauguin, his birthplace as Paris, the date of

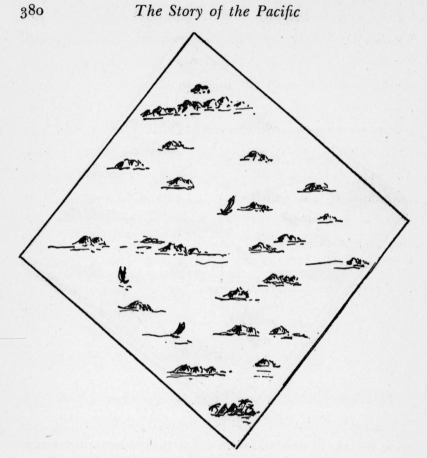

TO THE NATIVES, THE PACIFIC USED TO BE A
PLACE IN WHICH TO LIVE

his birth as June 7, 1848, and his profession as that of a
painter.

He was one of the pioneers of the great post-impression-
ist movement of the seventies of the last century, an excellent artist and one of the vilest creatures that ever drew the
breath of life.

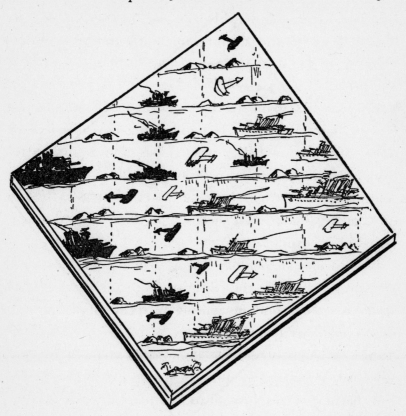

NOW THE BIG NATIONS HAVE TURNED IT INTO A BIG CHECKERBOARD
ON WHICH TO PLAY THE GAME OF INTERNATIONAL POLITICS

He had started his career as a bank clerk, a clever, schem-
ing manipulator of dishonest money. He ended it as a
broken-down wreck, whose remains were mercifully put
out of sight by the local French mission. From his Peru-
vian mother he had inherited an overpowering desire to
visit foreign lands where he would not be hampered in his
work by the petty prejudices of his middle-class French

background. Having left his wife and his children to their
own devices, he had set forth to find a spot that should
come up to the fever-stricken visions of his diseased body
and brain.

It was an ill day for the islands of the Pacific when he set
foot on their territories. The natives came to realize it. Even
today, after almost half a century has gone by, when the
sea wind brings them an occasional whiff of the over-ripe
copra that lies rotting along the water front, they look at
each other, shake their heads and say, "Ah, Monsieur
Gauguin is passing!"

But Europe, desperately trying to find some new form
of expression within the realm of its pictorial art, looked
at these strange and fascinating pictures of dusky Polynesian maidens that now began to come to them from
Tahiti and delightedly the fashionable element of Paris
absorbed the supposed spirit of native innocence, beauty
and charm that was brought to its attention by the terrible
author of *Noa Noa*.

All those saturated with the pleasures of an effete world
still encumbered with too many ancient traditions hastened
to this earthly paradise to spend the rest of their lives
among the wineshops and brothels of the Papeetian water
front. They were vicious but they had their glamour and in
a world gone glamour-mad, they felt that they were doing
something of great importance.

Within a surprisingly short space of time, they became

the subjects of a new sort of fiction that gained tremendous popularity. Thirty years afterwards the movies discovered them and thereupon the Pacific Ocean became a backdrop for the celluloid activities of Hollywood, and in this way,

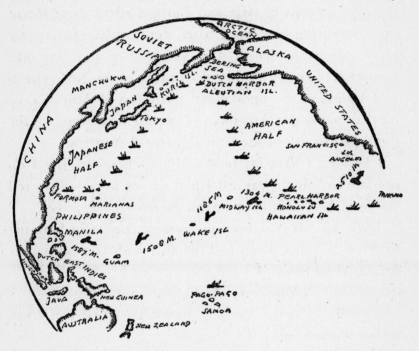

the Pacific Ocean brought itself for a third and last time to the attention of the Western world. But on this occasion, many of the natives must have smiled a smile of profound satisfaction and while watching the antics of the White Man they must have whispered to each other, "Behold! At last we have our revenge! They destroyed us. Now we destroy them, and the gods of the mountains can be contented."

And now, coming to the end of my little tale, I wonder what surprises this unpredictable ocean still holds in store for us and what the result will be of that terrible chess game now being played among its islands and atolls by the powerful nations of Asia and Europe, all of them intent upon acquiring new naval bases, new airplane bases, new army stations, so that at some future date they may take possession of the rich mineral treasures of the Netherlands East Indies, of the unoccupied territories of Australia, or for that matter (for Asia today is proving very strong) of the unlimited wealth of the United States of America.

I wonder. I have my fears and apprehensions, but I do not know. And anyway, all I had set out to do was to tell you how the Pacific happened to be discovered.

That task has now been performed. And right here my little book comes to an end, while I wish you pleasanter dreams than those of

Your very obedient servant,

HENDRIK WILLEM VAN LOON

*Nieuw Veere*
*Old Greenwich, Connecticut.*
10:10 P.M. *February* 17, 1940.

# INDEX

PAPEETE